GHOST IN SPACE

The comet's glowing tail was like a sequined curtain waiting for them to part its folds and enter the secret world of Wonderwhat.

The feeling of suspended reality slowly left Dawnboy. His gloved fingers checked the tools on his belt as he prepared to board the *Jealousy*.

Then the impossible happened. . . .

"So ye thought ye'd steal me treasure, eh?" A gravel-voiced roar echoed in Dawnboy's ears. "I'll blast ye all to the flaming pit o' cosmic hell first!"

Dawnboy looked up and gave a startled cry. Before him was the figure of a burly, black-bearded man . . . a man with a blaster gripped in each hand. *A man who had somehow returned from the dead to protect his treasure-laden ship!*

THE
TREASURE OF
WONDERWHAT

by Bill Starr

A Farstar & Son Novel
#2

A Del Rey Book

BALLANTINE BOOKS • NEW YORK

A Del Rey Book
Published by Ballantine Books

Copyright © 1977 by Bill Starr

Library of Congress Catalog Card Number: 76-13474

ISBN 0-345-28286-8

Printed in Canada

First Edition: December 1976
Second Printing: August 1979

Cover art by Darrell K. Sweet

Dedicated, with love and gratitude,
to my parents and grandparents, who
taught me that in all of life's
treasure hunts the true reward is
not the Treasure, but the Wonder.

*I will bring them through the fire,
and will refine them as silver is
refined, and will try them as gold
is tried.*

—Zechariah, 13: 9

1

"THAT SEEMS A fair offer," Dawnboy MacCochise remarked, as he read the huge letters that blazed forth in
full color against the blackness of interstellar space. He
was reclining in the copilot seat of the commercial starship *Gayheart* and peering at the forward bulkhead,
which appeared to be transparent. Actually the entire
bulkhead was the lens of an electron telescope capable
of bringing in scenes from up to five light-years away,
if there was no radiation or atmospheric interference.

"Wait till you see what's coming next," said Lulu,
the ship's biocomputer. "Newtonia seems to have a
little advertising war going on."

The words faded away and were replaced by:

1

HELP IN OVERCOMING THE GUILT OF SELF-TERMI-
NATION. FRANCHISES AVAILABLE TO DEALERS.

"See—they get you coming or going," Lulu said.

"I wonder if we have a third choice?" Dawnboy mused.

Dawnboy's father, Ranger Farstar, grinned at his son from the pilot's seat. "Don't let that silliness cause you to underestimate the Newtonians' intelligence. Like most scientists, they are only crazy within their own specialized fields. But it was only recently that advertising was declared to be an ethical exercise of free speech by physicians and other professionals, so they haven't quite got the hang of doing it in a sophisticated manner."

"Nothing could surprise me anymore." Dawnboy yawned with the vast wisdom of having lived nearly seventeen years and having just experienced his first space cruise. "Not after seeing how yer superrich friends on the business world o' Capitalia carry on."

"Don't be too sure about that," Ranger said. "It's a big universe. Even those of us who have done considerable traveling in it still find exciting new things occasionally."

"Well, I must admit I'm impressed by the way they broadcast those words so far out into space," Dawnboy said, reading an announcement about a method of factory automation recently developed by Biocybertech Industries. "How do they manage to do that?"

"I'm not too sure about that myself," Ranger confessed. "I think it's some complicated process of bouncing videowaves off of the planet's Van Allen radiation belt by a luxium-powered projector. When the waves hit cosmic dust in deep space, their energy charges release tremendously bright flashes of light. Is that about right, Lulu?"

"That's a fair summary of the basic theory," the biocomputer replied. "But I can give you a fully detailed technical description of the process from my memory banks, if you want. It will only take a few hours."

"Never mind," father and son said together.

"Just trying to be helpful."

"Thanks, but we have more pressing matters to take care of," Ranger said, then glanced over his glowing instrument panel. "Better run a double-check on our tow beam, Son. We don't want to risk losing the valuable cargo that we've hauled all this distance. Lulu, have you contacted the Director of the Darwin Institute yet?"

"Affirmative, Skipper. He seems most anxious to talk to you."

"I can believe it, considering what we're bringing him. Put him on the screen."

The photophonic visiscreen before Ranger brightened with the image of a stocky reptilian creature that looked vaguely humanoid. Its facial scales flushed violet with pleasure as it said: "Captain Farstar! Greetings from Newtonia. How pleased I am to see you again." The being spoke good Unilingo that was only faintly slurred by a vague hissing.

"Greetings, Dr. Clay. My blood temperature is increased by your warmth," Ranger said, using the semiformal greeting ritual of Cretacia, the director's native planet. "Did you receive my sub-ether message?"

"Indeed we did, and as you can imagine, it has stirred up no end of excitement in our dry old scientific minds. Have you really found such a marvelous technological artifact of the Vanished Ones?"

"Well, we found *something* that I had never seen the like of before," Ranger answered. "But it will be up to you fellows to determine if it was left by the hypothetical race of superintelligent beings that some people think traveled throughout the universe many thousand years ago. Lulu, give him a look at what we're towing."

The scene on the screen changed to exhibit what appeared to be a small moon. A powerful light beam from the *Gayheart* revealed the object to be roughly meteor-pitted and littered with cosmic debris. But here and there patches of a shiny metal surface showed through. A measurement scale in the corner of the screen indicated that the sphere was about five miles in diameter.

"Fascinating!" Dr. Clay hissed slightly. "You say it is a huge and powerful antigravity generator, designed to serve as an artificial moon and to control the tides on an Earth-size planet?"

"That's the only function that I could figure out for it," Ranger said. "The planet we found it orbiting was mainly a water world, with only one large island continent in a vast ocean. A natural, much larger, moon was attached to the planet and would ordinarily have caused gigantic tides to sweep over the continent. But this little satellite countered the big moon's gravitational pull, thus enabling land-dwelling life-forms to evolve on the planet."

Ranger went on to deliver a brief account of how he and Dawnboy had discovered, claimed and then lost the planet, managing to get away with only the artificial moon. Like most independent star traders, Ranger had always dreamed of finding the grand prize of space exploration—an uninhabited but humanly habitable planet that had not yet been claimed by any other intelligent species. Such desirable worlds were rare indeed and could be sold for fabulously high prices to land-hungry colonists from overpopulated societies. Finally Ranger had managed to get financial backing for an expedition to a remote part of the galaxy where he had good reason to believe such a planet might be found; and by a lucky coincidence, he was able to take Dawnboy along as a junior partner and apprentice spaceman.

They eventually located the planet, which Ranger tentatively named Dawnworld in his son's honor. But they had little time to enjoy their newfound treasure. Other parties seemed mighty anxious to gain possession of uninhabited worlds—especially the ruthlessly totalitarian astro-empire that went by the innocent-sounding name of the Interstellar Family of Intelligent Beings (IFIB). The IFIB starcruiser *Dzuntoy,* a war vessel commanded by Ranger's old friendly adversary, Autry

Lopezov, had trailed the *Gayheart* to Dawnworld. But Ranger had already filed his claim for the planet with the Sentient Species Association (SSA).

Lopezov waited patiently until Ranger went to investigate the small moon. Dawnboy, left alone on the planet's surface, was easily captured through IFIB treachery. Then, in order to save his son's life, Ranger was compelled to sign over his claim to Dawnworld. But first Ranger shrewdly bargained for the right to take the small moon with them when they left, by claiming it contained a small deposit of the valuable transuranic element luxium that Ranger hoped to sell for enough money to cover the cost of his expedition. Lopezov, unaware of the satellite's true purpose, had generously handed it over to Ranger and Dawnboy, who quickly departed with the knowledge that Dawnworld would soon be unsuitable for the penal colony that IFIB intended.

Now the *Gayheart* was approaching the science planet Newtonia, where Ranger was confident he could sell the antigravity satellite for a handsome profit. As Dr. Clay indicated, the Newtonian scientists were eager to study this first physical evidence that the ancient race they called the Vanished Ones had actually existed, something that up until then had been only hypothetically discussed. Ranger, by measuring the half-life of the luxium fuel in the artificial satellite, estimated it to be at least fifty thousand Earth years old, as he informed Dr. Clay.

"And I suppose you are going to demand some ridiculously high price for this piece of antique machinery," Dr. Clay said, flicking out his forked tongue in what was for his species a deprecatory gesture.

"Why, how can you suggest that?" Ranger asked innocently. "Just because Newtonia holds a virtual monopoly on the building, servicing and repairing of the best starships and we poor spacebums have to pay your exorbitant rates just to stay in business? In fact, because I am so unselfishly anxious to aid the cause of scientific advancement, I am going to let you steal this valuable artifact from me for a mere ten million stellars."

"T-ten million?" Dr. Clay spluttered, his scales turning from violet to chartreuse with shock. "You mean ten million Capitalian stellars?"

"Unless you know of a more reliable universal currency," Ranger said. "I'm not particular, as long as it's solidly backed by gold or some other precious element standard."

"But that's impossible!" the Cretacian snapped. "Such an expenditure would wipe out our entire budget for the rest of the fiscal year. We wouldn't even be able to pay our vital operating expenses."

"Such as your salary?" Ranger asked, holding back a smile. "Come on, Doc. I know that the institute has a special emergency fund. You'll just have to convince the Board of Trustees to open up their tight little fists on the purse strings. Or I'll peddle my wares elsewhere."

"Who else could you sell the satellite to?" Dr. Clay asked shrewdly.

"Oh, I know a few junk dealers who will buy almost anything," Ranger said casually.

The sentient reptile stared at him in horror. "You wouldn't dare! Not with such a priceless aid to scientific research. Why, this single object could possibly teach us more than centuries of experimentation. To destroy it would be worse than criminal. It would be . . ." Outraged indignation choked off his voice. Ranger was sure he would have blinked back angry tears, had he possessed eyelids.

Ranger studied his nails. "You're the one who called it priceless, not me. But then I can't pretend to have your refined sense of intellectual values. I'm just a stupid businessman who only understands profit and loss. So make me a reasonable offer and we can kick it around."

"Very well," Dr. Clay said more calmly. "If you insist on being crassly commercial about this, I think the institute could afford to pay—shall we say two million stellars? That should amply compensate you for your trouble."

"Yes, but it wouldn't do much for my greed. Nine million is the lowest offer I could possibly consider."

Ranger relaxed inwardly and settled down for some stubborn dickering. He knew better than to let Dr. Clay's acting the fuzzy-minded professor fool him. The natives of Cretacia had the reputation for being the toughest traders in the Lacerta constellation, as well as in most other parts of the universe they had reached. It was said that a Cretacian shed his skin once a year, but he was ready to skin others anytime.

Dawnboy listened with only half-interest to the bargaining between the two sharp business professionals. His father's recounting of their adventures on Dawnworld had brought back some painful memories that he wished he could forget. But at the same time, he realized that these were important episodes in his life and they had taught him some lessons that were well worth remembering. For instance, he had learned not to trust women, and that was a valuable discovery for a young man to make.

He grimaced at the bittersweet memory of Lieutenant Primary Grade Alexia Ustich, the Communications and Conditioning Officer of the *Dzuntoy*. Beautiful Alexia—so charming, so intelligent and so utterly dedicated to the strange ideology of Otherism, the psychological glue that held the IFIB empire together. Alexia's enchantingly treacherous wiles, more than anything else, had brought about his capture and the eventual loss of Dawnworld. Ranger had quickly forgiven his son and shrugged off their loss with the philosophical outlook of a seasoned businessman. But Dawnboy had still not gotten over the ego-crushing humiliation of having been outsmarted by a mere woman. But blaming and hating Alexia was no help, when he realized so clearly that she had just been doing her duty to the cause she had sworn to uphold. He had to give her his grudging respect for that, although he found it difficult to understand how she could willingly serve an organization that was so destructive to all the human values he had grown accustomed to cherish.

His thoughts drifted back to his first meeting with Alexia, some three months before. It had been on Capitalia at an elaborate dinner party given by Ranger's friend, the fabulously wealthy financier, Rothfeller Hughes. Alexia had been flatteringly attentive to Dawnboy then, and so had her counterpart Sub-Captain Alrik Bell-the-Cat, a member of a rival empire called the Protectors of Human Advancement and Purity (PHAP). In fact, for a while he had thought that totalitarian militarists were more interesting and more fun to be with than his father's stuffy business acquaintances. But that was before he learned how effectively collectivist movements stifle many of the individual freedoms he had always taken for granted.

Dawnboy's mind grew weary of trying to sort out all the confusing new information he had acquired in the past few months since he had been reunited with his father. He found it much more reassuring to think about his happy childhood on semi-barbarous Apache Highlands, his mother's homeworld. When he was five, his spacefaring parents had sent him there to be reared by the tough-fighting, hard-living MacCochise clan. Four years later word came that his mother, Gayheart, had been killed and that his father had been seriously injured by a destabilized light-energy converter on their ship.

So Dawnboy had grown up as a hearty, resourceful Apache brave, lovingly but sternly guided by his mother's sister Eve and by his grandfather Angus Mac-Cochise, Grand Laird of the clan. Like his space-pioneering Scots-Indian ancestors, he had learned from the hard school of experience the simple, manly virtues of honesty, courage, self-reliance, frugality, loyalty—and cunning deception in war and guarded friendliness in peace. Above all else, he had learned to safeguard his personal and family honor and freedom at any cost.

All things considered, that was probably the best early education that a future spaceman could receive.

Not that Dawnboy had ever seriously considered a star-voyaging career for himself in those days. When the clan heard nothing further from Ranger, he was presumed to have died and the boy fully accepted the rugged Apache Highlands way of life. He trained strenuously to become an outstanding warrior, dreaming of winning much glory in battle as a leading warchief. Perhaps the tribal elders would even elect him to be the next Grand Laird, upon his grandfather's death. Then one day a somewhat familiar stranger who called himself Ranger Farstar came back into Dawnboy's life, reawakening the lad's old romantic yearnings for the stars. . . .

Dawnboy glanced over at his father and shook off a sharp stab of homesickness for his clanspeople. Well, at least he had proved himself to be a competent beginning astrophile, as many star rovers laughingly referred to themselves. But he still wasn't sure if he wanted to make a lifetime vocation of it. He wondered if his father was ever bothered by the nagging feeling that perhaps he should have gone into some other line of work. Probably not, considering how much Ranger seemed to enjoy commanding his own ship in the risky pursuit of interstellar commerce. But maybe he had just never been tempted by another equally attractive profession, as Dawnboy had been drawn to a career of warring for the clan.

Ranger never talked much about his early life, but Dawnboy gathered that he had experienced an unhappy childhood on Alpha-Centauri's Old New America, the first human-colonized planet beyond Earth. For that reason he left home early, took an assumed name and lied about his age in order to join the Space Rangers—a respected but not very respectable band of mercenaries who roved the universe. They peddled their fighting skills to any warmaking power that was able and willing to pay their going rate; and they were seldom without work, given the nature of most sentient creatures. Ranger had not relished the wholesale killing his job had entailed, but at least his four years with the Space Rangers taught him to be a good starship pilot. By the time he was discharged he had saved enough money to buy a small cargo vessel of his own, and during one of his first trading cruises he had met Dawnboy's mother.

At first Dawnboy had thought Ranger was a pretty dull character, compared to the clan's more flamboyant warriors. But Ranger had quickly demonstrated that he could take care of himself in a fight, even though he seemed more interested in the mundane business of making money than in anything else. Gradually the youth was becoming aware that his father's level-headed, no-nonsense exterior concealed a strong boyish love of adventure and a gambler's urge to take big risks for big profits. That colorful side of Ranger's personality came to the fore during their recent planet hunt and even more so in the next venture that Ranger had proposed they undertake when they had completed their business on Newtonia.

Ranger had recalled an old half-factual and half-legendary yarn about lost treasure—the sort of wild tale that has fired adventurous men's imaginations since long before the first rocket blasted skyward. This particular story concerned the *Jealousy,* a Freedonian star-tramp laden with gold and precious stones that about three centuries ago had gotten trapped in the tail of an erratic comet called Wonderwhat somewhere between the Magellanic Clouds. That much of the story was known to be true, but there was no way of testing the frightening accounts of Wonderwhat's strange behavior and the mysterious disappearance of most of the star-ships that had gone searching for the *Jealousy.* The few astrophiles who had returned from such expeditions were too terrified and confused to speak coherently of their experiences. That part of the universe was still largely unexplored by Homo sapiens, thus making it an ideal refuge for space pirates. Additionally, the Magellanic Clouds contained the inhospitable worlds of the ZuJus, a warlike race so radically different from all other intelligent species that it was all but impossible for humans to communicate with them.

As Ranger had said, anybody who managed to recover the *Jealousy*'s treasure under those conditions deserved to profit from it. Dawnboy agreed. The dangers stemming from the uncertainty of the undertaking appealed to his young, reckless spirit. But the hope of obtaining the treasure was an even greater incentive because he and his father needed a great deal of money for a very special purpose.

2

"Six million is the lowest price I can accept without risking bankruptcy," Ranger insisted, with a quiver in his voice to let Dr. Clay know that he wasn't all that adamant.

"Five and a half is my final offer," the Darwin Institute director said firmly. "And I'll have to fight the trustees coil and fang to get a special appropriation for that much. Take it or leave it."

"There are always the junk dealers," Ranger threatened.

"That bluff won't work anymore," Dr. Clay said coolly. "You know that no one else would pay a fraction of what I am offering, and I know that you wouldn't destroy the satellite just for spite."

"Oh, all right. Five and a half million it is then," Ranger sighed, trying to sound disappointed. Actually the price was much higher than he had expected to get for the artifact. Dr. Clay must be slipping, or else his scientist's eagerness to get hold of the satellite had overpowered his businessman's cool-headedness. "You can deposit that amount in my account at the Astropolis branch of the Interstellar Travelers and Merchants Bank. My biocomputer will beam you a bill of sale record signed with my voiceprint."

"Agreed." Dr. Clay's scales turned violet again. "I'm glad to have the matter settled. Now, how soon can you deliver the merchandise?"

Ranger checked with Lulu, then reported: "Our estimated time of arrival at Newtonia is about sixteen hours from now. But we could reduce that considerably if you would send out a space tug to help us tow the satellite."

"I have already dispatched two tugs for that very purpose," Dr. Clay replied. "They will entirely relieve you of the towing, if you want to complete your voyage here at maximum speed."

Ranger laughed. "That's what I call confidence— sending out tugs even before you were sure I would accept your price. And I suppose the tugs have several scientific experts aboard to make sure that the satellite is what I claim it is?"

"Why, how could you suspect I don't trust you?" Dr. Clay hissed in a hurt tone. "True, several of our people insisted on going out in the tugs, but only because of their impatience to have a close look at the artifact. As a matter of fact, I had to fight off an urge to go with them myself."

"Well, as always it has been a stimulating and educational experience doing business with you," Ranger said, reaching for the photophone's cutoff switch. "I'm sure you won't be disappointed with your purchase."

"Likewise," Dr. Clay said. "And do come to visit us during your stay on Newtonia, if you can spare the time."

"Certainly. I'm curious to learn what you old testtubers discover about the satellite." Ranger ended the transmission and smiled at his son. "I hope you paid close attention to that little lesson in the fine art of star trading. Not that I claim to be a master of it, but it's something you had better learn quickly if you don't want to risk ending up someday with just a handful of comet dust for your work—or wind up shuffling around the Home for Retired Destitute Spacemen, on Nueva Brasil."

"I think ye did just fine," Dawnboy said with his thrifty Highlander's admiration for sharp bargaining. "Five and a half million stellars sounds like a powerful lot o' money to me."

"Ordinarily it would be. But by the time we've finished paying off the mortgage on the *Gayheart*, had her overhauled and outfitted for our next cruise and settled up other expenses, we won't have a great deal left over. Not nearly enough to endow the organ transplant research clinic that we discussed."

Dawnboy nodded soberly at the mention of a subject that was of utmost importance, but emotionally painful, to both of them. Searching for something more commonplace to discuss, he remarked: "I didna ken that the Darwin Institute director is a smart lizard. He looks more human than what I've seen o' them on Three-D tapes."

"I'm glad you're getting over your initial revulsion to nonhumanoid beings, Son," Ranger said. "But be careful of derogatory slang, as some species are very sensitive about that. Dr. Montezuma Clay is a sapientsaur, to use his humanized taxonomic classification. What he is called in his own language is unpronounceable by the human voice. If we tried to say it, it would probably sound even more insulting than 'smart lizard.' "

"I don't think he's so smart," Lulu chimed in.

"That's because you're a bigot," Ranger said.

"Not true," Lulu observed from the central compartment of the ship where her disembodied brain floated in a tank of cerebrospinal fluid. "I have equal contempt for all forms of intelligence that suffer the wretched handicap of being confined to physical bodies. When will you poor fools learn that my elevated state of existence is your only true hope of sentient fulfillment?"

"That's easy for you to say," Ranger retorted. "You didn't mind losing your body so much because you had had a long, satisfying life of—what was it, a hundred and thirty years? When the rest of us have gotten that much use from our present incarnations, we might be glad to join you."

"Please have some respect for a lady's right to keep her age confidential," Lulu scolded him. "Instead of making such wild exaggerations. I was only a hundred and twenty-six when Hirosaki's Disease destroyed my body."

"A mere lass." Dawnboy smiled. " 'Tis a wonder that yer mum even let you meet Hirosaki and catch his disease."

"Of course there are times when I wish I were still of the flesh," Lulu admitted. "Like when smart-aleck children need to be spanked."

Ranger laughed at their good-natured teasing. It was an improvement over their first several weeks together, when Lulu had tried to smother the youngster with grandmotherly affection. Dawnboy, a precocious adolescent anxious to prove his manhood, had resented her overprotectiveness as much as he had chafed under his father's gentle but firm discipline. Ranger was glad the three of them finally had managed to adjust so well to one another and to the demands of their work. He stood up and stretched, tired.

"Well, the tugs won't reach us for several hours, so we may as well have lunch and get some rest. Think you can handle things alone, Lulu?"

"Sure, Boss. It's all routine now. If I become too bored, I can always scan the Newtonians' ridiculous advertising for laughs."

"Just don't let it persuade you to go on a shopping spree for new gadgets when we get there," Ranger cautioned her, as he started toward the galley.

"Why not?" Dawnboy asked, following his father out of the ship's bridge. "We're rich now, aren't we?"

Eight hours later Dawnboy was again seated in the copilot seat, watching with great interest as they approached a binary consisting of a large K-class orange star and a smaller blue-white B-star. He had learned from Lulu that the double star was called The Curies, after the husband and wife team that had discovered radium. But because authorities could not agree on whether Pierre or Marie Curie had contributed the most to science, the binary's discoverer had diplomatically refrained from giving first names to the larger or smaller star.

"Deceleration to sub-lightspeed will begin in fifteen-point-eight minutes," Lulu reported, "at which time I will contact the Newtonian authorities for clearance to land. Do you want to talk to them, Skipper?"

"Not unless they specifically request it," Ranger answered, reclining lazily in the pilot seat. "You can take us in on autopilot, since you know the area so well."

"That's right. Newtonia was where ye were installed in the *Gayheart,* wasn't it, Lulu? I had almost forgotten about that," Dawnboy said.

"Uh-huh. And that's where my poor old bones lie a-moldering in their grave," Lulu said. "I could shed a tear at the sad thought, if I weren't so pleased with my new existence. And if I still had tear glands."

"Don't get too choked up over it," Ranger cautioned her.

Dawnboy went back to dividing his attention between the filtered view of the binary through the telescope lens and an educational tape of Newtonia that he was screening on his photophone. The planet seemed to be a pretty dismal piece of real estate, as were most of the worlds of the planetary specialization experiment that had been started by the SSA nearly a century ago. At that time it was believed that the accumulated knowledge of all intelligent species had become too vast and too complex for any single society to make proper use of it. So several worlds had been reserved exclusively for the leading sentient pursuits—Newtonia, for scientific research; Capitalia, for interstellar commerce; Musendowment, for artistic creation; Theoterra for religious meditation and so on.

Because all the known planets that could be easily reached and inhabited were in great demand for regular colonization, the planetary specialization experimenters had been forced to adapt to some rather harsh environments. In fact, the surface of Capitalia was made totally uninhabitable by its deadly atmosphere of ammonia and methane gases. So the wealthy Capitalians had built their homes and business establishments on the planet's asteroid rings. Newtonia had neither rings nor a natural atmosphere of any kind. But it did possess rich mineral deposits from which the ingenious scientists had extracted the materials to build their climate-controlled domed cities. A few had even started cultivating barren areas outside the cities, using the planet's heavy gravity to hold down the artificially created atmosphere in natural and excavated depressions. Such "countrified" districts made possible large-scale agrobiological research and reduced the Newtonians' dependence on imported foodstuffs. Furthermore, it was a pleasant relief for them to be able to look at fields and forests of growing things.

The scene on Dawnboy's photophone shifted to a large wheel-shaped object bristling with antennae, scanner disks, landing docks and other protuberances. It floated like a silvery, slowly rotating chandelier against the space-dark backdrop high above Newtonia's stark surface. This was Astropolis, the star city, that served as Newtonia's only large satellite. Originally it had been intended as an astronomical observatory, but later technological advances had enabled the stargazers to perform most of their work more efficiently from the planet's surface. So now it served primarily as Newtonia's administrative and commercial center. The outer rim was largely occupied by shipyards and other heavy industries, since the work of building and repairing spacecraft was more easily performed in zero gravity.

Dawnboy glanced up to find that they had drawn

close enough to their destination to see Newtonia through the telescope—a fuzzy globe that appeared motionless in its wide orbit around The Curies. He blanked his photophone screen and watched the planet grow larger and clearer as Lulu reduced their speed. With her acute instinct for timing, she kept the ship on star-drive until it seemed that they would overshoot their target. Then at the last possible split-second, she cut out the light-energy converter, switched over to antigravity drive and swung into a tight orbit that perfectly set them up to rendezvous with Astropolis without a wasted iota of time or energy.

"Good job," Dawnboy complimented her. "I'm glad to see that ye have na lost yer touch."

"Not so loud," Lulu said. "If your skinflint father thinks I'm still in good shape, he might decide against having me overhauled when we dock; and I'm so looking forward to loading up with the latest equipment."

"Don't worry, I think we can afford to dress up our favorite gal in the latest electronic finery," Ranger said. "That is, if you don't smash us all to atoms against Astropolis at this speed."

"Don't be such a scaredy-cat," Lulu chided. But she quickly fired braking rockets as they orbited the planet and saw the satellite city come rushing toward them. "Everything's under control."

"Except my heart," Ranger said shakily. "Did you get landing clearance?"

"Affirmative."

"That was simple," Dawnboy remarked. "The Newtonians do na seem as anxious to guard their space as the Capitalians were."

"They have strong defenses, too," Ranger assured him. "They're just more subtle about it. They have spy-beams that can penetrate ships' hulls at a thousand light-years and can count every hair on the back of your hand. So they know exactly who we are and what we have aboard."

Dawnboy watched curiously as Lulu further reduced their speed until they seemed to be barely creeping around the rim of Astropolis. Everything in view was fascinating, but he was particularly interested in the sprawling shipyards with their work crews of vacuum-suited men and robot machines swarming over many different kinds of vessels in varying states of construction. Some of the newest passenger models were many times the *Gayheart*'s size, and their sleek lines made her look dumpy in comparison.

Ranger also studied the ships with professional interest. His attention was drawn to a large, older-model vessel with a gold cross emblazoned on her hull—or rather what was left of a gold cross. The ship seemed to have suffered serious damage and was in the process of being repaired. "Is that the old *Wherewithal?*" Ranger asked Lulu. "Wasn't she the missionary ship of the Church of Divine Capitalism?"

"Affirmative," Lulu answered. "According to a news report I monitored, she is in for repairs after getting shot up while trying to carry the Word to the heathens on Fabrica, in the Denebola system."

Dawnboy eyed his father skeptically. "Is there really such a religion as that?"

"You bet your grandfather's favorite tomahawk there is. Matter of fact, an old buddy of mine from the Space Rangers became a preacher in it, when he got tired of killing people and decided to uplift their souls instead. I've never gone into it very deeply myself. Basically its purpose is to help people overcome their guilt feelings about wanting to acquire large amounts of money—a far greater psychological problem than you might imagine. The Divine Capitalists believe that money and free enterprise are God's gift to the advancement of all intelligent beings. So they send missionaries all over the universe to try to win converts and promote the advantages of capitalist individualism over the collectivism of people like our IFIB and PHAP friends."

"And I suppose the church's headquarters are at Capitalia?" Dawnboy said. "None o' the people I saw there seemed to feel any guilt about being rich."

"No, surprisingly enough, the religion has never been very popular among Capitalians, although they contribute generously to its charitable work," Ranger replied. "I guess people who are busy making and spending money don't have much time or inclination to talk or think about it. But if you're interested, I think we have a tape of their bible: MONEY IS THE ROOT OF ALL GOOD."

"Maybe I'll look into it when I have time," Dawnboy said. "I reckon 'tis only logical, after people have worshiped money for so long, that they should eventually get around to making a formal religion o' it."

"Don't knock it," Ranger said. "At least the Divine Capitalists are peaceful, and their beliefs are no crazier than the IFIB's philosophy of Otherism, which teaches that everyone should live for the benefit of others instead of for himself."

Dawnboy couldn't argue with that.

3

RANGER AND DAWNBOY quickly cleared Customs after docking at the Astropolis space terminal. Then they found themselves surrounded by a small army of scientists excitedly firing questions about the exotic satellite they had sold to the Darwin Institute. Finally Ranger managed to distract the crowd by asking the spaceport officials to project some of his videotapes onto a large wallscreen. That diversion even captivated the attention of the aggressive news reporters from Newtonia's 3-D networks, so that Ranger and his son were able to slip away unnoticed.

They went first to the Goddard-Jarles Astromotive

Research and Development Company, which operated the largest spaceship yard in Astropolis. Ranger ordered a complete, no-expense-spared overhaul and servicing job for the *Gayheart,* to be done according to Lulu's specifications. When the two men prepared to leave the yard, Lulu came as close to tears as is possible for a sentimental biocomputer and naggingly urged them to take care of themselves. Ranger promised her they would be careful and would keep in touch with her via the microcommunications transmitters and receivers implanted in their throats and ears. Dawnboy was still not fully adjusted to those marvelous devices, which his father had had installed in him shortly after he joined the *Gayheart*'s crew. They were controlled by flexing the facial muscles, and Dawnboy occasionally found himself unintentionally broadcasting after a careless laugh or cough.

The first order of remaining business was to find convenient lodgings for their stay on Newtonia. Astropolis boasted many fine hotels, but both father and son were anxious to have firm ground under their feet again after having been so long in space. So they decided to travel down to Aristotleville, location of the Darwin Institute. Dawnboy would have liked to try out the new matter-transporter rapid-transit system. But Ranger, despite his belief in scientific progress, had an old-fashioned spaceman's reluctance to having his molecules separated, beamed through space and reassembled at their destination. Instead, he insisted they take a self-service antigravity taxi down to the planet's surface. Dawnboy enjoyed the view of the barren landscape made colorful here and there by transparent domed settlements and cultivated valleys, although that was about what he had expected from watching tapes of Newtonia.

Arriving at Aristotleville, they checked into the Armillary, a moderately priced hotel of the type favored by new arrivals who needed time to adjust to the startling devices that Newtonians always seemed intent upon springing on otherworlders. Ranger had stayed at the inn before and he liked its comfortable but mainly nonfunctional accommodations. The whole building was fully automated and efficiently serviced by cybernetic robots, and its rooms contained photophones for communications and playing videotapes. But it did not offer beds that rocked one to sleep and awakened one with a gentle nudge, tables that electronically analyzed a diner's dietary needs and served him accordingly, liquor containers that told a drinker when he had had enough and the other ultramodern conveniences that some Newtonian hostelries provided.

Among the more pleasing features, Dawnboy especially liked the natural-grass carpet and living wall-flowers, which gave the indoors a refreshingly outdoors atmosphere. He kicked off his shoes and savored the luxury of running his toes through the tickling grass blades, his wild Apache heart surging at the thought of curling up in a blanket on the floor, instead of suffering the civilized confinement of a bed. When he went into the sanitation chamber he noted that the soniclaver was similar to their shipboard facilities, as was the waste-disposal unit which used radiation to kill bacteria and recover usable chemicals. The unit itself was basically the same shape as every other toilet he had ever seen, including the crude privies on Apache Highlands. For some reason he found it reassuring to know there was at least one human function that not even advanced science could change very much.

After enjoying a light meal on their terrace that overlooked the hotel's lobby-courtyard, Ranger and Dawnboy got on with their task of provisioning the *Gayheart* for their treasure-hunting cruise. Ranger ordered tape catalogs from the leading developers of electronic probes, vac-suits, new weapons and other useful equipment for space explorers. Like greedy children, they indulged themselves in drooling over the most novel and attractive items, such as Galvanic Laboratories' individual force-field pack. The compact unit weighed only fifty pounds and was guaranteed to make its wearer indestructible by anything short of a small nuclear blast. Unfortunately the battery that powered it weighed two hundred pounds and carried a charge of only ten minutes' duration. That was about long enough, Ranger remarked, for a man to compose himself to meet death gracefully.

"But we may as well order a couple anyway," he decided. "They will be easy to carry in the weightlessness of space or in a vehicle when we enter a gravity field. Even if we never use them, it will be worth the investment to have them along as insurance."

While his father made selections and placed orders, Dawnboy fell to browsing haphazardly through the catalogs. Along with the listings of fascinating items for sale were bits of interesting background information about the Newtonian establishments. It seemed that just about any sort of crackpot activity that could conceivably be called a science was tolerated here because no one knew when an apparent charlatan might turn out to be an "Edison"—the local term for a gifted amateur experimenter who made discoveries that were overlooked by the professionals. Such an individual had been Dr. Epicurus Felixer, founder of Felixer's Fine Pharmaceutical Company, whose advertisement Dawnboy had read while still in space.

Felixer was a lovable old quack, who had become famous around the turn of the century by inventing panacillin, which for a while had seemed to be the long-sought-after universal cure for all human diseases. But eventually the axiom that research chemists invent remedies for sicknesses that haven't yet been found proved true. Suddenly the natural defensive antibodies of Felixer's patients combined with his wonder drug's ingredients to produce brand-new superbacteria that weren't curable by panacillin or by any other drug. That in a way was good for Felixer, who was guaranteed repeat business as he kept inventing new treatments for the new diseases his old treatments created. But deep down Felixer was a true scientific genius who had continued his search for the elusive cure-all even after he had become fabulously wealthy. After his death his successors had carried on his work, and now the Felixer Clinic's expanded facilities embraced nearly every known aspect of medical research. Dawnboy was particularly intrigued by the clinic's advanced work in human organ transplant research.

Just as he was starting to think about that, another item in the catalog caught his attention—an item that had been around a long time on Newtonia, though there was nothing quite like it on Space Highlands. It was called a Sonarvision device, and its makers claimed that it enabled the blind to "see" with sound waves. Worn as a headband, the device sent out ultrasonic waves that struck nearby objects, echoed back and became audible to the wearer. Like a bat navigating in darkness, the Sonarvision wearer could tell from the varying pitch of the echoes he received the direction, distance, shape and size of the objects around him. Dawnboy immediately thought of how helpful the device would be to Chief Chatto MacNair.

Chatto was a close friend and adviser to Dawnboy's grandfather, Laird Angus, and he had been Dawnboy's tutor in many things while he was growing up. As young men, Angus and Chatto had been deadly enemies in a war that had cost the life of Angus's favorite son. When Chatto had finally been defeated and captured, Angus had blinded him in an uncontrollable fit of vicious fury. In time they became friends. Chatto then forgave Angus and devoted the rest of his life to scholarly pursuits which he claimed were more satisfying than war. But, even so, the cruel act remained a shameful memory for Laird Angus.

Angus had offered to pay for an operation to restore Chatto's sight, if that was possible, and since leaving Apache Highlands, Dawnboy had learned that the delicate art of laser surgery could reattach and regenerate severed nerve endings. But Chatto had grumpily said that he had adjusted to his blindness and it wasn't worth the trouble of going off-world to have it cured. However, Dawnboy didn't think the old chief would refuse the Sonarvision if it were sent to him as a gift. He was also sure that in this case Laird Angus would gladly overlook the clan's laws against importing any product of advanced technology that might threaten their stubborn devotion to ancient tradition.

When Dawnboy mentioned his idea to his father, Ranger readily agreed and even suggested that he select gifts for all his family members and friends. They would make up a package and leave it at the spaceport's General Trans-shipment Department, where it would be picked up by the next commercial vessel bound for Apache Highlands's sector of the universe. That planet was far off the regular starlanes, but eventually a tramp star trader would deliver it there, as long as the freighting costs were prepaid.

"And that reminds me," Ranger said. "I should have checked with the local ISTA hall for the latest news when we landed at Astropolis. They could even be holding some mail for us." He cleared his photophone screen to make the call.

Independent star traders were by nature and by necessity a ruggedly competitive lot who didn't trust one another as far as they could jump on Jupiter. But experience had taught them the value of cooperative action in solving problems that were of concern to all of them. So the Independent Star Traders' Affiliation had been formed to promote ethical business practices and to help the members safeguard their lives, property and rights in an unpredictable and often dangerous universe. Although sometimes mistakenly referred to as a space-merchants' guild, the loose-knit ISTA had always been prevented from becoming a rigidly exclusive professional protective organization by the rebellious individualism and profit-hunger of its members.

The ISTA charter did contain a clause pledging all members to boycott any planet where a brother member had been overtaxed or otherwise treated unfairly by government authority. But the affiliation had no power to enforce such a boycott and in practice it usually wasn't long before a bold, greedy trader would risk a furtive run to the blacklisted world in hope of turning over a high profit and getting away with it. By such actions, commerce and communication were maintained between the far-flung inhabited worlds of the universe, in spite of the efforts of some of their governments. As always, the free market was of far greater benefit to those who did not understand it, distrusted it, hated it and wished they could have gotten rid of it, than to those who bore the expense and responsibility of operating it.

Ranger had never cared much for the dull professional discussions and social functions that the more gregarious ISTA members often staged in their halls. But he faithfully paid his dues for the other useful services provided by the affiliation, such as furnishing free meals and lodgings to members who were down on their luck—a condition to which he was no stranger. Primarily the halls served as clearinghouses for the latest information on astronavigational hazards, on what commodities were most in demand on various worlds, on dangerous political situations and on other data of special interest to star traders. Because a star trader's work kept him constantly on the move—frequently to remote areas beyond the reach of communications beams—the ISTA's mail-forwarding service was his only means of eventually receiving personal messages.

The automated cyber-clerk system at the ISTA hall replied to Ranger's query that it was indeed holding a videotape letter for the *Gayheart*. But it was addressed to First Mate Dawnboy MacCochise, from Apache Highlands.

"How can that be?" Dawnboy wondered. "There are na video recording facilities on the entire planet, let alone the clan's territory."

"Probably a wandering trader called there to do business in one of the cities," Ranger surmised. "And your family took advantage of the opportunity to send you a message."

"But what it must ha' cost them!" Dawnboy sighed. "When just to pay for sending a written letter all this distance is enough to make any true Highlander weep blood. Grandsire Angus must still be gnashing his teeth."

"Then don't you think you should find out if it was worth it?" Ranger smiled.

"Aye, sir!"

Dawnboy rushed into his adjoining room and opened another photophonic channel to receive the letter, while Ranger left his photophone on to record the latest ISTA bulletins.

Both men watched eagerly as the letter opened with a long shot of MacCochise Castle on the bank of River Glasgow, with the clan's rolling farmlands in the background. It was a clear day, and in the far distance could be seen towering Skull Mountain and other peaks of the southern Whipsaw Range, which brought back poignant memories to both father and son. The scene dissolved to the interior of the castle's main parlor—a large room that was luxuriously furnished, compared to the clan's general Spartan simplicity. Several of Dawnboy's kinspeople were crowded into the room around a sofa upon which perched Grand Laird Angus, looking excruciatingly self-conscious as he tried to tuck his knobby knees under his kilt.

Dawnboy's Aunt Eve sat beside the old laird with her daughter Kathleen, a saucy fourteen-year-old who had made Dawnboy's life miserable with her tag-along tomboyishness. Chief Chatto MacNair stood behind the sofa along with other high-ranking officials, including Father Jamieson, the castle chaplain. About the only important clan member not present was Ravenslayer Lochnagar, the leading warchief. He was an uncle two or three times removed to Dawnboy and an implacable enemy to Ranger.

"Hello, Son. We hope ye receive this soon," Eve said nervously, evidently responding to an off-camera cue to begin. "Ye've only been gone from us for a few weeks, but as we do na ken when we will ha' another chance to send ye a message, we want to do it while Captain d'Saudi's ship is here."

"D'Saudi? Is that old pirate still alive?" Ranger exclaimed. "I haven't seen or heard of him in years."

"*Shhhh!*" Dawnboy hissed, staring raptly at the screen.

Eve picked up haltingly and proceeded with the usual family news: they were all fine; they missed him a great deal, but they hoped he was enjoying his first space cruise. As always, Ranger was struck by the beautiful, raven-haired woman's resemblance to Gay, who had been her sister as well as his wife. He and Eve had had their differences, but during his last visit to Apache Highlands he was sure he had felt a strong attraction between them. He was grateful to her for the way she had reared Dawnboy as her own son, and perhaps if things had been different . . . He harshly told himself to stop thinking such useless thoughts.

When Eve was finished she turned the camera over to Kathleen and to Dawnboy's best friend, lanky Duncan Melrose of the Mescalero-Stuart Tribe. They chattered away about their activities and about the other youths and maids that Dawnboy had grown up with. Duncan had just taken his first scalp, in a clash with some Mongol-Sioux raiders, and he proudly showed off the gruesome trophy.

After them came Tessie, an ex-slave of the clan, whose freedom Ranger had helped purchase. The golden-haired beauty stood boldly before the camera, her former cringing servility replaced now by the firm confidence of a full-fledged clanswoman. After paying her fondest respects to Ranger and Dawnboy, she said that someone they knew had an announcement to make. Tessie stepped back into the crowd and led forth a blushing, tongue-tied young giant whom Ranger recognized as Charlie MacCarthy, a tough warrior who seemed to have met his match at last. Sheepishly Charlie blurted out that he and Tessie were betrothed and that he wished that Ranger and his son could attend their wedding.

Ranger smiled sympathetically as Tessie proudly led Charlie away, a possessive hand on his arm. He could well understand how Tessie's ample charms had captivated the easygoing Highlander, but Charlie was no doubt in for some radical changes in his carefree lifestyle now that he had acquired such a driving and socially ambitious wife.

Finally, Laird Angus was persuaded to say a few words, and once started he didn't seem to know how to stop. He rambled on about clan politics, the weather, the prospect of harvesting bumper crops this year, of how Teelget, Dawnboy's favorite pegasus, missed his young master, etc., etc. He said the clan continued to enjoy prosperity and peace with most of its neighbors, despite occasional rumblings from the Hebriden Kingdom to the south. From Londonburg, the capital, came rumors that old King Lawrence III (Larry the Louse, he was called contemptuously behind his back) was dying. His probable successor, young Prince Hector, was hungry for conquest and might prove to be a problem, but the clan's warriors needed exercise anyhow.

At that point Chief Chatto broke in with his usual gloom and doom prophesies about the clan's days being numbered. He predicted that soon the surrounding nations would become so large and industrially advanced that they could make short work of the clan's relatively few warriors, who would be armed with primitive weapons. "Mark me words, Prince Hector will be a bad enemy to us," Chatto announced ominously.

Angus called him a nincompoop for using the word "bad" with "enemy." "How can there be any such thing as a good enemy?" he demanded.

"A good enemy is one that loses his battles agin ye, as Larry the Louse did. A bad enemy is one that wins them," Chatto answered with the homespun wisdom that had made him famous.

The two old men started to renew their long-standing argument, but Eve pointed out that they were nearing the end of the tape. She quickly sent love and kisses to Dawnboy; then everyone present joined together in bidding him a fond farewell, to which even Ranger's name was kindly added. Just as the group shot started to fade, Kathleen pushed forward and called out: "Remember, Uncle Ranger, ye promised to take me wi' ye into space the next time ye come here!"

"Well, that was a nice letter," Ranger said, squeezing Dawnboy's shoulder. "You're lucky to have so many people who care about you."

"Aye," Dawnboy said soberly. "D'ye mind if I play the tape over again? I might ha' missed something."

"Go ahead. I want to study the ISTA bulletins anyway." Sensing that his son wanted to be alone for a while, Ranger stood up and left the room, discreetly closing the door between them.

Dawnboy thoughtfully reviewed the tape with feelings of homesickness mixed with the mild contempt of a semi-sophisticated young man who was rapidly outgrowing all that had previously been near and dear to him. Even Duncan's bragging about his prowess in battle seemed embarrassingly childish, although Dawnboy knew that just a short while ago he would have envied the kilt off him for being the first to count scalp-coup. Everything about the clan seemed so petty and backward, now that he had gotten a little education and had a glimpse of the universe's myriad other societies. Maybe his grandfather had been right in warning him that if he left Apache Highlands he might become so changed by his experiences in space that he could never fit back into the clan's culture, even if he wanted to.

That thought was most depressing, especially as he wasn't yet sure if he wanted to devote his life to space-faring, either. The suspicion that he might have lost his old life without gaining a new one filled him with a gloomy despair that dragged down his spirits for the rest of the day. Even at bedtime he was not much cheered up by the prospect of stretching out Apache-style on the grass floor, although it was to prove to be the best night's sleep he had had in months.

4

THE FOLLOWING MORNING Ranger and Dawnboy took a taxi through Aristotleville's narrow, hygienically clean streets to the Darwin Institute. As Dawnboy looked over the institute's huge, sprawling complex, he wondered how people managed to find their way around it.

In the institute's main reception hall, an electronic cyber-receptionist extended Dr. Clay's apologies for not being there to greet them in person. He was tied up in a conference and would not be free to see them for another hour. They could wait in his office, the machine's voice politely continued. Or, if they wished to look around the institute, an antigravity shuttlecart would be put at their disposal. Ranger accepted the offered transportation, then inquired about a specific part of the institute, causing Dawnboy to look sharply at him.

"We may as well get our personal business out of the way while we are here," Ranger explained. "Not that we can do anything, but ..." His voice trailed off awkwardly.

Dawnboy nodded understandingly as he gazed around at the vast array of science exhibits in the large room. "I would na ha' believed so much knowledge could be concentrated in one place."

"Yes, and it's constantly increasing," Ranger said. "Every time I come here I see something new. The institute's original purpose was the study of universal biology. But since nearly everything affects life in some way, the facilities have expanded to include nearly everything."

"I can well believe that," Dawnboy said, looking at the stark white walls that gave the room the uninviting appearance of a warehouse. "I canna say I much admire their taste in architecture, though."

"Well, scientists have never been too strong on artistic appreciation," Ranger replied. "But they'll probably get around to prettying up their surroundings when they can afford it. Up till now, it has taken nearly all of Newtonia's income and credit resources just to get them established here and import the materials they need for their work. Oh, this looks like our vehicle coming now."

A two-seater shuttlecart glided silently up to them and hovered a few inches from the floor. The two men stepped into the cart and the cyber-receptionist programmed it to take them to the destination Ranger had requested.

The cart carried them swiftly and smoothly across the room and down a long hallway, its electronic guidance system steering it around other vehicles and pedestrians. The interior of the institute was even more confusing than the impression Dawnboy had gotten from its exterior. After they had turned several corners and dropped down to a lower level, even Ranger admitted that he was hopelessly lost. Dawnboy decided to leave the driving to the cart and stared curiously at the countless human and other beings they moved past. Having spent most of his life on an all-human world, it had taken him awhile to adjust to the shocking appearances of some aliens. Now he felt that he was entirely unprejudiced and tolerant of other intelligent species, although it still bothered him to see them in positions superior to humans.

At last the cart halted before a closed door deep inside the institute's main building. At Ranger's spoken command, the door slid open and the cart took them into a long room filled with ranks of electronic equipment. Upon some of the machines sat transparent, liquid-filled tanks containing wrinkled grayish objects. Wires connected the tanks to the machines, which hummed busily as they went about their work.

The cart stopped before one of the tanks and settled to the floor. Ranger and Dawnboy dismounted from the cart and peered uneasily at the thing in the tank. It looked no different than the brain of any human or similar creature. But it was what they had come to see. It was the last living remnant of Gayheart MacCochise Farstar, Dawnboy's mother.

Dawnboy stared at the brain, trying to find some feeling of kinship toward it within himself. But he felt nothing. It was just a lump of protoplasm to him, with no special identity or personality. His mother was only a vague memory, so much like his Aunt Eve that the two women had become inseparably mingled in his mind. He supposed he loved his mother in the same way that he loved Aunt Eve, though that would have been hard to prove from the way he felt just then.

But that was not important to the goal he had set for himself, when his father first told him that only his mother's body had been killed in the accident that had destroyed their ship. He had solemnly vowed then that he would do all he could to help restore his mother to full life, regardless of what the task might cost him. That was the sort of romantic gesture any emotional adolescent boy might make and then soon forget, but a brave of Apache Highlands does not commit himself to such a pledge lightly.

Ever since her accident, Gayheart's brain had been kept alive and in good health by the institute's scientists. To prevent tissue atrophy, the organ was employed in simple computer work that required only the subconscious mind. It was never stimulated to full consciousness, as was Lulu's brain. The scientists feared that awareness of her helpless condition might inflict an unendurable emotional trauma on someone as youthful and passionately in love with life as Gayheart had been. So Ranger had made the anguished decision to have the essence of his wife held in abeyance here until it could, hopefully, be provided with a new body by a surgical team with the knowledge and skill to make a successful brain transplant.

Dawnboy glanced at his father and was shocked by Ranger's pale, tight-lipped expression as he stared at the electronic screens that registered the organ's brain waves and other life signs. Until that moment, Dawnboy had not guessed what a great emotional strain it must be for his father to be so close to all that was left of the woman he had loved so deeply. Obviously he still loved her and had never stopped blaming himself for her present condition.

Like Dawnboy, Ranger had sworn to do all he could to help give Gay a new life, but he held few illusions that the resurrection would benefit him personally. He realized that what Gay had gone through might have altered her personality so drastically that she would no longer care for those who had once been dear to her. So Ranger's effort to provide her with a new body was merely the last act of love that a considerate husband could perform for the memory of a cherished wife.

Here was an example of marital devotion that Dawnboy was still too young to appreciate fully. But he did admire his father for clinging to so fragile an ideal and he wished he could do something to relieve Ranger's inner turmoil.

"Uh, maybe we ought to come back some other time, Dad," Dawnboy said, trying to draw Ranger away from the encased brain.

Ranger shook off his hand. "It's all right. I'm just . . ."

He turned sharply at the sound of approaching footsteps behind them. Dawnboy followed his gaze and saw a chubby, swarthy-skinned man of late middle age coming toward them.

"Captain Farstar?" the man inquired. "I just learned of your arrival from the receptionist. I'm Dr. Mark Hoosier, a selfologist with the Felixer Clinic's organ-transplant division. Recently I've been doing research work on these brains and . . ." He broke off and stared in surprise at the life-signs screens above Gayheart's tank. "Now whatever could be causing that?"

Ranger and Dawnboy looked up and saw that the previously rhythmic light lines across the screens were now fluctuating wildly.

"It's as if the brain is being given powerful stimuli to test its receptivity," Dr. Hoosier mused, coming forward to inspect the dials on the panel of the brain's life-support system. "No, everything is normal here, and in its present unconscious state . . ."

"Please stop referring to *her* as it." Ranger reacted sharply.

"Oh, I'm sorry." The doctor flashed an embarrassed smile, then resumed studying the screens. "It's almost as if she is aware that . . ." He peered speculatively at the two visitors. "No, that's impossible! Still, I wonder . . . Would you two mind stepping back a few paces? Just far enough to be outside of her field of perception. There, that's fine."

As Ranger and Dawnboy moved away from the brain case, Dr. Hoosier watched the screens' lines return to their normal even rhythms. "Fascinating!" Hoosier adjusted a dial. "Now move forward again, please."

"No!" Ranger snapped. His face had turned dead white and he was trembling. "Obviously she somehow knows who we are, even if you don't think that's possible. I'm not going to allow you to agitate her further just to satisfy your curiosity."

"Very well," Hoosier said apologetically. "Please forgive my lack of consideration. I don't suppose experimentation along these lines would yield much new data anyway."

"Good. Then let's go someplace where we can talk," Ranger suggested.

Hoosier nodded and turned away from them. "Come into the office that I am using while I'm here. I don't have all of my files with me, but I think I can explain your wife's case pretty well."

The scientist led the way to an adjoining small room

that was sparsely furnished with a desk, some chairs and two photophone wallscreens. Hoosier seated his guests before the desk, then offered a box of smokeless cigars to Ranger, who politely declined. Hoosier stuck a cigar between his teeth and puffed it to ignition as he lounged in his desk chair. A cherubic smile made his plump face look even rounder.

"I'm very glad to meet you, gentlemen," Hoosier said, after Ranger had introduced him to Dawnboy. "We can learn a great deal by studying the brains here, but talking with their relatives and friends helps, too."

"I've heard that there have been some important new discoveries made in organ-transplant research," Ranger said, coming directly to the point. "Is it possible for you to place my wife's brain in another body now?"

"Of course that's possible," Hoosier replied casually. "We've done it several times. The only problem now is to learn how to do it successfully."

"Ye mean that yer patients ha' na survived the operation?" Dawnboy asked.

"Some of them have survived, after a fashion." Hoosier leaned back and savored his cigar. "The practice of transferring organs from one body to another has a long, colorful history. Some scholars even think it dates back to ancient Earth before the Space Age. But so few records of that period have survived that we can't be sure. Probably the practice is one of the so-called lost arts that have been discovered and rediscovered by many different cultures, only to be forgotten when their civilizations were destroyed by wars or other catastrophes."

"Never mind ancient history," Ranger said impatiently. "Tell us what today's scientists know about it."

Dr. Hoosier's placid smile only became more relaxed in response to Ranger's urgent tone. "I'm coming to that. But don't underestimate the importance of studying the history of medicine. It has taught us many things and saved much time and energy, not to mention several lives that probably would have been lost if we had had to learn everything from direct experience. That was why I spent most of last night searching through the artificial satellite you just sold to the institute. I was hoping—actually it was wishful thinking—that the Vanished Ones had possessed medical knowledge far superior to ours and that they had left some records of it in the satellite."

"Did ye find anything?" asked Dawnboy, pleasantly excited by the thought that his work with Ranger might help his mother in a totally unexpected way.

"Not yet, I'm afraid," Dr. Hoosier replied.

"Well, you never know what might turn up in that thing," Ranger said hopefully, although he seriously doubted Hoosier would make such a lucky find. "But aside from that, what are the chances that you will be able to do anything for my wife in the near future?"

The doctor took his cigar out of his mouth and frowned at it. "How much do you actually know about our work, Captain Farstar? Do you know what a selfologist does?"

Ranger shrugged disinterestedly. "I always thought that was just a fancy title for a psychologist."

Hoosier smiled at his cigar and stuck it back in his mouth. "Ah, yes, psychology, from psyche, an ancient Greek word meaning soul. Did you know that in some societies we are actually called soul healers or spirit doctors? I think those are much more straightforward terms, though not as impressive as psychologist or psychoanalyst. But it really doesn't make much difference what you call those of us who study and try to treat the metaphysical essence—psyche, soul, self, personality or whatever it is that makes an intelligent being more than just an animated mass of atoms. It is all steeped in so much mysticism that it's hard to tell where faith leaves off and science begins."

Ranger shifted uneasily in his chair. "You make it sound like witch doctoring."

"How very astute of you!" Hoosier laughed. "As a matter of fact, we have learned a great deal from the study of primitive folk medicine. Our backwoods medical colleagues may lack our modern instruments and wonder drugs, but they make up for it by becoming shrewd judges of character. Many of them have developed their intuitive understanding of the soul's problems to a fine art that would be the envy of any modern selfologist. When it comes to performing a brain transplant, I would rather be assisted by an ignorant but sensitive witch doctor than by a brilliant but unimaginative scientist."

"Ye canna really mean that," Dawnboy scoffed. Back on Apache Highlands he had regarded the village priests and sorcerers with fear-inspired reverence. But now that he was acquiring a scientific education in his father's starship, he did not like to be reminded of his benighted childhood.

"I never meant anything more seriously in my life," the selfologist assured him. "Here, let me show you something."

Dr. Hoosier touched a button on his desk to activate one of the viewscreens on the wall. "When we started performing the operation on intelligent beings, we learned that transplants between identical twins worked best. As you can imagine, cases are very rare in which one twin will suffer total brain damage and the other total body destruction. But in a universe of several thousand billion more or less rational creatures, even such freakish events as that happen frequently enough to provide us with experimental specimens."

On the screen a creature appeared that seemed to be a combination of a human and a wolf. "I'm sure you recognize her as a young female Lycanoid of Wereworld, in the Lupus Constellation. She was originally twin sisters, and our first intelligent patient to survive a brain-transplant operation. Her recovery seemed to be so successful that she was allowed to go home after eight months of postoperative therapy. Three months later she committed suicide."

Dr. Hoosier changed the scene to show a human boy about twelve years old. He sat motionless in a chair, staring blankly at the camera. "We were more cautious with this patient. We kept him under treatment for nearly two years after his operation, until he too seemed to have made a healthy adjustment to his new condition. But shortly after his discharge from the clinic, he started displaying symptoms of schizophrenic withdrawal from reality. He soon lapsed into a catatonic trance and so far has not responded to any treatment."

The selfologist blanked his viewscreen. "I could show you several other examples, but they are all basically the same. Physically and mentally our patients seem to come through the operation in fine shape. But then they are possessed by self-destructive drives that neither they nor we can do anything about. Not one of them has been able to live a normal life without constant supervision and protection."

Ranger tore his gaze away from the wallscreen and tried to erase the sickening image of the boy's face from his mind. A few minutes ago he had been on the verge of calling Hoosier a fake and demanding that another doctor be put in charge of Gay's case. But peering into the boy's glassy eyes, so utterly empty of all emotion except hopeless resignation to his fate, had filled Ranger with a terrible dread. He knew he could never risk having Gay end up like that.

Dawnboy cleared his throat and asked in a subdued voice: "What makes them like that? I mean, is there na anything ye can do to help them?"

Dr. Hoosier sadly shook his head. "A witch doctor would explain it by saying that the body is still inhabited by its original soul, which resents being taken over by the new brain, which presumably brings its own soul along when it moves in. Two souls cannot peacefully occupy the same individual simultaneously, so they must constantly battle one another for dominance. The struggle causes so much inner agony that the patient is driven to end it with death or withdrawal from consciousness."

"Cut out that mumbo jumbo about souls," Ranger ordered. "There must be a scientific explanation for what has happened to those patients. You don't have that problem when you transplant other organs, do you?"

"No," Hoosier answered. "We can swap two people's hearts, livers, arms, legs, even eyes without much difficulty. But the brain is something special. It is the most important part of the nervous system, which extends throughout the entire body. Impressed upon that system are all the memories, feelings and individual traits that make up an intelligent being's self or personality or soul or whatever we agree to call it. So when we perform a brain transplant, we force two partial personalities to occupy one complete nervous system. A situation like that is bound to cause violent clashes."

"That does na sound much different from the witch-doctor theory about two souls in one body," Dawnboy remarked.

"I know, but it's the best theory I've been able to come up with," Hoosier said defensively. "It seems to be supported by the fact that we never have any of those problems when we attach a disembodied brain to a computer or any other machine."

Ranger got out of his chair and started to prowl restlessly about the office. Three paces brought him to the nearest wall, and he spun around abruptly, feeling irritated and confined by the smallness of the room. But he knew that was not the real cause of his frustration.

"All right, so you think you know the cause of the trouble. Then why aren't you trying to do something about it?" Ranger demanded of Dr. Hoosier.

"I am," the selfologist replied patiently. "I have been experimenting with a new method of postoperative treatment to help patients survive the trauma of brain transplants. A telepathic Brainsponge puts me in mental contact with the patient and I explore the connections between the brain and the body's remaining nervous systems. If I can get the patient's conscious mind to recognize where the trouble originates, then he may be able to overcome it. So far I've had some promising results, but it will be a long time before I can hope to perfect the method."

"How long?" Ranger asked.

Hoosier thrust his cigar butt into an ashtray and shrugged his round shoulders. "How should I know? Years, decades, centuries—who can say? I am trying to find my way through unexplored territory. There's no telling how many times I might become lost and have to start over again."

"Even if ye do make yer method work, it will na help my mother," Dawnboy said gloomily. "She has no twin sister to provide her with a new body."

"We are working on that, too," Hoosier said. "Eventually we hope to be able to make successful brain transplants between unrelated individuals. But that also will require much time and experimentation." He held out his open hands and pouted like a child begging for candy. "Time, that's what I need more than anything else! Find a way to add more hours to my days, Captain Farstar, and I promise I'll have your wife whole and healthy again."

Ranger smiled at the harried scientist. "Time is important to all of us," he said gently. "So we won't take up any more of yours, Doctor. I just want to spend a few moments alone with my wife before we leave, if you'll excuse me."

"Of course," Hoosier said with an answering smile. "It's been a pleasure meeting you, Captain." He stared thoughtfully after the tall spaceman as he left the office.

Dawnboy made no effort to join his father. He had seen all he wanted to see of his mother for one visit. He remained in his chair and peered narrowly at Dr. Hoosier. "I didna understand most o' yer talk about the soul and the self and whatnot. But just between the two o' us—d'ye believe any o' it yerself?"

"I believe in *everything*," the selfologist replied sincerely. "That is a special privilege we physicians enjoy, because medicine is as much an art as a science. And I think I just learned the answer to a question that theologians and other students of the soul have debated for ages."

"What's that?" Dawnboy asked.

"Whether or not the soul is divisible. Unless I miss my guess, a sizable piece of your father's soul has become permanently attached to your mother's."

Dawnboy did not know what to make of that, so he said nothing.

5

DR. MONTEZUMA CLAY was waiting for Ranger and Dawnboy when they returned to the Darwin Institute's reception hall. Dawnboy could tell that his father was still morosely preoccupied with thoughts about Gayheart, but Ranger managed to put on a cheerful smile for Dr. Clay's benefit. When the introductions were made, Dawnboy was impressed by the sapientsaur's strong handshake. There was nothing slimy or repulsive about him, despite his reptilian appearance.

"From Apache Highlands, are you?" Dr. Clay asked with what Dawnboy took to be a twinkle in his unblinking eyes. "Then you must be accustomed to seeing creatures like me crawl out from under rocks."

"Oh, no, sir," Dawnboy said uneasily. "Matter o' fact, some of my best . . . Uh, that is . . ."

Ranger came to his rescue with a laugh. "Actually, his favorite mount at home is a pegasus. That's sort of a snake with wings. I don't believe you have anything like that on Cretacia."

"No, but I have examined preserved specimens," Dr.

Clay said. "Not much family resemblance between them and my species, I'm happy to say."

"Cretacia seems a fascinating place, from what I've heard tell o' it," Dawnboy said. "Is it true that yer pet teddysaurs there sometimes become so overly affectionate that they gobble up their masters?"

"I'm afraid that's just an old spaceman's tale," Dr. Clay replied. "Teddysaurs are actually docile vegetarians about the size of Earth elephants. They were domesticated as draft animals but they became pretty useless after our Industrial Age. For pets, most of us prefer sanswits. They are quite gentle and loving, although so stupid and ugly that . . . Oh, pardon me!" It was his turn to look embarrassed, to Dawnboy's puzzlement.

"Sanswits are humanoids who look a lot like us," Ranger explained, "but they are less intelligent than chimpanzees."

"Oh," Dawnboy said thoughtfully.

"Well, now that we've done our bit to promote good interspecies relations," Dr. Clay said, "I suppose you are curious to hear what we've learned about your artificial satellite. So let's go talk to some of the people who have been working on it."

Ranger and Dawnboy eagerly followed the sapient-saur as he moved swiftly across the room to the nearest wall. But Ranger hesitated when he noticed they were approaching a boxlike metallic structure festooned with coils of electronic wiring, dials and switches. "I, uh, don't suppose there is some other way we can get there?" Ranger asked uneasily.

"We could take a shuttlecart," Dr. Clay answered. "But the matter-transporter is much quicker and it is perfectly safe."

"Yer na afraid o' it, are ye, Dad?" Dawnboy taunted. "If ye are, I'll go first."

"No, it's just that . . ." Ranger shrugged helplessly. "Well, I guess I'll have to try it sometime. But I can't get over my old starship jockey's prejudice for having a solid vehicle around me."

"Of course, that's a much more natural way to travel," Dr. Clay said dryly. "But we can't fight progress. Here, let me show you how simple it is." He adjusted a couple of dials, threw a switch and stepped into the chamber. His body started to glow brightly, then quickly faded from view.

"Well, if he can do it, I guess we can," Ranger said, taking a deep breath to steady his nerves. He and Dawnboy stepped into the chamber together.

Dawnboy, for all of his scientific curiosity and adventuresome spirit, shared his father's misgivings about using the transporter. What if something went wrong and their molecules became hopelessly scrambled? He knew the machine had been highly developed and was used commercially for short trips, but that was not much comfort when *his* safety was involved with its operation. His knees trembled as he braced himself for whatever sensation the process might cause. But a moment later he was stepping forward into another room, feeling no differently than if he had passed through an ordinary doorway.

"See—nothing to it," Dr. Clay said, standing before them.

Dawnboy glanced at his father, who grinned sheepishly as he looked them both over to make sure everything was as it should be. "Easiest trip I ever took," Dawnboy said casually. "We should buy one o' these things for the *Gayheart*."

Ranger grunted noncommittally and looked around. They were in a large room nearly half-filled with computer banks and other electronic equipment. One entire wall was a window that looked out on the airless world beyond the city's dome. About five hundred meters away the satellite rested on a cradle of steel girders. Several figures climbed over the curved shell in vacsuits and magnetic boots, while others moved in and out of an open hatchway.

"Here are some people I want you to meet," Dr. Clay said, leading them toward an automatic serving table where two figures sat. One was a bald human male who looked a lot like an aging bullfrog. The other was younger and wore a flower-petal-shaped hairstyle that Dawnboy recognized as a traditional rank-symbol of a female marsupial humanoid from New Aussieland. She turned to the newcomers with a wide smile that Dawnboy found most charming, in spite of the severe flatness of her face and figure, which were considered signs of great feminine beauty among her own species.

"Well, Falla, I'm glad you managed to drag Wage away from his labors long enough for a citroffee break," Dr. Clay said.

"Yes, but don't keep him too long or he'll start to twitch with anxiety," the New Aussielander said, nodding fondly at her companion.

Dr. Clay ordered the table to serve cups of citroffee to Ranger and Dawnboy, and then began the introductions. Dawnboy accepted his cup eagerly. He had developed a liking for the tangy, stimulating brew from beans native to Nueva Brasil.

"This is Dr. Falla Thurban, our best xenoarchaeologist," Dr. Clay introduced the female. "And this is Dr. Wage Gitlow, the new head luxiumwright. I think you knew his predecessor, Tevo Landing."

"Of course," Ranger said. "What's become of Dr. Landing? Did he retire?"

"No, he died," Dr. Gitlow said flatly. "High time, too. The stubborn old coot never would have stepped down and given somebody else a crack at his job."

"You're lucky to have caught him in one of his sweeter moods," Dr. Thurban informed Ranger.

"Excuse me, sir," Dawnboy said. "But I thought the study o' luxium was called luxiumology."

"It is officially," Gitlow said. "But the field has several specialists—luxiumradiologists, luxiumthermologists, luxiumchronologists and what-have-you. Basically the discovery of luxium was to the space age what the invention of the wheel was to ancient man. We use it to power star-drive engines, matter-transporters and for countless other things requiring tremendous amounts of energy. So those of us who are primarily concerned with the practical application of luxium have borrowed our title from the old-time wheelwrights."

"Oh, I see," Dawnboy said.

Ranger looked out at the satellite. "I hope you've managed to learn more about that thing than I did. I was able to figure out how to turn a few basic switches on and off without blowing the whole thing up, but that was all."

"We haven't gotten much further than that so far ourselves," Dr. Thurban said. "If this really is an artifact of the Vanished Ones, it doesn't appear that we are going to learn much about them from it. It was easy to get a rough idea of their language by computer analysis, but all of the records aboard seem to be strictly technical in nature. They tell us exactly how the satellite functioned, but that's about all." She sighed sadly. "It's very frustrating to get just a teasing taste of something we've hungered after for so long."

"Maybe some of the other specialists will uncover some valuable clues," Dr. Clay said hopefully. "Don't give up hope so soon."

"Well, I doubt if it holds much more interest to me, anyway," Dr. Gitlow said. "Samples of the fuel from it that I've examined are just ordinary, run-of-the-cyclotron luxium 437. That's a long way from being the hyper-charged stuff I had hoped to find. But I still think such an element exists in natural objects like the comet Wonderwhat, if we could just find a way to get hold of it."

"Wonderwhat?" Dawnboy exclaimed. "But that's what we . . ." He broke off with a guilty look at his father.

"That's all right," Ranger said. "We don't have to keep it secret that we're planning to go searching for the treasure of the *Jealousy,* since everybody thinks only crazy people do that anyway."

"Don't tell me you're going chasing after that old cosmic will-o'-the-wisp," Dr. Clay laughed. "I thought you had better sense."

"You seriously intend to try to find the treasure

ship?" Dr. Gitlow asked, squinting intently at Ranger. "Just the other day I spoke to someone who had the same plan. I asked her permission to install some analyzing and recording equipment on her ship in order to gather data about the comet. But she turned me down. Was quite snooty about it, in fact."

"Really? Who is she?" Ranger asked with interest.

"Archguardess Eythine dara Gildenfang, widow of the Vampirian nobleman who was lost on a similar expedition to Wonderwhat. I suppose you know about him?"

"Yes, I remember the news he made when he set out from here two years ago," Ranger replied. "But when nothing further was heard from him, I assumed he had disappeared like so many others who searched for the *Jealousy*."

"That was the generally held opinion," Gitlow said. "But about six months ago a sub-ether message torpedo arrived here from Archguard dara Gildenfang, addressed to his wife. Its message tapes were programmed to self-destruct if tampered with by anything but her voice speaking secret code words that only she and her husband knew. Our authorities passed the tapes on to her, and she claimed they reveal that her husband actually found the treasure ship. But before he could board it, he was attacked by a pirate ship. In the following fight he destroyed the pirate, but his own vessel was badly damaged and he was mortally wounded. He had just enough time and enough strength left to send off a message to his wife."

"Which told her how to find and recover the treasure?" Dawnboy guessed.

"So she says. Evidently she has faith in her dead husband's words, because she has gone to a lot of expense to outfit another ship to chase after the *Jealousy*."

"I would certainly like to talk to her about it," Ranger said. "If she hasn't blasted off yet."

"I think she's still here," Dr. Gitlow said. "She was staying at the Soyuz Hotel in Astropolis with her young stepdaughter. But she is most secretive about her late husband's message. That's understandable, considering how many other treasure hunters are willing to do anything for a bit of information about the *Jealousy*."

"Well, it won't cost me anything to ask her," Ranger said. "Thanks for telling us about her."

"Don't mention it. Frankly, I think the whole lost-treasure story is poppycock. Even if the treasure really exists, it would be insignificant compared to some reliable data about the comet itself. That reminds me, would *you* like to aid science by taking my equipment along on your search for Wonderwhat?"

"I don't mind," Ranger replied. "As long as the apparatus doesn't require too much space or take very long to install."

Dawnboy placed his cup on the table for a citroffee refill and took a hot sweet roll from the food compartment. "What makes Wonderwhat seem so valuable to ye, Dr. Gitlow?" he asked. "I ha' na learned much about it yet, except that its wildly erratic, unpredictable course makes it difficult to approach."

Dr. Gitlow peered longingly out at the satellite, and was about to rise. But Dawnboy's question about one of his favorite topics of discussion caused him to settle back into his chair. "The comet's unusual behavior is precisely what intrigues me," he answered. "I strongly suspect that whatever is influencing Wonderwhat's course might contain the key to the most important discovery since the downfall of the Paleoscientific Age."

Dr. Thurban smiled at Dawnboy's puzzled expression. "That is his personal term for Old Earth's twentieth century A.D.," she explained. "Which he thinks of as a time of degenerate backsliding for science."

Dr. Gitlow glared aggressively at her. "What else can you call a period of devastating wars, brutal totalitarian regimes, massive enslavement, insane ideologies, the virtual substitution of nature worship for industrial progress and even attempts to wipe out the differences between the sexes—all done in the holy name of science?" he demanded.

Dr. Clay looked at Ranger and Dawnboy with amusement showing in his pink-tinted scales. "Dr. Gitlow keeps us on our toes with his unconventional opinions," he said. "He is our resident maverick from the USA."

"The Unified Systems o' Aquila?" Dawnboy asked interestedly. "Is that na where Lulu is from, Dad?"

"Yes, she was originally from New Tokyo, the second planet in the Altair system," Ranger answered.

"Nearly a neighbor. I'm from Altair's third planet, New New America," Dr. Gitlow said. "But the real problem with the Paleoscientific Age . . ."

"Please, can't you find something more relevant to discuss?" Dr. Thurban asked in a bored voice. "I know you are proud of your vast knowledge of the history of science, but I'm sure our guests aren't eager to hear a lecture about it just now." Then she smiled and patted Gitlow's hand to take the sting out of her rebuke.

The luxiumwright's stern expression melted into a shy smile at her touch. "I guess I do tend to be a bore at times," he confessed. "Sorry about that."

"But a lovable bore," Dr. Clay said kindly. "Excuse me; my office is calling me."

Dawnboy noticed for the first time the tiny lump of an earphone implanted under the skin below the sapientsaur's left auditory opening. Dr. Clay cocked his head to the left and listened attentively for a few moments, then said:

"All right. Transfer the call to the photophone in here, please." He looked at Ranger with his facial scales expressing something between amusement and dismay. "It's for you, Captain Farstar. The technicians overhauling your ship have a problem and they couldn't reach you through your own earphone because Astropolis is orbiting on the planet's opposite side. It seems that your biocomputer has locked their foreman in a compartment and is threatening to shut off his oxygen supply."

6

"WHAT?" RANGER CRIED, nearly leaping out of his chair.

"But that's impossible!" Dawnboy protested. "Lulu would na harm anyone."

"Not only wouldn't, but couldn't, according to the first law of conditioning biocomputers and robots," Dr. Thurban said. "They are strictly forbidden to take aggressive action against any intelligent being, unless commanded to do so by their human superiors. Isn't that right, Captain?"

"That's the law," Ranger agreed. "But Lulu was never one to let even the fear of deactivation prevent her from doing something if she is convinced it's right. So this must really be . . . Well, I'll soon find out what she's up to."

He rose and moved swiftly over to where the photophone screen was suddenly activated among the banks of electronic equipment. Dawnboy and the others followed close behind.

The screen brightened with the furious visage of a man who identified himself as a vice-president of the Goddard-Jarles spaceship yards. Before Ranger could speak, the executive broke into an angry tirade about a crazy biocomputer that was endangering human lives. Ranger interrupted him with a demand to be put in contact with Lulu immediately. The vice-president said he would be delighted to do that and transferred the call to the interior of the *Gayheart*'s bridge, where everything appeared to be in order.

"Lulu, are you there?" Ranger inquired anxiously.

"Of course I'm here," Lulu's voice replied crossly. "Where else would I be?"

"What the devil is going on up there?" Ranger demanded. "Did you really lock up one of the technicians?"

"Yes, here he is." Lulu changed the scene to show them a heavyset man in a blue coverall lying motionless on the Sick Bay examining table.

"Oh, my God!" Ranger gasped. "He isn't dead, is he?"

"Just dead drunk. I told him to have a drink of medicinal brandy to calm his nerves and he polished off the entire bottle."

"Why did ye lock him up?" Dawnboy asked. "Tell us what's wrong, Lulu. We want to help ye."

"Then tell these glorified screwdriver pushers to have some respect for my privacy," Lulu said, with a girlish pout in her voice.

"Your *what?*" Ranger and Dawnboy exclaimed in amazement.

"You know that I'll stand for just about anything that you think is good for the ship," Lulu said. "But I draw the line at having another brain plugged into the computer banks with me, prying into my innermost thoughts and feelings. It's ... it's an unnatural relationship!"

Ranger's features suddenly relaxed. "Oh, now I understand what's bothering you. You don't want the new cerebral linkage assembly that I ordered installed. That's nothing to worry about. I only had it put in as a possible emergency device, should we ever have a problem that requires the wisdom of two or more brains. But we will probably never use it."

"Honestly?" Lulu asked. "You weren't planning to couple me with another brain against my will?"

"Of course not. It would be an unnecessary expense for the ordinary operation of the ship. Besides, it takes all of my patience just to put up with you. Now cut out that foolishness and let those people get on with their work."

"Well, all right, if you say so," Lulu said reluctantly. "But I warn you, if you ever bring another brain aboard this ship except for an emergency, I'm walking out."

"Now that's something I'd like to see," Dawnboy laughed.

"Sorry I didn't think of explaining this to you before we left you there," Ranger said soothingly to Lulu.

"And I'm sorry I made such a fuss about it," Lulu said. "Go on and enjoy the rest of your stay on Newtonia. I won't bother you again."

"Everything is going to be fine," Ranger assured her. "But try to sober that guy up before his friends find him and decide to join the party." He switched his transmission back to the angry vice-president and reported that the trouble with Lulu had been settled. Then he signed off and apologized to the scientists for bothering them with his personal problems.

"No bother at all," Dr. Clay said graciously. "I am sure that we all enjoyed having a look at your ship. And I must say that life with Lulu certainly seems ... interesting."

"Never a dull moment," Dawnboy assured him.

They all returned to their seats, and Dawnboy looked expectantly at Dr. Gitlow. "Ye were going to tell me about Wonderwhat's scientific value," he prompted.

"Oh, yes." Gitlow cast another longing glance at the satellite outside, then settled down with a patient sigh. Like most real professionals, he could never resist an opportunity to talk about his work. "I don't know if you have enough physics to understand a full technical explanation, so I'll try to keep it confined to basics. To begin with, you know how a starship's light-energy converter works, don't you?"

Dawnboy nodded, eager to show off his knowledge. "Thousands o' tiny photonic cells on the ship's hull collect starlight, which is fed into the luxium reactor via laser beams. The reactor has already split highly refined luxium fuel into subatomic particles. The light striking those particles converts them to anti-matter in the combustion chamber, which is supplied with an equal amount o' matter from the other side o' the reactor. The matter and anti-matter particles totally annihilate each other, releasing vast amounts o' energy."

"Which provides the thrust that enables starships to travel at many times the speed of light," Dr. Gitlow said, finishing Dawnboy's description of the process. "It is basically a very simple operation, which we use in a slightly more complicated form to power matter-transporters."

"I still do na understand how *that* works," Dawnboy said.

"Neither do I," Ranger admitted.

Dr. Gitlow muttered something uncomplimentary about the ignorance of laymen and explained: "In matter-transportation the converting of light and luxium into thrust power is the same. But in addition to that, the atoms of the person or object to be transported are transformed into argon, an inert gas. That's why people who travel by matter-transportation are often called Argonauts, in case you have ever wondered about that. Then luxium-generated neutrinos are combined with the argon's subatomic particles to produce superneutrinos, or sutrinos as we call them. Just as neutrinos can travel unhindered through any solid object, sutrinos can pass unaffected through *anything*, even time. Thus the transported sutrinos arrive instantaneously at their destination, where the process is reversed to restore the traveler to his original composition."

Dawnboy stared at Gitlow in amazement. "Ye make it sound so simple!"

Dr. Thurban handed a fresh cup of citroffee to Gitlow and said, "You didn't explain how all of that information relates to Wonderwhat, Wage."

Gitlow gestured impatiently with his cup, splashing some of the hot liquid onto his hand. "I was getting to that," he claimed, pressing his hand down on the porous tabletop, which automatically absorbed the spilled citroffee. "Because of Wonderwhat's extraordinary peculiarities, I have concluded that the head of the comet must be composed of some element that is far more powerful than luxium. I have a personal theory—mostly guesswork, actually—that the element consists of matter and anti-matter particles arranged in such a way that they do not entirely annihilate one another. Instead, the partial destruction of electrons and positrons creates the power that drives the comet through space, enabling it to pick up new particles to replace the annihilated ones. That would explain why Wonderwhat has always been reported to be the same size every time it has been sighted over the centuries."

"That's right," Ranger said, prodding his memory. "Didn't you publish a tape, several years ago, in which you speculated that Wonderwhat could have been created by a collision between a matter star and an anti-matter star? If that was what actually happened, it would prove the old theory that our universe co-exists with a similar universe made up of anti-matter."

Gitlow beamed happily at Ranger, convinced that anyone with the good sense to have studied his science tapes could not be all bad. "Exactly! That is why I want to gather more data on the comet. If we can discover how its energy source functions, we may be able to duplicate it and use it to greatly extend the range of our matter-transporters. We may even be able to find a way to travel safely through VIP's and learn if an anti-matter universe does indeed exist on the other side. Wonderwhat has been observed to enter and emerge from VIP's unharmed, so it must project some sort of protective energy field."

"What are VIP's?" Dawnboy asked.

"That's Newtonian jargon for Very Interesting Phenomena," Dr. Thurban replied. "It can mean just about anything, but generally it refers to what you star sailors call cosmic vortexes or spacesuckers."

Ranger turned to his son and reminded him: "I've told you about those. So far we've been lucky enough not to encounter any, but they are reported to be fairly common between the Milky Way and the Magellanic Clouds. That is another reason why the treasure of the *Jealousy* is so hard to recover."

"Oh, aye," Dawnboy said. "They are sort of gaps in deep space. Anything that blunders into one is evidently disintegrated, because it is never seen or heard from again. Many starships were lost in them before Tocsin Doubleknight on Aldebaran Two or Hittyl, as some people call it, invented the lepton scanner to detect their presence."

"That's the usual textbook description," Gitlow said. "But we don't actually know very much about VIP's because we haven't yet been able to devise instruments to analyze them. The Doubleknight scanner tells us only that VIP's exist and that they move around unpredictably. So I am hoping that the equipment I install in your ship will pick up some significant new data about VIP's, as well as Wonderwhat."

Dawnboy stared wistfully into space. "Would it na be a glorious thing, Dad, if we could go up to Wonderwhat, snatch a bit o' its matter/anti-matter fuel and bring it back here for the scientists to study?"

"I don't think that would be very practical," Ranger laughed. "Even if we got hold of the stuff, how would we carry it? We would be like the alchemist in the old fable, who invented a universal solvent but couldn't keep it because it dissolved every container he put it in. Just the matter/anti-matter explosions produced in our ship's engine are so destructive that the synthesteel linings of the combustion chambers have to be replaced every few months. I hate to think what damage something far more powerful than luxium could do."

"Yes, that's another problem that we'll have to work on," Dr. Gitlow said, with the careless air of a man who did not like to be bothered with minor details. He tossed his empty cup down the serving table's disposal chute and rose to his feet. "I don't want to seem inhospitable, Captain, but we really must be getting back to our work on the satellite out there."

Ranger stood up and said he and Dawnboy had to

be getting on with their business, too. He told Gitlow
that he could have his equipment placed aboard the
Gayheart whenever he wished. Then he added: "On
second thought, why don't you come with us? I'm sure
you could learn much more from personal observation
of Wonderwhat than from the study of records brought
back by machines."

The luxiumwright's face brightened for a moment,
then he sadly shook his head and gazed out at the artificial satellite. "Thanks for the invitation. I would love
to take you up on it, but I have too many duties holding me here. Besides, I've become too intrigued by the
artifact you brought us, although I doubt that I'll learn
much from it."

"Then we'll be on our way," Ranger said, with a polite bow to Dr. Thurban. "It has been a pleasure meeting you, Doctors, even if your director here did cheat
me scandalously on the price of the satellite."

"I hate doing business with a sore loser," Dr. Montezuma Clay said, with a reptilian smirk.

7

RANGER AND DAWNBOY spent the remainder of the
morning sight-seeing around Aristotleville, then returned to their hotel for lunch. Dawnboy was glad to
see that his father's normal good humor had been
restored, after the unsettling experience of visiting his
mother's brain. The young Apache hoped they would
be too busy for the rest of the day for Ranger to dwell
on depressing memories. Dawnboy had learned, during
their brief time together, that his father's active mind
and body did not take well to idleness.

When they finished their noon meal, Dawnboy reminded Ranger of Archguardess Eythine dara Gildenfang, the woman whom Dr. Gitlow had said was also interested in the *Jealousy*'s treasure. Ranger put through a photophone call to the Soyuz Hotel in Astropolis and asked for the lady's rooms. The call was answered by an attractive teen-age girl with blonde hair and pixie-like ears.

The girl identified herself as Shvanne dara Gildenfang, the archguardess's stepdaughter. She said her stepmother was out just then, but when Ranger explained the purpose of his call, she cordially invited him to join them for dinner that evening in the Soyuz dining room. Ranger thanked her for the invitation and promised that he and Dawnboy would be there at seven-thirty.

Ranger ended the call and watched Shyanne's image fade from the screen. "Pretty little thing, isn't she?" he remarked to Dawnboy. "I've heard that of all the humanoid races, Vampirians are the most attractive and compatible to humans. She appears to be about your age, too."

"Really?" Dawnboy asked disinterestedly. "I didna notice."

His father regarded him with raised eyebrows. "Now don't tell me I'm going to have to have a long talk with you about *that!*"

Dawnboy laughed and was about to retort that he knew as much as the next man about women, but he thought they were pretty much a waste of time. He was interrupted by a call from the hotel's cyber-clerk announcing that two visitors were on their way up to the Farstars' rooms.

"Why didn't you show them to us on the screen first?" Ranger demanded. "To make sure it was all right to send them up?" The computer replied that it was not programmed to answer that question and offered to put Ranger in contact with a sentient official, if he so desired. "Never mind," Ranger muttered. "It serves me right for staying at an old-fashioned hotel without a decent security system."

"Who d'ye suppose it is, Dad?" Dawnboy inquired.

"I haven't the faintest idea. I'm not acquainted with very many people here on Newtonia, aside from those we've already seen. I just hope it isn't more news reporters with questions about the artificial satellite."

"D'ye na like being a famous celebrity?" Dawnboy grinned. Then he glanced out the open doorway to their terrace and uttered a startled cry at the sight of an attractive young woman rising on an antigravity beam from the lobby courtyard below.

A moment later, Dawnboy was out on the terrace receiving a warm welcoming hug from Helen-of-Troy Hughes-Orfo, daughter of Rothfeller Hughes. They had last seen her a few months ago, at her father's Capitalian estate, on the evening her husband died.

"Helen! Where in the cosmos . . ." Ranger blurted in surprised delight as he followed Dawnboy out of the room. Before he could think of what to say next, a short man with an incredibly thick body and muscular arms came over the terrace railing, grabbed him in a powerful embrace and swung him around as lightly as a doll, all the while grinning so broadly that his round face seemed split into hemispheres.

"Slim! You here, too?" Ranger gasped. *"Owww!* Watch my ribs, will you? Put me down, you silly fool."

"Not till you say what's the best damned fighting outfit in the universe," the short man roared.

"The Ninth Tactical Scouts of the Second Ranger Dragoon," Ranger replied promptly.

"And don't you ever forget it!" The short man stood Ranger on his feet and pumped his hand with a crushing grip, slapping his shoulder nearly hard enough to knock him down. "Snowy, you old son-of-a-spaceape! You don't look any older than the day we enlisted. How do you do it?"

"Clean living," Ranger grinned, freeing his hand to pat the man's broad shoulder affectionately. "You should try it sometime."

"Snowy?" Dawnboy inquired over Helen's head.

"My hair was a lot whiter when I was younger," Ranger explained. "Son, meet Slim Hinterwald, from Gargantua. That's a heavy gravity planet where everybody's brains turn to muscle."

"Yeah, but it makes us irresistible to women," Slim said, going over to squeeze Dawnboy's hand to a pulp. "Your old man and I served together in the Space Rangers, kid. I always had to look after him, wipe his nose and give him dry pants when the action started."

"And later he was my first mate when I had my own cargo ship," Ranger related. "Just before I met your mother."

"A fine woman. Sorry to hear about her death," Slim said seriously to Dawnboy. "Look me up sometime when you have a few days to spare and I'll tell you what a heller old Snowy used to be, before she tamed him. Like the time our scout team had leave on Freedonia and a bluenose innkeeper refused to serve us after closing time. So we all chipped in and bought the joint, then drunk it dry."

"He doesn't want to hear about that sort of thing," Ranger said, as Helen went over to give him the same greeting she had given Dawnboy.

"Want to bet I don't?" Dawnboy challenged.

Ranger held Helen out at arm's length to exchange smiles with her. "It's great to see you again," he said happily. "How are your father and the twins and David Goliath? And what are you doing here on Newtonia? How did you know where to find us? Are you staying long? When did you meet Slim?"

Helen laughed merrily at him. "Let me see if I can answer all of those questions in order. Dad is fine. So are the boys, who are with me. I am staying at the visiting executives' apartment of the Goddard-Jarles Company. Dad's a major stockholder, as you probably know. David also came with me, to undergo additional surgery at the Felixer Clinic. I am here primarily to take care of some business matters for Dad, and I will be leaving tomorrow. It was almost impossible for me not to learn that you two are here, with all the news stories about you bringing in that artificial satellite. So I called the ISTA hall and found out you were staying here at the Armillary."

"I was hanging around the hall when she called," Slim put in. "When I heard her mention your name, I introduced myself and we decided to look for you together. You weren't here everytime we tried to call you. So we finally decided to come over here, after lunch, and wait for you to show up."

"Well, I'm sure glad you did," Ranger said. He seated his guests and insisted on calling room service to send up refreshments.

Dawnboy sat next to Slim. "Are ye still a spacemon, Mr. Hinterwald?" he asked, trying to turn the conversation to matters of more interest to him.

Slim nodded. "Unfortunately, I never learned a more reliable way to make a living. For the past several years I've been flying for the Transastro line."

"That's right," Ranger said. "Didn't I hear recently you were about to be made their Chief Pilot?"

"Yeah, but instead one of the owners' relatives got the job," Slim replied. "So I told them where they could shove their whole damned line. Now I'm on my way to an instructor's job at the Merchant Space Academy on New New America."

"God help the poor academy," Ranger sighed. "Too bad we aren't headed that way or we could offer you a ride. But maybe you'll want to come with us anyhow, if searching for lost treasure appeals to you."

Slim gave Ranger a disdainful look. "So there really is some truth in the rumor that you've become stupid enough to go after the mythical treasure of Wonderwhat. No, thanks. I'm too old for that nonsense. So are you, even if you won't admit it."

"All right, but don't come around trying to borrow money from me if we do find the treasure." Ranger turned sympathetically to Helen. "I'm sorry we had to leave Capitalia so abruptly after Juan's death. We would have stayed to offer whatever help we could, but there was so much pressure on us . . ."

"I understand," Helen said. "And I'm afraid I was in no condition to accept condolences then. It was such a terrible shock . . ." Her voice choked off and an expression of painful sorrow clouded her violet eyes. But she quickly snapped out of it and brought back her usual gay smile. "But those of us who are still here must go on with the business of living. Especially the business part. Which is one of the reasons I wanted to see you. When I leave here, I'll be going on to Eldor. Have you ever heard of it?"

Ranger, Dawnboy and Slim looked blankly at one another, then shook their heads.

"That's not surprising," Helen went on. "It is a rather recently discovered planet out beyond the de-Rizzo Sector that was colonized about fifty years ago by a strict religious sect who wanted to maintain a simple way of life uncontaminated by industrial technology."

"There have been a lot of idealistic colonies like that founded," Slim said. "But most of them don't work out the way they were planned."

Helen nodded. "Neither did this one. Now a younger and more progressive generation is taking over there and they are looking for outside investments to help develop the planet's rich natural resources. Dad's advance men out there have sent back enthusiastic reports about Eldor's tremendous commercial potential; now I'm headed out there to look the situation over. Not many other businessmen have gotten there yet, so we have a chance to invest early in what could be the biggest economic boomworld in years."

"Sounds promising," Ranger agreed. "And just the sort of thing I would like to get into, if I weren't otherwise occupied just now."

"I was kind of hoping we would be able to go there together," Helen said, trying to hide the disappointment in her voice. "But if you are so anxious to go treasure hunting, I won't try to talk you out of it. However, if you have any surplus capital that you don't mind gambling with, I'll be glad to see if I can find some high-return investments for it. That is, if you trust my business judgment enough."

Ranger laughed. "I doubt if I'll ever have to worry about that. Do you really think this Eldor thing could be that big?"

Helen shrugged. "Anything is possible in business. But you know how cautious I am with other peoples' money. If an on-the-spot inspection doesn't convince me that we have a good chance of at least doubling our investments within six months, I won't put a single stellar in it."

"That's good enough for me," Ranger said. "I think we have about a hundred thousand stellars that we can afford to do without for a while. I'll have the bank set up a special account giving you power of attorney over it."

"A hundred thousand!" Slim looked greedily at Ranger. "Oh, man, if I had that much money, I'd retire and look up five or six women I've been thinking about marrying."

"Who are you trying to kid?" Ranger snorted. "Even if you ever found a woman who could stand to live with you, you know you'd never let her tie you down."

Slim grinned slyly. "Yeah, but I wouldn't have to tell her that." He cocked an appraising eye at Helen. "How about you, honey? Do you think a poor little rich gal like you could find happiness with a broke but overpoweringly charming starship pilot, for a little while?"

Helen boldly returned his frank stare. "The question is, are *you* willing to risk being trapped by an ugly widow with two kids?"

Slim reacted with an exaggerated expression of horror, and they all laughed at him. It seemed to Dawnboy that Helen's gaze had lingered speculatively on Ranger, not Slim, when she replied. But then Dawnboy supposed he must have been mistaken when Helen returned briskly to her conversation.

"By the way, Ranger, Juan mentioned you in his

will. He felt guilty for having betrayed you to the IFIB and PHAP agents, so he left you his share of his family's farming lands on HeyRube, the agricultural planet where he was born."

"That was a foolish thing for him to do," Ranger said. "Of course I'll sign it all over to you and the boys."

Helen made a definite negative gesture. "No, we don't need it. Besides, I want to keep my memories of Juan unchanged. If I owned anything on his home-world, I might be tempted to go there, and then I might learn things about him that I would rather not know."

Ranger nodded. "All right, if that's the way you want it."

"Anyhow," Helen went on, "I don't know if the property will ever be of any use to you. Some of Juan's relatives have claims on it, so it may take a long time to straighten out the legal technicalities."

"Maybe it would be a good place for you to retire," Slim needled Ranger. "I always thought you were a better farmer than spaceman."

"Yeah, and if I need a strong, dumb animal to pull my plow, I'll let you know," Ranger shot back.

The refreshments arrived then, and the four friends settled down to reliving old times and filling one an-other in on their latest exploits. When Ranger and Slim fell to discussing their early military experiences, their ridiculous exaggerations soon had Helen and Dawnboy helpless with laughter.

8

"I STILL DON'T trust these things," Ranger complained as he stepped out of the Astropolis matter-transporter that evening, just behind Dawnboy and Slim.

"You better learn to like 'em," Slim warned. "Because they're gonna replace starships one of these days, if the scientists can ever find a way to lower their high operating cost and extend their range."

Ranger gave his old friend a disapproving frown. "How can you be so cheerful about something that would put space jockeys like us out of work?"

Slim replied with an indifferent shrug of his massive shoulders. "That wouldn't bother me. I never cared very much for pushing space vehicles around the galaxy anyhow."

"Then why did ye become a starship pilot?" Dawnboy asked.

"Because it was the best way to keep ahead of jealous husbands and single women with marriage on their minds," Slim replied.

Ranger spotted an electronic directory of the space city several paces away and led his two companions over to it. Astropolis was composed of a dozen concentric metal rings with connecting tubes radiating out from their common center like spokes from a wheel's hub. The matter-transporter station was located in the hub, which also contained the city's power plants and the central terminal of its internal transportation system.

After learning that the Soyuz Hotel was in the eighth ring out from the hub, the three men went up to the second level to catch a pogobus to the stop nearest the hotel. Dawnboy was fascinated by the ingenious simplicity of the bus system. The bus itself was merely a long metal cylinder that was shot by a catapult through a resistance-free vacuum tube. At its destination, the bus was caught by another catapult and eased to a stop, the braking action cocking the catapult for its next launch.

"I still do na see how ye can be so sure that this lady will welcome our company on her treasure hunt," Dawnboy remarked as they took seats on the bus.

"Just leave everything to me," Slim said with a confident smile. "I'll start out by telling her how dangerous that part of the universe is, compared to the civilized Aquila systems that she's familiar with. Then I'll turn on the charm and convince her that she needs two strong, capable he-men like you and Snowy to escort her ship to the Magellanic Clouds and back."

Dawnboy looked doubtfully at his father. "D'ye think he can really do it, Dad?"

"I suppose he must be a great lady's man," Ranger said archly. "I've never been able to find anything else he's good for."

"Fortunately for you, I'm immune to the jealousy of lesser men," Slim blandly informed Ranger. Then he winked at Dawnboy. "Watch my style carefully, kid, and you'll never have to worry about being unpopular with the fair sex. If Archguardess Gildenfang has an ounce of real red-blooded womanhood in her, I'll soon have her glowing like an illumination strip plugged into a luxium dynamo."

Dawnboy agreed that such a performance would be well worth seeing. He and the two older men had by then developed a strong interest in the Farstars' feminine rival for the treasure of Wonderwhat. That afternoon, after Helen had finally been called away on business, Ranger and Slim turned to discussing the practical aspects of the treasure hunt. Ranger remarked that it would be most helpful if they could learn more about Archguardess Eythine dara Gildenfang before meeting her that evening. Slim had already assumed he was part of the dinner party.

Old news tapes from the public library provided considerable background data on the lady, and Slim managed to obtain even more from the ISTA hall's records department, where a friend of his was conveniently employed. They learned that she was, like the luxiumwright Wage Gitlow, a native of New New America, the capital world of the Unified Systems of Aquila. She was a few years younger than Ranger and was a qualified, experienced starship commander in her own right. Her father had owned a small fleet of cargo vessels that operated within the USA, and she had gone to work for him at an early age. Upon his death five years ago, Eythine inherited the line and ran it successfully for more than a year. Then she married Archguard Ramislaus dara Gildenfang, a handsome but impoverished aristocrat from the bleak world of Vampiria.

Theirs had evidently been a happy marriage, as unions between humans and humanoids go, although Eythine's new husband appeared to have been unduly interested in her inheritance. At his urging, she sold the business and used a large portion of the money from it to finance his ill-fated attempt to find the long-lost *Jealousy* and recover her rich cargo.

When Eythine learned of her husband's death, she became determined to use the secret information he had sent her to finish his work. With Shyanne, Ramislaus's daughter by his first wife, she came to Newtonia and purchased a late-model starship which she christened the *Ram's Revenge*. She had spared no expense in having the ship outfitted and provisioned for a cruise to the Magellanic Clouds, and Ranger was not overjoyed to learn that the vessel was nearly ready to blast off. The *Gayheart* would not be fully spaceworthy for several more days. With a sizable headstart and all her other advantages, the archguardess stood a good chance of finding and taking possession of the treasure ship well before Ranger and Dawnboy could even begin their search for it.

What most disturbed Ranger, however, was the news that Eythine planned to undertake her hazardous voyage with the assistance of only Shyanne and her ship's biocomputer. Ranger, a firm believer in the equality of the sexes, knew that a good skipper could easily handle a fully automated starship alone. But even so he still retained enough male chauvinism to doubt that two women could survive such a dangerous venture without some masculine help. Slim agreed with Ranger. That was the main reason he had volunteered to accompany Ranger and Dawnboy this evening. He would use his overpowering charm to persuade Eythine to wait until the *Gayheart* was ready to blast off with the *Ram's Revenge*. Of course the fact that Eythine's pictures revealed her to be an unusually attractive woman had nothing to do with his unselfish offer, Slim insisted.

When the pogobus reached their stop, the three men stepped out into a narrow thoroughfare between commercial compartments, their way lighted by overhead strips of solar energy. Dawnboy glanced fondly over at Slim as they walked toward the Soyuz Hotel, a few dozen meters away. The youth had taken an instant liking to this happy-go-lucky Gargantuan and he hoped his father would be able to talk Slim into joining their expedition. Aside from his outstanding qualifications as a spacehand, Slim was marvelous fun to be with. Dawnboy thought he would never tire of listening to Slim's wildly improbable yarns about his even more improbable adventures.

Most of the Soyuz Hotel's services were automated, but the dining room was still staffed by waiters and waitresses of more or less human appearances. That was because most Newtonians, who spent much of their time working and living with machines, had more than the average intelligent being's impatience with such devices. They occasionally liked to be able to complain to something that could answer back intelligently when things did not go according to their wishes.

One of the waiters, a four-armed humanoid from Shiva in the Aldebaran System, greeted Ranger, Dawnboy and Slim. When Ranger mentioned Archguardess dara Gildenfang's name, the waiter nodded and escorted the three men over to a table near the observation window that looked down on Newtonia's nightside.

The girl Shyanne was seated between a man and woman at the table, sipping crimson liquid from a tall glass. Dawnboy had only glanced at Shyanne's image on the photophone that afternoon. Now he studied her more closely and saw that she was indeed about his age and rather pretty, though a bit on the thin side. Even her slightly nonhuman features—needle-sharp canine teeth, pointed ears and catlike slitted green eyes—did not detract from her fresh adolescent beauty. She wore a cutely ruffled short-pants suit and was neatly groomed, except for her hands, which had the rough, broken-nailed appearance of a mechanic's. Dawnboy approved of that. He figured that a girl who wasn't afraid to work with her hands might be interesting company after all.

Dawnboy recognized the woman beside Shyanne from her pictures. Archguardess Eythine dara Gildenfang was all human—and all woman. A stunning brunette with a lovely oval face and large gray-blue eyes, she had the kind of figure that made men glad that clinging, low-cut evening gowns had never gone out of style among more civilized races. She smiled up at Ranger, Slim and Dawnboy with the calm, self-assured air of someone who knew exactly what beauty, intelligence and wealth could do for a woman. Dawnboy wondered how Slim was going to go about trying to outcharm her.

The man seated across from the two ladies also displayed a strong self-confident manner, as if he were accustomed to assuming command automatically. He was a large handsome man about Ranger's age, with skin and hair as black as starless space. Despite his plain civilian suit, Dawnboy was instinctively sure that he must be a spaceman or a military official of some sort. Something about him reminded the young Apache of the highly sophisticated barbarians of the IFIB and PHAP empires he had met. Dawnboy instantly liked, but distrusted him.

Ranger introduced himself, Dawnboy and Slim while the waiter's four hands pulled out chairs for them at the table. Eythine greeted them warmly and introduced the black man as Fletcher Zairundi, master of the *Seven Deadly Sins,* an independent startramp from New Black Harlem. Dawnboy was seated beside Slim and directly opposite Shyanne, who was studying him with discomfiting frankness.

"I am delighted you could join us," Eythine said brightly to Ranger. "When I heard through shipyard gossip that you are also interested in the Wonderwhat treasure, I knew we would meet eventually. So I am glad to have this opportunity to refuse in advance any proposal you might make that we join forces. I mean nothing personal by that; I have just told Captain Zairundi the same thing. Since I don't think either of you have as much to contribute to a partnership as I have, I prefer to go it alone and retain full claim to whatever I find. But thank you very much anyway, if that is what you were about to suggest."

Ranger and Slim stared blankly at Eythine, their mouths half-open. Dawnboy hid a smile behind his hand and whispered to Slim: "Do na· look now, but I think somebody just switched off yer dynamo."

"Well, uh . . ." Ranger grinned self-consciously, then turned to Zairundi to cover his confusion. "Are you going looking for the *Jealousy,* too?"

"No, I couldn't afford such an expensive expedition, even if I believed in fanciful tales of lost treasure." The black man spoke in a deep, lazy drawl that belied the piercing attentiveness of his brown eyes. "I was a friend of Mrs. Gildenfang's late husband. When I arrived here yesterday and learned of her plans to embark on the same sort of mad venture that caused his death, I felt compelled to look her up and try to talk her out of it. Failing that, I offered to accompany her in my ship and provide whatever protection I could against pirates, ZuJu raiders and the other dangers of that wild part of the universe. You just heard her reply to that offer."

Ranger turned back to Eythine with a helpless shrug. "Well, if you have your mind all made up about this, I'll spare you the long argument I had prepared to convince you that the cruise is too dangerous for a lone woman."

"She won't be alone," Shyanne said, still eyeing Dawnboy speculatively.

Ranger cast a startled glance at the girl, then regarded Eythine with a disapproving frown. "So you really are taking your stepdaughter with you? Don't you think she's a little young for that?"

Shyanne gave Ranger a defiant look. "I'm old enough to take care of myself," she informed him with a note of weary exasperation that made Dawnboy instantly sympathize with her. He was not surprised to learn that the universal conflict between the young and their elders had many striking similarities among the varied intelligent species.

Eythine gazed fondly at her stepdaughter. "I doubt if she is much younger than your son, Captain Farstar. Besides Vampirians mature early. So far she has proved herself to be an excellent student of everything I've taught her about spacefaring. But I still haven't entirely made up my mind about taking her along on this cruise."

"You'll take me," Shyanne said confidently. "Because you know it's only fair that you should. I have as much right to my father's information about Wonderwhat as you do, even if you won't share it with me."

"When two people know a secret, it isn't a secret anymore," Eythine smilingly reminded the girl. "Don't gulp your pseudoplasma, Shyanne. You have better manners than that." She looked apologetically at Ranger. "I never had any children of my own, so it isn't easy for me to get used to looking after a self-willed teen-ager."

"I know exactly how you feel," Ranger replied, with a meaningful look at Dawnboy, who stared back with baby-faced innocence.

Then Dawnboy looked at the red fluid in Shyanne's glass and remembered what he had learned about the eating habits of Vampirians. Unable to digest solid food, they lived on a liquid diet which in olden times they had drunk straight from their hosts, including humans. After learning how to synthesize palatable liquid proteins from vegetables, they had become much more popular among their fellow humanoids. But even so, knowledge of what Shyanne was drinking ruined Dawnboy's appetite.

"Excuse me for rushing through my dinner before the rest of you have even ordered," Shyanne suddenly interrupted. "But I have to take off soon. Another old friend of Father's called as we were about to leave our rooms this evening. He said he has something that my father gave him to give to me. He tried to deliver it to me on Vampiria, but we had already left for Newtonia by the time he arrived. Now he is sick in a hospital in Aristotleville, so I will have to go down there to see him."

Captain Zairundi started to rise. "I must be going, too. Since you are determined not to accept my offered assistance, Archguardess, I won't trouble you any longer."

Eythine stopped him with an outstretched hand and appealing expression. "Please stay. There's no reason why we all can't have a pleasant evening together. I've been so busy recently that it is a rare pleasure for me to be able to relax with people again."

Zairundi hesitated uncertainly and Slim looked up at him from the mountain of muscle that was his body. "You heard the lady. Now sit down and enjoy yourself, or I'll break your legs," Slim said jovially.

Zairundi laughed and sank back into his chair. "I can hardly refuse an invitation like that. But I'll stay only on condition that you all agree to be my guests for dinner."

"We can fight over the check when it comes," Ranger said.

Shyanne finished her drink and stood up. "Well, *I* have to be going now. But I'll try to get back early."

Ranger turned to Dawnboy. "Why don't you go with her, Son? It will give you kids a chance to get better acquainted, without us old folks to bother you." He looked inquiringly at Eythine. "That is, if it's all right with you for this roughneck to be alone with your stepdaughter."

The beautiful woman laughed and looked up at Shyanne. "I am sure she is old enough to choose her own companions. What do you think of him, dear? He looks like a perfect gentleman to me."

"Whatever that is," Shyanne added, coolly appraising Dawnboy with her eyes. "Well, I guess I could do worse."

Dawnboy squirmed uneasily under the women's bold stares. He was puzzled by his father's apparent desire to get rid of him for a while, although the prospect of spending some time alone with Shyanne was far from unpleasant. The only reason that occurred to Dawnboy was that perhaps Ranger wanted him to try to learn something from Shyanne about Eythine's treasure-hunting plans. Then Dawnboy sternly told himself that it was just his suspicious Apache nature to attribute such underhanded motives to a man as honorable and straightforward as his father. Still, it wasn't a bad idea.

"All right, I'll go wi' ye," Dawnboy said to Shyanne as he got to his feet. "If ye do na mind having me along."

"Of course not. I'll appreciate your company," Shyanne smiled, starting to lead Dawnboy away from the table.

"Wait. I'll go with you," Slim said, heaving his bulk out of his chair. "I don't want to stay with these old folks, either."

Ranger started to ask Slim to stay, then decided it

really did not make any difference if he went or stayed. Slim was hardly the ideal chaperone, but at least he could keep the two youngsters entertained if they found that they did not actually like each other.

"Well, we certainly cut our party down to size in a hurry," Eythine said. "I hope they won't be away too long."

Zairundi watched Dawnboy and Shyanne walking side by side across the dining room. "They do make a handsome couple," he commented.

"Yes, it brings out the matchmaker in me," Eythine said, smiling at Ranger. "Isn't it a pity that we can't mate our children as carefully as they do farm animals?"

Ranger laughed. "On some worlds they do. But I haven't noticed that it improves the stock very much."

9

"WHAT IS IT that this mon wants to give ye?" Dawnboy asked as he, Shyanne and Slim walked out of the hotel and headed for the pogobus stop.

"He didn't say exactly," Shyanne answered. "Something in a locked strongbox that my father left with him. Probably old jewelry or some other family heirloom. A few things like that are about all that are left of the once-great dara Gildenfang fortune."

Slim regarded the girl sympathetically. "Your family has fallen on hard times, huh? I figured that had to be the reason why your old man went treasure hunting. Otherwise somebody as high-ranking as an archguard would stay home and help his local Paramount rule his territory."

"So you know something about our way of life?" Shyanne asked Slim. She smiled wistfully. "Yes, once the dara Gildenfangs were among the highest nobility of Nekronis, the largest dominion on Vampiria. Many of my ancestors held important government posts and were rewarded for their services with extensive land grants and lordship of the workers living on them. But the last few generations of the family have produced degenerate wastrels who squandered their inheritances until there wasn't much left for my father and me except the famous dara Gildenfang charm."

Dawnboy tried to recall what he had learned about Vampirian social and political practices. Feudalism had prevailed over most of the planet until humans discovered it some four centuries ago. Since then there had been much industrial and democratic progress, but many of the old ways still lingered. The leading aristocratic families continued to enjoy high social status, even though they had lost many of their traditional powers. That would account for Shyanne's haughty self-confidence that at times bordered on arrogance.

"So ve think ye are loaded wi' charm?" Dawnboy teased Shyanne.

"I know I am," she answered matter-of-factly. "But it's nothing to brag about. It is just something that some of us are born with, like curly hair or a cute nose. My father was really the great charmer of the family. He had a superb gift for making rich, beautiful women fall in love with him."

"That sounds a lot like me," Slim said, as a bus drew up before them. "Reminds me of the great love affair I had with the high priestess of the vegetable people of Floradora. What a beautiful head of leaves she had! What shapely limbs! I never tired of nibbling her lovely cauliflower ears and kissing her tender rose petal lips. We were blissfully happy together and we might even have settled down to raise a family of little sprouts, if it hadn't been for our tragically different life-styles."

Dawnboy managed to stifle his giggles. That Slim was really too much.

They boarded the bus and seated themselves for the trip back to the hub of Astropolis. "I ken I'll probably hate myself for asking," Dawnboy said to Slim. "But what made yer life-styles so tragically different?"

"She went dormant every winter," Slim replied. "And I had to carry her around in a pot. I didn't mind that, but then one evening at dinner I absentmindedly ate her head for the salad."

"How horrible!" Shyanne cried.

"I'll say," Slim affirmed. "It gave me the worst heartburn I ever had. Of course she grew another head in a few weeks, but somehow things were never the same between us."

Shyanne bit her lips to keep from laughing at Slim's woebegone expression. "Is he always like this?" she asked Dawnboy.

"My dad says he gets even worse if we do na humor him," Dawnboy answered. "Tell us more about yer father. I'm interested in why he went searching for the *Jealousy*."

"For the treasure—what else?" Shyanne replied. "He married my mother for her money. Then when that was all spent and she was conveniently dead, he went out and hooked Eythine. But he decided not to throw away her inheritance on high living. Instead he threw it away on an expedition to find the treasure of Wonderwhat. He had a crazy dream of using the treasure to restore the dara Gildenfang estates to their former glory. Now Eythine is determined to finish his job and make his dream a reality. She thinks that will be some kind of a monument to him, as if that really matters anymore."

"Ye do na seem to approve o' yer stepmother very much," Dawnboy observed.

"Oh, don't get me wrong," Shyanne said quickly. "I like Eythine. She is a wonderful person, for a human, and I know that I'm better off with her than I would be with my relatives on Vampiria. They still think that a well-born young lady should only learn the social graces and how to catch a rich husband. But I want a more meaningful life. Eythine can help me get it, with her technological experience."

"Ye want to be a starship captain, like her?" Dawnboy asked, glancing at the girl's work-roughened hands.

"I did at first. But what really interests me is matter-transportation. That will be the major transportation industry of the future. Anyone who gets into it now can look forward to a highly rewarding career."

"You're a pretty smart gal to think of that," Slim complimented Shyanne. "But if you are serious about it, you should stay here on Newtonia. Some of the schools here have excellent courses in matter-transportation technology."

"I know," Shyanne responded. "But I can look into that later. Right now I think it is more important for me to go along with Eythine and give her whatever help I can. This cruise can give me a lot of valuable experience. I'll also have plenty of spare time to study up on luxiumology and the other sciences associated with matter-transportation. I may even be able to learn if Wonderwhat actually does hold the key to long-range matter-transportation."

"If that interests ye so much, 'tis a shame that yer stepmother didna allow the luxiumwright to put his equipment aboard her ship," Dawnboy said. He told Shyanne about his meeting with Dr. Wage Gitlow that morning.

"Yes, that was disappointing," Shyanne said. She blinked her limpid cat's eyes and smiled coaxingly at Dawnboy. "But now tell me about the artificial satellite that you and your father brought in. I've been dying to hear the full story. Is it actually an artifact of the Vanished Ones? The news reports were so confusing. Did you really have to fight your way through an IFIB battle squadron to get it?"

"Well, it was na a full squadron," Dawnboy said modestly, pushing the memory of the single IFIB starcruiser to the back of his mind. Like most normal young men, he could resist anything except flattery from a pretty girl. With just a few improvements on the truth, he related to a raptly attentive Shyanne and a secretly amused Slim how he and Ranger had discovered Dawnworld and gotten away with the satellite.

Dawnboy was just winding up his story when their bus reached the city's hub. The three of them disembarked and walked down to the level where the matter-transporter was located. There was no traffic through the transporter just then and Dawnboy saw the reason for that as they approached the machine. A man wearing a green coverall with HERETHERE TRANSPORTATION SERVICE, INC., lettered across its back stood beside one of the transporter's dozen booths. He had removed a panel from the side of the booth and was working on a confusing maze of electrical wiring and mini-transistors with delicate instruments from a toolbox at his feet. The man looked up as they approached, his gaze fixing on Shyanne with such unconcealed intensity that Dawnboy was tempted to tell the shameless lecher to mind his manners.

"Sorry, folks, but the machine is out of order just now," the repairman informed them. "We had complaints about some of the booths sending people to the wrong destinations, so I've had to shut down the whole thing while I look for the cause of the trouble."

"How long will it take you to fix it?" Shyanne asked. "We have to get down to Aristotleville right away."

"We can use an antigrav taxi," Slim suggested. "That won't take us more than an hour to get there."

"I hate to waste that much time," Shyanne said impatiently. "I promised Eythine I would be right back." She gave the repairman a melting smile. "Can't you please let us go through? It's very important."

"Well, I dunno . . ." the man replied doubtfully. Then he brightened as he plucked a mini-transistor from the transporter with a long, tweezer-like tool. "Wait, I think I've found the bad part after all. Maybe I can get this booth back in action in a few minutes."

They watched while the man, whistling softly through his teeth, slipped a new mini-transistor into the machine and directed the needle-thin beam of his photon torch to weld it in place. Shyanne critically studied the man's work.

"Are you sure that's the right part?" Shyanne asked. "I mean, that's part of the transporter's directional system, isn't it? I think that requires a fifty-volt transistor, instead of . . ."

The repairman gave Shyanne the kind of tired, long-suffering look that all professionals reserve for meddling amateurs. "Lady, if you want my job, you're welcome to apply for it first thing in the morning," he said flatly. "Until then, how about letting me do it?"

"Sorry," Shyanne mumbled, her cheeks glowing at the rebuke. "I was only trying to be helpful."

Dawnboy stepped protectively between Shyanne and the repairman, an angry challenge on his lips. But Slim put a restraining hand on the young Apache's arm. "Easy, kid. He didn't mean anything personal," the burly Gargantuan said soothingly. "He's just trying to do his work. So let's let him get on with it."

Dawnboy nodded and stepped back to Shyanne's side. He was grateful to Slim for preventing him from committing a rash act that he would later regret. But at the same time, he felt disappointed for not being allowed to put the insolent repairman in his place. Not that he wanted to impress Shyanne by defending her honor, of course. No mere woman was worth that much trouble, especially one who was not even human. So he tried to ignore the warm feeling of pleasure that swept through him when the girl flashed him an appreciative smile.

"Okay, that should do it," the repairman finally said, putting down his tools. "Where do you want to go?"

Shyanne gave him the name of the hospital where her late father's friend was a patient. The repairman set the transporter's dials for the booth nearest her destination.

"I'd better go first, to make sure it's safe," Slim said, stepping forward.

"No!" The repairman stepped swiftly in front of Slim. "No offense, sir, but I think you might be too heavy for the beam to carry. I've just got this thing jerry-rigged for temporary use, because the young lady said she is in a hurry. Since she has the least mass to be transported, she should go first."

"Well, I am na much heavier than she is," Dawnboy said, eager to win another smile from Shyanne. "I'll go first."

Dawnboy moved quickly around Slim and the repairman, who made a desperate lunge to block the youth, but he was already disappearing into the transporter booth. Slim brushed past the repairman and stepped into the booth, with Shyanne at his heels. The repairman glared angrily at them as they faded from view, then he rushed in after them.

Dawnboy's momentum carried him several paces out of his reception booth before he could stop and look around. He saw at once that he had not reached his desired destination. Around him stretched the barren, rocky floor of a small valley, sparsely dotted with short leafless plants. Floodlights illuminated the area, and overhead the harsh, star-riddled blackness of Newtonia's atmosphereless sky looked coldly down on him.

Even as Dawnboy's mind reeled in confusion, he thought he knew where he was. This must be one of the planet's newer cultivated areas. Agronomists had pumped enough oxygen into the valley to support the hardy, primitive plants, which would in turn produce more oxygen as they grew. Eventually the valley would have an atmosphere in which humans could live and work comfortably. But that pleasant condition was still far from being a reality, as Dawnboy learned when he tried to inhale a deep breath.

His mouth gaped open and his lungs labored futilely to suck in enough of the thin air to replenish his blood's dwindling oxygen supply. At the same time, he became conscious of the deadly coldness of the valley.

With so little atmosphere to hold the sun's heat, the nighttime temperature here must be well below zero. All in all, this was not the sort of place where Dawnboy cared to stay very long. Gasping and shivering, he turned around to go back into the transporter booth, only to find his way blocked by two men wearing heavy clothing and face masks with hoses attached to oxygen tanks on their backs.

Peering more closely, Dawnboy saw that only one of the figures was human. The other had the curling horns and goatlike features of a Satyr from one of the Capricorn worlds. Dawnboy wondered where they had come from. They must have been standing beside the booth when he emerged from it, as if they had been expecting him. But that was impossible, since he had obviously been sent here mistakenly by some malfunction in the Astropolis matter-transmitter.

Dawnboy decided not to waste time trying to figure out the situation that had suddenly become too complicated for his rapidly vanishing strength. Since the two beings were probably scientists working here, they would understand just how important it was for an unprotected human to get out of this brutal environment. Dawnboy staggered toward them on rubbery legs, expecting them to step out of his way or even help him into the booth. Instead, the human raised a gloved fist and struck the young Apache on the jaw.

It was a light blow, but in Dawnboy's weakened condition it seemed to land with the smashing force of a pile driver. For a moment he blacked out entirely, reviving to find himself sprawled on his hands and knees before the two creatures. He stared up at them in shock, more than a little angry and more than a little frightened. They peered down at him with what appeared to be disappointed expressions behind their oxygen masks.

"What's he doing here?" the Satyr asked in a whining voice. "I thought it was supposed to be a girl."

"Yes, that fool Daran sent us the wrong one," the man replied angrily.

"Oh. The Arrow isn't going to like this," the Satyr said uneasily. "I hope he doesn't think it was our fault."

The man turned on his heel. "Don't worry about that. Come on. Let's get back to the ship and find out what they want us to do now."

"What about him?" The Satyr gestured at Dawnboy.

"Leave him," the man said carelessly. "He won't last long enough for anybody to find him alive."

Dawnboy's pain-blurred vision followed the strange pair to the transporter booth. The man adjusted the destination dial, then they both stepped into the booth and vanished.

Dawnboy knew how right the man had been; he would not live very much longer if he remained here. The matter-transporter was his only hope of survival. Desperately he tried to crawl toward it, but his powerless limbs collapsed and he fell on his face in the dirt, nearly losing consciousness again. He lay full length with his chest heaving violently for one agonizing breath after another. If he just remained motionless, he thought he might be able to obtain enough oxygen to stay alive. But what good would that do him if he froze to death?

Besides, he had to get back to Astropolis and warn Shyanne of the danger she was in. Even his fuddled mind was able to conclude that this had been an unsuccessful attempt to kidnap the girl by what appeared to be a gang of rival treasure hunters. Evidently they had planned to use Shyanne to force Eythine to give them her secret information about Wonderwhat. Even now the gang could be making another effort to abduct the girl.

Dawnboy's cold-stiffened fingers clawed at the frigid ground, dragging him inch by precious inch toward the transporter booth. Sickening black waves of unconsciousness washed over him and the scene before him wavered in and out of focus like the cruel teasing of a nightmare. At times he thought he was actually dreaming and he yearned to relax and sink deeper into the warm dark comfort of sleep. . . .

Somehow he always managed to rouse himself and make a little more tortuous progress toward his nearby-yet-so-hopelessly-distant goal. The first raw shock of the cold had passed, leaving his flesh so deeply chilled that he was no longer troubled by goose pimples or tremors. His face was too numb to hurt when he scraped it against sharp stones in the soil. He stared blankly at his hands as they poked out like blocks of wood in ground that he could no longer feel, pulling him along at a speed he knew could only be measured in centimeters per minute.

What's the use? his mind whimpered, full of self-pity. *I'll never make it all the way to the transporter. I may as well give up and die here.*

But from an older and deeper level of his being came the command: *Keep going! I am an Apache brave of the MacCochise clan. I was born to die gloriously in battle, not sniveling in the dirt like a worm.*

The irony of thinking about battlefield glory in his present condition made him want to laugh, if he could have spared that much energy. Did he really think he could fool himself with that childish claim? He was no longer a savage warrior. He had become civilized, too softly civilized to hope to survive this demanding ordeal. So why didn't he just . . .

Suddenly his head struck something that felt even harder than the rocky ground. He looked up and saw that it was the base of the transporter booth. For a full minute he stared stupidly at his numb right hand lying inside the booth. Finally he stirred himself with the knowledge that he had made it after all. Now he had only to crawl inside the booth and . . .

No! The unknown man had moved the dial. Somehow Dawnboy would have to reach up and turn it back to the setting for the Astropolis station. The sight of the dial about four feet above his head made him want to weep with frustration. He could not possibly get on his knees and reach that high. But he *had* to do it. If he transported himself to the place the man and Satyr had gone, they would be able to kill him easily in his helpless state.

To spur himself to make the mighty effort of drawing his knees up under him, Dawnboy thought again of Shyanne in danger. Panting and gasping against the dark waves, he slowly rose to his knees. He braced his body against the side of the transporter and inched his hand up toward the dial. A dull roar filled his ears and he knew his consciousness was fading fast. But there was no way that he could hurry his hand. With agonizing slowness his stiff fingers slid over the cold metal, touched the dial, slipped away and made the painful journey back to it.

The dial stubbornly resisted his efforts to turn it. Unable to close his hand, he jabbed the dial with his fingertips, tearing skin and drawing blood from the unfeeling flesh. Slowly the dial clicked back—one, two, three, four—that was it!

The transporter was now set to send him back to Astropolis, as soon as he could drag himself into it. He sank back down on all fours, but was unable to stop there. The ground came up and hit him in the face with a cold, hard note of finality that told him he would not rise again. This time he let go of his awareness and gladly plunged into the welcoming darkness.

10

EYTHINE'S SLIM WAIST fitted snugly in the curve of Ranger's arm as she moved lightly to follow his awkward lead around the dance floor. Except for an occasional grimace at what was happening to her toes, she was polite enough not to refer to his difficulty in keeping his feet in time with the music. It was her own fault for insisting that he dance with her, Ranger thought, but that didn't make him feel any less foolish. He had never been much of a dancer, and lately he had even forgotten how pleasant it was to hold an attractive woman in his arms. It was nice to become reacquainted with the feeling.

"What exactly do you know about Zairundi?" Ranger asked, glancing across the room to where the black captain sat at their table, sipping his drink.

"What?" Eythine looked blankly up at him. "Oh, not much more than what he has told me, actually. He said he met Ram in the course of business and they became good friends."

"That's not much of a reason for him to feel obligated to be your protector. Did your husband ever mention him to you?"

"No, but I should imagine there were a lot of things in Ram's past that he didn't tell me about."

"It seems too much of a coincidence for this chap to show up here just as you're about ready to blast off for Wonderwhat," Ranger mused. "Claiming to have been a friend of your husband makes a convenient way for someone to worm his way into your confidence and probe for information about the treasure ship."

"Well, if that was his intention, it hasn't done him much good," Eythine said. "I know how to keep my mouth shut with strangers." She flashed him a pained smile. "Even good-looking strangers who try to dance their way into my heart."

Ranger chuckled and tried harder to avoid her toes, which only made him more awkward. "That's right, you have no reason to trust me, either. But I think I'll do a little checking of my own on Zairundi tomorrow, if you don't mind."

"Not at all. Let me know if you find out anything suspicious."

The music trailed off and they made their way back

to the table. Eythine limped slightly, but she insisted that she had enjoyed the dance immensely. Zairundi welcomed them with a warm smile. "You two also make a handsome couple. If dancing were one of my better skills, I'd ask for the honor of having the next one with the lovely lady."

"Thanks, I'll try to be satisfied with your compliment instead," Eythine said with a relieved sigh. Under the table, she slipped off her shoes and massaged one aching foot with the other.

Zairundi signaled the waiter for another round of drinks. "I hope I'm not bringing back painful memories about Ram, Archguardess. But I have been wondering, did he ever finish his book on space pirates?"

Eythine looked sharply at Zairundi. "Ram told you about that? He hardly even mentioned it to me. He called it his secret vice, because writing is not considered a manly activity for Vampirian nobles."

"I know," Zairundi said. "He only revealed it to me when he learned that I shared his interest in the subject."

Ranger waited attentively to see if the black man would take advantage of this casually offered proof that he had indeed known Eythine's husband intimately.

"Ram and I thought it strange that the ancient practice of piracy had continued even into our age of scientific enlightenment," Zairundi went on after the fresh drinks were served. "Did you know that as far back as the nineteenth century, our Earth ancestors optimistically predicted that science would eventually eliminate all criminal impulses from human behavior?"

"That was a foolish hope," Ranger said. "They should have known there would always be some people who want something for nothing so badly that they don't care who they hurt to get it. The only places where science has been used thoroughly to wipe out crime are the totalitarian societies, where criminals have taken over the governments and robbed everybody else of their freedoms."

Eythine smiled at Zairundi and quoted: "When freedom is outlawed, only outlaws are free. Being plagued by a little crime is part of the price we have to pay for living under governments that protect the individual's rights. But even in free societies crime can be kept down to a tolerable level, as we've shown in the USA, if the majority of the people have high moral conduct and are willing to support efficient police forces."

Under the table Eythine's right foot, still rubbing her left, slipped and bumped softly against Ranger's right calf. Ranger jerked his leg away, hoping that his expression did not reveal his shocked surprise. He could not determine from her innocent face if the nudge had been an accident or an amorous overture, so he tried to cover his confusion with a laugh.

"Don't you Aquilans ever stop boasting about being the torchbearers of good old Yankee democracy?" Ranger asked Eythine. "I grew up on Old New America, which was founded on pure one hundred percent Americanism straight from Old Earth. But even that didn't save us from the slow degeneration that seems to be the fate of all civilizations."

"You're just jealous because your people made mistakes that mine have learned to avoid," Eythine retorted, keeping her tone as light as Ranger's. Then she said to Zairundi: "I don't see anything strange about space piracy. Criminals have preyed on all transportation systems, from stagecoaches to jet passenger aircraft. I guess things are easier to steal when they are being moved from one place to another."

Ranger nodded in agreement. "That is especially true of a starship in the lawless reaches of deep space. A pirate who gains possession of a cargo ship can easily pose as an honest trader when he reaches a remote world where the people are too anxious to buy his goods to ask any questions."

The ivory slash of Zairundi's smile against his black face was as startling as bone showing through flesh. "And that is precisely why criminals continue to pros-

per—because so many so-called honest folk are eager
to do business with them." He sipped his drink. "It will
be interesting to see how criminals manage to take advantage of the newest means of transportation, the
matter-transporters. Did you see on the news that two
transporter booths were stolen from the Herethere
Transportation Company today?"

Ranger and Eythine made negative movements with
their heads. "I don't see how the booths can be of
much use to the thieves," Eythine remarked. "They require so much power to operate that the authorities' instruments could easily pinpoint their positions."

"But that takes time," Zairundi pointed out. "A
clever gang of crooks should be able to pull off a few
jobs before police pressure forces them to move on to
another world."

Ranger had to admit that the black captain was
probably right. "How do you think they will use the
booths?" he asked. "As a means of making quick geta-
ways from the scenes of their crimes?"

"Perhaps," Zairundi replied. "Or, if they learn of a
valuable item being matter-transported, they may be
able to use their booths to intercept it."

"I thought the booths have safety devices," Eythine
said. "So that if the electrical field of the transmitting
booth isn't exactly aligned with the receiver's, nothing
will be transported."

Zairundi selected a few salted nuts from the appe-
tizer tray and said: "What some sentient minds have
devised, other sentient minds can find ways to outwit. I
just wish I were staying here long enough to find out
how the stolen booths will be utilized for dishonest
purposes."

"Then you plan to leave Newtonia soon?" Ranger
queried.

"An idle starship gathers no money," Zairundi
quoted. "I have been offered a high hauling fee to take
a cargo of parthenogenetic equipment to Sappho. I
may as well take it, now that the archguardess has re-

jected my offer to accompany her on her treasure hunt."

"Please call me Eythine." Eythine insisted. "The title rightfully belongs to Shyanne, although I can legally use it until she comes of age."

"Sappho, the all-woman planet?" Ranger asked. "I don't envy you going there."

Zairundi laughed. "I'm not looking forward to it either. But I understand that the Sapphons no longer torture men to death as sacrifices to their Goddess."

"So those silly females have finally discovered that men can be put to a better use?" Eythine wondered with a suggestive smile. "I hope that means they are getting over their rabid sexism."

Ranger's legs had gradually relaxed when Eythine's foot made no further effort at contact. He concluded that her touch had been unintentional; perhaps she had even been unaware of it. Ranger could not determine if that knowledge made him feel relieved or disappointed.

"I think it's good that man-hating women have a planet all to themselves," Ranger opined to Eythine. "There should be exclusive worlds like that for every extremist group, to prevent them from bothering the rest of us."

Eythine said he had a good point, but Zairundi disagreed.

"The trouble with extremists," the black captain said, "is that they tend to discriminate against their nonconformist members far more severely than they themselves were treated in normal societies. I had some experience with that when I was growing up on New Black Harlem. Even my own family never fully accepted me, because I wasn't black enough to be a true Afro."

"You look plenty black to me," Eythine said, carefully studying Zairundi's face. "Except for your teeth and the whites of your eyes."

Zairundi smiled wanly at her. "Thanks for the compliment. But you overlooked one important detail." He held out his right hand, showing the pale, pink-tinted palm. "A thousand years of selective breeding has given my people total blackness, even there. Only rarely does a throwback like me come along to remind them of their shameful ancestry of partial whiteness."

Ranger mentally filed away that bit of information about Zairundi for further consideration, wondering if it offered a clue to understanding the man's personality. "I have heard that New Black Harlem is one of the few human worlds where racism still persists," he said. "It seems a pretty stupid custom, now that even prejudice against other species has become unfashionable."

"Stupid perhaps, but understandable," Zairundi replied. "Remember, the Ethnic Migrations that helped populate so much of our galaxy were humanity's last great expressions of racial pride. A lot of people believed that many good ethnic traits were being lost as the races intermingled their genes. My ancestors were especially anxious to preserve their black heritage after the racial trauma they had suffered from centuries of slavery and discrimination. In those days blacks had tried to rise from their degradation by imitating their white masters. So it was hardly surprising that they went to the opposite extreme when they obtained a world of their own."

"What a pity they couldn't have been content just to live their own lives happily," Eythine said wistfully. "Instead of thinking they had to prove they were superior to their former oppressors." She craned her neck to look around the room. "Speaking of people living their own lives, I wonder how my headstrong stepdaughter is getting along down in Aristotleville. I should have gone with her."

Ranger smiled reassuringly at Eythine. "Don't worry about her. I'm sure my son and Slim Hinterwald are taking very good care of her."

11

SLIM HINTERWALD'S REFLEXES were far better conditioned by experience than Dawnboy's at responding to the unexpected. Therefore he was able to halt and crouch in a defensive position on his third step out of the matter-transporter booth. A quick glance around at his new but not unfamiliar surroundings told him that he was in the cargo hold of a starship. He could not resist wondering curiously what ship this was and how he had gotten here, even as his pilot's caution told him not to worry about those details until he had determined how safe or how dangerous his situation was.

Slim quickly spotted three bipedal beings standing several meters away from him. Two were human males of nondescript appearances, and the third was a towering gorilla-like humanoid from Nonith in the Praesepe Cluster. Evidently they were as surprised as Slim was by his sudden arrival, for they froze in the middle of an animated conversation and stared incredulously at the powerfully built Gargantuan.

In the split second it took for the three sentients to react, Slim judged their expressions to be unfriendly and he thought it best that he and Shyanne beat a hasty retreat back through the transporter. They could think about finding Dawnboy once they had secured their own safety. But as Slim started to turn around to warn Shyanne, the unsuspecting girl blundered into his back and uttered a startled cry. An instant later the man in the repairman's uniform appeared behind Shyanne and grabbed her roughly.

"There's been a mix-up!" the repairman called over

to the other two men and the Nonithian. "But I've got the girl. You three take care of this guy!"

Slim started after the repairman as he dragged the struggling Shyanne away. But from the corner of his eye Slim saw that the other three had already gone into action, and he swung back to meet their attack. The smaller of the two men sprang forward and launched himself in a flying tackle at Slim's legs, while the slow-witted Nonithian lumbered along behind him.

The other man hurried toward a low bench against the bulkhead. On the bench Slim glimpsed an object that he recognized as an Artelian synapse disrupter. Slim knew he had to stop the man before he could bring that weapon into play. Even a mild discharge from a disrupter would render any creature with a central nervous system unconscious, and Slim doubted that these thugs would care very much if he was never revived. But first Slim had to deal with the man who was rushing to tackle him. That did not prove to be much of a problem.

The man struck Slim's left leg with his shoulder and wrapped his arms around it. He might as well have tackled a marble statue, for all the inconvenience he caused the thick-muscled Gargantuan. Slim shook the man off with a powerful kick that sent him skidding across the deck. The hulking Nonithian loomed up before Slim with outstretched arms, its long yellow fangs bared in a threatening snarl. Slim's body was not built for speed, but even he had no difficulty dodging around the awkward Nonithian and keeping out of its grasp.

Slim raced after the man who was making for the synapse disrupter. The man reached the bench and snatched up the disrupter, spinning around just as Slim charged full speed into him. Slim's left hand knocked the weapon from the man's grip as the ex-ranger's huge right fist slammed against his jaw, driving his head back into the synthesteel bulkhead. The bulkhead rang dully as the man bounced off it and crumpled into a limp heap at Slim's feet. Slim looked around for the disrupter, saw it on the deck about three meters away, and at the same time, observed the repairman dragging Shyanne toward an open doorway at the end of the hold. The girl was fighting bravely with her nails, knees and teeth, but her captor was too strong for her.

Slim hesitated momentarily between going after the disrupter and going to Shyanne's rescue. By the time he decided the weapon was most important, the man he had kicked away was back on his feet and racing him for the disrupter. The man pounced upon the disrupter an instant ahead of Slim. Before the man could turn over, the edge of Slim's hand chopped down on the back of his neck, knocking him senseless. The man's body covered the disrupter. As Slim tried to roll him off, a massive hairy paw suddenly seized his shoulder and flung him against the bulkhead.

Grunting painfully, Slim peered up into the Nonithian's glaring red eyes as the creature advanced to grapple with him. Slim lurched away from the bulkhead swinging, but his blows glanced harmlessly off that monster's rock-hard bulk. Slim knew that not even his considerable strength stood a chance of winning a wrestling match with the savage Nonithian. His only hope lay in trying to outmaneuver the humanoid with fancy footwork and to break away at the first opportunity.

It was a good plan, but the Nonithian refused to go along with it. Effortlessly absorbing Slim's furious punches, the Nonithian shuffled forward, relentlessly forcing Slim back against the bulkhead. Slim realized he was being cornered. No matter which way he turned, there was a long, hairy arm to block his escape. When Slim's back touched the bulkhead, he decided he had nothing to lose and rammed his shoulder into the brute's chest in a final attempt to escape. The Nonithian flinched slightly at the impact, then its arms closed around Slim's thick body in a crushing embrace.

Slim squirmed and kicked desperately as he tried to work one hand free to gouge the Nonithian's eyes. But the brutal hold was as unbreakable as it was painful. Like a steel cable being winched taut, the Nonithian's mighty arms steadily squeezed the breath from Slim's lungs in a choking hiss. Slim's vision blurred and he knew that a little more pressure would snap his ribs like dry sticks. He did not doubt for a minute that the Nonithian was capable of exerting that additional pressure.

Then suddenly and inexplicably the creature's grip loosened. Slim gratefully gulped a deep breath and mustered his remaining strength to thrust himself violently backward, pressing his palms against the Nonithian's chest for leverage. The Nonithian held on stubbornly for several agonizing moments, then its arms abruptly flew apart and Slim slipped away biting the air in quick gasps. His wobbly legs felt almost too weak to support him and he edged away with his back braced against the bulkhead.

As Slim moved out of danger, he saw what had briefly distracted the Nonithian's attention from him. Shyanne stood behind the Nonithian, her pale face set grimly as her small fists pounded the humanoid's broad back. Across the hold, the repairman writhed on the deck clutching his groin, painfully indicating how Shyanne had gotten away from him.

What a gal!

The sight of the tiny girl trying to fight such an overpowering opponent would have been laughable, if Slim had not been aware that he owed his life to Shyanne's courageous attack. Now it was time for him to repay the favor, as the Nonithian turned angrily to face its new challenger. Slim dashed forward and caught Shyanne's arm, whirling her around to run with him toward the transporter booth. He paused only long enough to flick on the machine's transmitting switch, then he thrust Shyanne into the booth and leaped after her.

They emerged at the Astropolis station before the startled eyes of a man and woman who had been about to use the booth. Slim rudely brushed the couple aside and switched off the transporter to prevent their attackers from pursuing them here. He glanced at the other booths and saw that they were all deactivated with their *Out of Service* signs on.

"W-w-what ..." Shyanne stammered breathlessly. "Who were those men? Why did they ... ?"

"We can talk about that later," Slim snapped. "Right now we have to find out what happened to Dawnboy."

Shyanne looked around quickly. "He isn't here anyplace."

"I know. He must still be wherever the transporter sent him," Slim surmised. "We'll have to get a real repairman here to figure that out."

The man whom Slim had pushed aside stepped forward indignantly. "Say, what do you think you're ...?"

"Sorry, folks, but we've got an emergency here," Slim interrupted. "Please keep out of the way. Or, better yet, run to the nearest police signal box. We may need their help."

The man hesitated uncertainly, then nodded and hurried away. The woman asked if there was anything she could do to help. Slim asked her to use a nearby photophone to call the transporter company for a service technician. Shyanne had moved over to the opened side of the transporter booth where the repairman had been working. "This doesn't look much different from the diagrams of transporter workings that I've studied," she murmured, peering at the complex circuitry. "Maybe I can trace where Dawnboy was sent."

"You'd better not ..." Slim began, then changed his mind. "Oh, go ahead, if you think you can sort it out without messing up anything. We don't know what danger Dawnboy might be in right now."

Shyanne looked in the repairman's toolbox and found the instruction manual she had hoped would be there. By glancing at the book's diagrams, she carefully traced a visual path through the tightly packed jumble of wires and mini-transistors. Her pretty face puckered thoughtfully as she mused: "It looks like ... Yes, I think that's it."

"Have you found out what happened to Dawnboy?" Slim asked.

"I think so. It looks like I was right when I told the repairman he should use a fifty-volt transistor instead of a twenty-volt one. The twenty was too weak to carry the full load for more than a minute or two. It burned out after one transmission and the beam was switched to another circuit. That's why you and I were sent with the repairman to a different destination than Dawnboy's.

"So that must be why he was so anxious for you to go through the transporter first," Slim deduced. "Evidently, this was an attempt to kidnap you, Shyanne. The repairman was to send you first to wherever Dawnboy went. His friends would be waiting there to render you helpless and take you on to the starship hold where we were eventually transported. That way, your disappearance would have been attributed to a transporter malfunction and no one would suspect that a crime had been committed until they had searched all over the planet for you."

"That was a pretty clever plan," Shyanne said with grudging admiration. "It probably would have worked, too, if Dawnboy had not acted so chival . . . impulsively."

Slim nodded grimly. "The kid has more guts than brains, just like his father. Can you tell which transporter station he was sent to?"

"It should be the last one that the transmission dial was set for." Shyanne glanced at the dial and read: "Station B-12. I don't know where that would be on Newtonia."

"And we don't have time to look it up," Slim said. "Dawnboy must need help or he would have come back here by now. I have to go to him as soon as we can fix this . . ." Slim broke off and slapped his forehead. "What's the matter with me? I can use one of these other booths. The repairman only had them turned off to make us use this one." He rushed to the next booth, switched it on and set the transmission dial to B-12.

"Don't you think you should wait for the police?" Shyanne asked. "You have no idea what might be waiting for you at B-12."

"We can't waste any more time," Slim replied. "If I'm not back before the police get here, send them after me. I'll try to get Dawnboy and bring him back with me. So stand by to switch off the booth as soon as you see us, in case anybody tries to follow us."

Slim gave the girl a reassuring grin, then stepped into the booth. Shyanne watched the stocky Gargantuan fade from view and nervously pressed her knuckles to her lips as the seconds dragged slowly by without any sign of his reappearance. This was far more nerve-racking than the ordeal she had experienced in the starship hold. She had been too busy then to realize how frightened she actually was. Now she had nothing to do but wait and worry about her new friends who could be in danger on her account.

Not that she was to blame for what had happened to Slim and Dawnboy, Shyanne reminded herself. However she could not deny that having two good-looking men fighting for her was rather pleasing to her feminine ego. Vampirian folklore contained many exciting tales of stalwart heroes who bravely vanquished wicked enemies to win the favors of fair damsels, and Shyanne was still young enough to enjoy her own romantic fantasies. She thought that Dawnboy would make a good champion for a lady's honor, if only he were older and more like his father.

Shyanne tried to remember everything she had learned about the Apache youth during their brief acquaintance. She thought he was kind of cute in the way he tried so hard to act grown up. It was a pity that girls matured so much faster than boys, although she supposed they could still be friends in spite of that. Then she remembered that Dawnboy and Ranger were going to be competing with her and her stepmother for the treasure of Wonderwhat. If the rivalry became serious enough, she and Eythine might even be forced to blast the Farstars' ship out of existence.

But it was pointless to worry about such a possibility now, especially since there was a good chance that Dawnboy might already be dead. At that grim thought Shyanne's vivid imagination turned sober with anticipatory grief. How terribly tragic it would be for such a nice boy to die for her! She would honor his memory by mourning him in the Vampirian tradition, even to the point of slashing her earlobes, as if he had been her brother or sweetheart. Then, in the years to come, everyone who saw her tiny sorrow scars would know what a great loss she had suffered and they would understand why she always looked so sad and withdrawn.

Sudden movement in the transporter booth snapped Shyanne out of her morbid daydream. She hurried forward as Slim stepped out of the booth with Dawnboy's motionless form cradled in his arms.

"Is he alive?" Shyanne whispered.

"Just barely," Slim grunted. "Where I found him, it was cold enough to rattle a polar bear's back teeth. He was huddled at the foot of the booth, too weak to drag himself into it. Probably the heat of the booth's motor was all that kept him from freezing."

"We'll have to get him to a hospital," Shyanne said. She touched one of Dawnboy's hands and cried out at the shocking coldness of his flesh. *"Oh, the poor thing!"* She pressed her body to Dawnboy's and vigorously rubbed his hand with both of hers.

Slim looked past the small crowd of curious onlookers gathered around them and saw two uniformed police officers in antigravity boots hurrying toward them. Then he felt Dawnboy stir slightly in his arms and he peered down at the lad's pinched features.

Dawnboy's eyes opened slowly and he looked from Slim to Shyanne, then back at Slim. His lips parted in a faint smile and he whispered: "Do na worry about me. I always do things like this to make the lassies fuss over me."

Shyanne smiled tearfully back at Dawnboy, and Slim

chuckled deep in his barrel chest. "Just like your old man," he muttered fondly.

"Now, how about some food?" Dawnboy wailed, suddenly remembering that he had followed Shyanne from the restaurant before he had had dinner.

12

EYTHINE SLIPPED A détente capsule into her mouth, swallowed it with a sip of brandy and sank down wearily on her bed. She hoped the tranquilizer would enable her to sleep soundly, after the busy day and nerve-racking evening she had experienced. Tomorrow would be even more hectic because she was determined to blast off from Newtonia as soon as possible. But as she tried to relax, her gaze jerked guiltily to the closed door to the adjoining bedroom, where she knew Shyanne lay quietly sobbing herself to sleep.

Shyanne had been bitterly disappointed by Eythine's decision not to allow the girl to participate in the search for the lost treasure ship. Secretly, Eythine also regretted the decision and she had been deeply hurt by Shyanne's angry protests. The girl had accused her stepmother of callously deserting her because Eythine did not want to share the treasure with her. Hadn't she proved that she could take care of herself, Shyanne insisted. Look how she had helped Slim and Dawnboy thwart her would-be kidnappers. It was just not fair, Shyanne argued stubbornly, to use the kidnapping attempt as an excuse to leave her in a boarding school in Aristotleville.

"I worked just as hard as you did to get our ship ready for the cruise," Shyanne claimed, exaggerating the truth only slightly. "And I have as much right as you have to everything my father left us when he died. If he were still alive, you wouldn't dare treat me this way!"

Eythine had adamantly endured the girl's furious outburst, replying calmly that she was only thinking of Shyanne's safety. Finally Shyanne broke down and tearfully begged not to be left behind. It had taken all of Eythine's willpower to resist the maternal urge to gather the disappointed child in her arms and grant her her wish. On the verge of joining the girl's weeping, ing such a young and inexperienced girl along on so Eythine had brusquely left Shyanne alone in her room.

Now as Eythine reviewed the scene in her mind, she concluded that she had done the right thing. Shyanne's narrow escape this evening had made Eythine realize how foolish she had been to have ever considered tak- dangerous an expedition. A chill suddenly went through her as she recalled her fright when she and Ranger were summoned by the police to the hospital where Dawnboy was being treated for minor frostbite injuries.

Captain Zairundi accompanied Eythine and Ranger to the hospital, where the three adventurers were giv- ing an account of their exploits to a rather bored- looking police inspector. When Ranger learned what had happened, he had drawn the inspector aside out of Zairundi's hearing and expressed his suspicion that the black spaceman was somehow involved with the kid- nappers. The inspector promised to investigate that possibility, but complained that he did not have very much to work on. Slim and Shyanne had no way of knowing to which of the many nearby starships they had been transported. Nor were their descriptions of the kidnappers very helpful. The criminals could have been wearing pseudoderma disguises, the police officer pointed out, and beings of their descriptions were con- stantly coming and going in a busy interstellar port like Newtonia.

At the time, Eythine was so relieved to learn that

Shyanne had come safely through the ordeal that she had not seriously thought about Zairundi's possible connection with the kidnappers. Reconsidering the matter now, she saw how easily the mysterious Afro could have arranged for the abduction to take place at the exact moment he was in a position to insinuate himself into her confidence. As Ranger had remarked, it was an unlikely coincidence that Zairundi had just happened to come into her life at this time. But, on the other hand, the same thing could be said of Ranger. Eythine knew as little about him as she knew about Zairundi. The rough treatment Dawnboy had received from the kidnappers strongly supported his father's innocence, unless that too was part of the plot to draw suspicion away from Farstars. But if that was the case, then why did Ranger's friend Slim fight to rescue Shyanne from the hold of the unknown starship?

Eythine's thoughts became so confused that she decided to leave the detective work to those who were trained for it. The détente capsule was beginning to spread a warm, drowsy sensation through her and she smiled at the memory of how pleasant the evening had been until she was called to the hospital. This was the first time she had been able to relax and enjoy the company of attractive men since her husband's death, and the experience had aroused some old feelings within her that she had thought had died with Ram. She did not think that Ram would object to her innocent flirting with Ranger and Zairundi. She chuckled as she recalled Ranger's embarrassed expression when her foot had accidentally bumped his leg under the table. Fortunately Ranger was enough of a gentleman not to interpret the touch as an invitation to more intimate contact.

For just a moment Eythine's drug-inspired imagination dwelled on what might have happened if she and Ranger had been able to spend some time alone together . . . Then she pulled her thoughts back to reality, reminding herself that practical-minded, self-disciplined starship commanders did not waste time on pointless daydreaming. Perhaps someday she would recover enough from her grief to become seriously interested in other men. But for now her mind was still dominated by Ram's memory and his dream that she had vowed to realize for him. First she had to recover the treasure of Wonderwhat and restore the greatness of the dara Gildenfang family on Vampiria. After that she could think about making a new life for herself.

Eythine almost laughed at the casual way she had come to think about finding the treasure of Wonderwhat. That was a bad habit she would have to break in a hurry. Even with the secret information about the comet that Ram had sent to her, she knew that she had a rough and dangerous voyage ahead of her. She thought of contacting Tombolo, her ship's biocomputer brain and asking him how soon he thought they would be able to get underway. Tombolo had spent most of his long life as a dara Gildenfang retainer, so when he learned that his body was dying he had requested that his brain be allowed to continue in the family's service, if that were possible. Eythine appreciated Tombolo's sage advice and she often liked to hear him reminisce about Ram's early life. But now she was growing too sleepy to talk to anyone.

As always, remembering Ram and the all-too-brief happiness she had savored with him left her with a sick, empty feeling. It was going to be a long, lonely cruise to the Magellanic Clouds and back, without even Shyanne along for companionship. Thinking of that reminded Eythine what a great comfort the girl had been to her while she was recovering from the shattering news of Ram's death.

Not surprisingly, Shyanne had intensely disliked her stepmother at first. Eythine had assumed that was merely the expression of an only child's resentment of another woman's attempt to take her dead mother's place and draw some of her father's attention away from her. But after Ram had departed on his treasure hunt, Eythine's patience and friendliness gradually won over the girl. Shyanne finally confessed that she had felt more contempt than hatred for Eythine, because the older woman had been foolish enough to fall in love with a man who only wanted her money.

Shyanne's shrewd observation made Eythine feel even closer to her. Eythine realized then how much the Vampirian adolescent was like herself, with her beauty, brains and energetic drive to get what she wanted out of life. Like Shyanne, Eythine had been reared by a gruffly affectionate father after losing her mother at an early age. Eager to please her remaining parent, Eythine had worked diligently to master his trade. Before she was twenty, Eythine was serving as a competent Second Officer in the flagship of her father's small fleet. At twenty-five she became one of the youngest licensed starship commanders in the Unified Systems of Aquila.

Eythine had been justifiably pleased with her accomplishments, but her greatest reward was her father's glowing pride in her success. Only after his death did she realize how much she needed the emotional support of a man's approval. Unfortunately, there was no other man close enough to her to take her father's place in that respect. Her busy career and the new demands of running the family business had left her with little time for romantic involvements. Therefore, when the dashing and gallant Archguard Ramislaus dara Gildenfang strode boldly into her life, she was particularly vulnerable to his winning ways.

Not that Eythine had been entirely swept off her feet by Ram's overpowering charm. She was aware of his interest in her money and she knew she would have only herself to blame if he exploited her. As her wise, much-wed Aunt Gwenda had often warned her: "Any woman who waits until she's over thirty to fall in love deserves what she gets."

But none of that had seemed important to Eythine when she accepted Ram's proposal. She knew she was deeply in love with him and she hoped that in time she could develop his fondness into an equally strong love. It was a gamble, she realized, but one that she felt was well worth risking her fortune and future on. That was something that Eythine had been unable to explain to Shyanne, who looked at life through the cynical sophistication of youth. The girl would have to learn in her own way, as Eythine had done, the fantastic lengths to which a woman will go for a man who can make her feel like a real woman.

Now Eythine was about to demonstrate that ancient truth to herself and it was not fair for her to expose Shyanne to all the dangers and hardships that that would entail. The girl would be much better off here on Newtonia, where she could satisfy her desire to study matter-transportation technology. The police had promised to keep close watch on Shyanne, although it was unlikely that those kidnappers would bother her again. Probably they would try to follow Eythine to the treasure ship, and she was confident that her astronautical skill could easily dispense with that nuisance. That left the treasure hunt itself as her only major problem, and she had learned to reduce that one to manageable size by taking everything one day at a time.

The thought of how much she was going to miss Shyanne once more intruded on Eythine's consciousness, but she brushed it aside as she sank gratefully into the comforting fog of sleep.

13

THE FOLLOWING MORNING Ranger and Dawnboy returned to the *Gayheart* to expedite the work being done on the ship. They were happy to be back among familiar surroundings, even though the vessel would not be entirely spaceworthy for several more days.

That situation was even more frustrating when, that afternoon, they learned of Eythine's sudden departure in the *Ram's Revenge*.

"D'ye reckon there's any point in us even going out there?" Dawnboy asked. "Wi' the lead she has on us and her secret data about Wonderwhat, she may get the treasure and be on her way back before we are even clear o' this galaxy. That is, if the treasure really exists and if 'tis possible for anyone to recover it."

"Well, I don't like to quit a game until I've played my last hand," Ranger replied, as they watched a technician install their new lepton scanner. "We'll give the lady some tough competition, even if we don't finish in the money. Besides, we've promised Dr. Gitlow that we would take his instruments along and see if they detect anything new about Wonderwhat. If nothing else comes from our expedition, we can always write it off as a contribution to science."

"Too bad we canna spend that," Dawnboy remarked, his thrifty Scottish ancestry coming to the fore.

They continued with their work and were somewhat cheered an hour later by the news that Captain Zairundi's ship the *Seven Deadly Sins* had shoved off for Sappho with its cargo of parthenogenetic equipment. Ranger's inquiries about Zairundi had thus far only revealed that he appeared to be just the sort of honest businessman he claimed to be. His ship was properly registered in Heathcate's Universal Registry, his ISTA dues were paid up and his credit rating was good. Ranger could find no record of his involvement in lawsuits or any other legal trouble. Nor did any of his half-dozen crew members fit the descriptions of the thugs who had tried to kidnap Shyanne.

"At any rate, we've seen the last o' him for a while," Dawnboy said. "Sappho lies a good many light-years off in the opposite direction from the Magellanic Clouds."

"I sure hope you're right," Ranger said, still unable to shake off his uneasy feelings about Zairundi. "We'll

probably have enough trouble on this cruise as it is."
He looked closely at Dawnboy, who was resting after
making an inspection tour of the ship's hull in a vac-
suit and magnetic boots. "Do you feel all right, Son?
You look rather pale."

"I'm fine," Dawnboy assured him. " 'Tis just that my
tissue that got frostbitten last night is still a wee bit
numb. I'll spend some more time under the protoplasm
regenerator to take care o' it."

"It serves you right," Lulu scolded, "for not using
your throat mike to call me for help when you found
yourself in that freezing valley."

"I didna think o' that until it was too late," Dawnboy explained. "I was too busy trying to get back to
help Shyanne and Slim."

"A mistake like that could cost you your life," Lulu
said, miffed by Dawnboy's resistance to her efforts to
fuss over him. "I think we should leave him here where
it's safer, Skipper. You and I can handle the ship without him."

"I thought about that," Ranger said, "when I heard
that Eythine had decided to leave Shyanne here."

"Aw, Dad, ye canna do that to me!" Dawnboy protested.

Ranger smiled reassuringly at the boy. "I only said I
had thought about it. But I can't treat *you* as a child.
You've proved that you can do a man's job, and as
long as you continue to act like a man, I'll let you
make your own decisions."

"Ye already ken what my decision is in this case,"
Dawnboy said, trying to conceal the glow of pride he
felt at his father's words.

As they were about to return to work, they were
pleasantly interrupted by the arrival of Slim Hinterwald. The burly Gargantuan chided Ranger for not
being on hand to see Helen-of-Troy Hughes-Orfo off
when her ship left Astropolis that morning.

"I somehow forgot all about her," Ranger said with
a guilty blush. "I hope she didn't mind it."

"Naw, she was a good sport about it," Slim

said. "That's a great little woman, Snowy. You ought to lock onto her and her old man's money, before some low-down fortune hunter like me does it."

"That's what I say," Lulu put in.

"I can manage my love life without your help," Ranger curtly informed them.

"What love life?" Dawnboy asked, drawing an icy glare from his father.

"Ah, yes, what is more beautiful than romance among the stars?" Slim sighed. "Reminds me of the time I nearly married the ex-Virgin Queen of Symbion. She was called the Virgin Queen, until ten minutes after I got there."

"What took you so long?" Ranger asked.

"Why, you don't think I'm rude enough to do anything to a lady without a proper introduction first, do you?" Slim demanded. "Anyhow, it turned out they had this custom that if a man kissed a woman without her permission, she had the right to either marry him or to sell him into slavery."

"And the queen chose to marry ye?" Dawnboy asked.

"She wanted to, but she needed the money even more," Slim answered. "So she started to auction me off. By then all the other women were so anxious to buy me that a riot broke out and I was able to escape in the confusion."

"We _had_ to ask," Ranger groaned, turning away from Slim. "When will I learn not to encourage you and your tall tales?"

"Never, I hope," Slim answered, instantly launching into another of his far-fetched yarns.

They were spared the ordeal of listening to it by Lulu's announcement that Ranger had a call from the police department. Ranger switched on his photophone screen and faced Inspector Bothwell, the official who was investigating the attempted kidnapping. Bothwell reported that the police had not made much progress toward learning the kidnappers' identities. He wondered if Slim or Dawnboy had been able to remember any other details that might help him with the case. Slim replied that he had already told the Inspector everything he knew about the experience.

"Wait, I do remember something else," Dawnboy interrupted. "The mon who hit me called the fake repairmon Daran. And the Satyr with him referred to someone or something as The Arrow."

"Those were probably false names that they assumed to confuse any witnesses," Inspector Bothwell said. "But we will check them out with our files of known criminal aliases. The Arrow could be a code name for their leader."

Ranger had another idea. "Did you find any evidence to connect Zairundi with the kidnapping or with the theft of the two matter-transporter booths? I'm sure that one of them must have been the booth in the starship hold where Slim and Shyanne were transported. And it couldn't have been just coincidence that Zairundi mentioned the stolen booths to me at exactly the time the kidnapping was taking place."

Inspector Bothwell shook his head regretfully. "If Captain Zairundi was involved with either of those crimes, he was clever enough not to leave any traces behind. I tried to get a warrant to search his ship before he left, but I had no evidence to convince the court of his probable guilt. I couldn't even hold him here as a material witness, without violating his civil liberties."

With a touch of irony, Ranger recalled what Eythine had said about having to put up with a little crime being part of the price they had to pay for living under governments that protect the individual's rights. He chewed his lower lip in exasperation and muttered: "Damn it, I *know* Zairundi is mixed up in this somehow. All the time I was with him last night I had the impression that he was toying with Eythine and me, that he was deliberately telling us of his guilt with the arrogant confidence that he could always stay a few steps ahead of us."

"It looks like he was right about that," Slim remarked.

Ranger unhappily agreed with Slim. He wished there was some way they could keep track of the *Seven Deadly Sins*. He had a nagging suspicion that they had not yet seen the last of Zairundi.

In the busy days that followed, Ranger had little time to worry about Captain Zairundi or about anything beyond the immediate task of getting the *Gayheart* in shape for a long cruise. Dawnboy was eager to help with the work, but his father insisted that he take time off to see more of the wonders of Newtonia. Ranger wanted the lad to make the most of this opportunity to further his scientific education, because he did not know when they would be able to visit the planet again.

Dawnboy enjoyed rambling around the fascinating world, especially when Slim accompanied him. The instant liking between the oddly matched pair had been forged into a deep friendship by their struggle with the kidnappers, and Slim took the youth under his muscle-bound wing like a fond uncle. Dawnboy soon learned to appreciate the keen mind and vast store of knowledge that the Gargantuan's jovial exterior concealed. At first Dawnboy could not understand why a man of Slim's superior abilities went to so much trouble to impress people as being merely a lighthearted fool. Ranger explained that Slim had never believed that the unpleasant necessity of working for a living should interfere with life's true purpose—having fun.

One day Dawnboy and Slim called on Shyanne at her boarding school and took her on a sight-seeing tour of Aristotleville's industrial research area. The girl seemed to be getting along well in her new environment and she was particularly pleased to have been admitted to a course on matter-transporter technology taught by Dr. Gitlow, the leading authority in that field. She was the only girl in the class, and she rather enjoyed that distinction. But in spite of that, Shyanne still resented her stepmother. She had every right to go along on the treasure hunt, the girl stubbornly insisted. It had been grossly unfair of Eythine to treat her like an irresponsible child, Shyanne claimed, with a winsomely childlike pout.

So convincingly did the pretty Vampirian argue her case that Dawnboy sympathetically agreed with her. Then suddenly it dawned on him that she was hinting that he should help her stow away on the *Gayheart*. At that point, Dawnboy hastily changed the subject. He could hardly wait until he and Slim could get away from the girl. *Great space; is there no limit to the underhanded deviousness of women?* he wondered. It seemed that no matter which way a man turned, there was always a conniving female to take advantage of him. Yet, strangely enough, when he and Shyanne were not together he found himself missing her. He did not know what to make of his mixed emotions toward the girl. Nor was he enlightened or amused by Lulu's grandmotherly advice that he should take a cold shower and forget it.

The work on the *Gayheart* proceeded rapidly, with Ranger urging the workers on and Slim entertaining them with his uproariously incredible stories. Some of Slim's romantic claims were so outrageously bawdy that even Lulu was scandalized, as she hung on every word. Dawnboy was especially anxious to hear the chunky Gargantuan tell about Ranger's wild youth, much to the latter's discomfort. During one such reminiscence, Slim suddenly broke off and said:

"Oh, that reminds me. Snowy, do you by chance remember Nation Flintlock, the ranger scout pilot who joined the Church of Divine Capitalism after our discharges?"

"Yes, I mentioned him to Dawnboy when I saw the Church's missionary ship in port for repairs. What about him?"

"We just missed seeing him. He was aboard the *Wherewithal* when she docked. But he went on to Puerto Miami the day before I got here."

"Too bad he didn't stay a little longer," Ranger said. "I would have liked to see him again. I always thought it was ironic that he was the one who turned religious, after being the most rowdy and cynical disbeliever in our old gang."

"Yeah, it was a shame the way you and he led me astray," Slim said accusingly. "When I was such a moral, clean-cut kid. The skipper of the *Wherewithal* told me that old Flint almost became a martyr for his faith, when they got into trouble on Fabrica. The Fabrican authorities didn't want their people to hear sermons about the sacredness of private property and other subversive capitalist ideas. So they tried to blast the missionary ship out of their space. When she was damaged, Flint took a lifeboat out and decoyed the Fabrican ships long enough for her to escape. Then he shook them off and rejoined the *Wherewithal*. So I guess he hasn't lost his touch at the controls."

"Nor his courage," Ranger said with admiration. "He was the most iron-nerved combat pilot I've ever known. I thought for sure he would make a career of the Space Rangers or some other military force. Just goes to show how wrong you can be about people."

"I remember hearing about the High Intender o' Fabrica, in Rothfeller Hughes's Currency Museum on Capitalia," Dawnboy said. "He used to issue letter-o'-credit tapes that his creditors thought were as good as gold, until they discovered that the tapes erased themselves when presented for payment. Fabrica is a funny name for a planet. Why is it called that?"

"For the logical reason that it was fabricated," Slim answered. "It's an artificial world."

"*Artificial?* Aw, come on!" Dawnboy demanded.

"He's telling the truth, for a change," Ranger said. "Lulu, you'd better explain it to Dawnboy. I'm not too keen on the history of that part of the galaxy."

"Not much to tell," Lulu began. "About eighty years ago there was a political dispute that led to civil war on Gnomondia, a human-inhabited planet of Deneb. The losing side, led by the High Intender, was driven off the planet and took refuge on several large asteroids. The High Intender got the bright idea that all of the planetoids could be brought together to form a single planet with enough gravity to hold down a life-supporting atmosphere. So he contracted with several world-development companies to do the job, paying them with his infamous letter-of-credit tapes. When the contractors complained of being cheated, the High Intender had them executed and passed a law against any form of capitalism on Fabrica. You can get the death penalty just for speaking the word there."

"That explains why the ruler of Fabrica is called the High Intender," Ranger added. "Like most people who borrow heavily to finance lofty ideals, he had high intentions of paying off his debts someday. But he didn't like to be pestered for payment in the meantime."

"That's what I always tell my women," Slim said. "Sure, honey, I intend to get married and settle down someday. But don't pester me about it."

Dawnboy tucked the story of Fabrica away in his mind, marveling anew at the intriguing variety of intelligent societies scattered throughout the known universe. They had moved into the galley during their conversation and Dawnboy sliced three sizable wedges from a chocolate cake while his father brewed a fresh pot of citroffee. Dawnboy placed the largest helping of cake on the table before Slim and asked, "What made ye think o' yer old friend Flintlock just now?"

"Oh, yeah," Slim said around a mouthful of cake. "I was going to tell you about the time that Flint and I and some of the other boys introduced your Dad to the mysteries of love."

Ranger stared uncomprehendingly at Slim. "What the devil are you talking about?"

Slim gave Ranger a reproachful look. "Don't tell me you've forgotten your passionate evening with Lady Mary on Jernia! Not that you were in any condition to remember anything then, but . . ."

"Oh, for Mars's sake!" Ranger exclaimed, his

puzzled expression turning into a painful grimace. "You're not going to tell that absurd story!"

"Why, Boss, you're actually blushing," Lulu accused Ranger. "This story must *really* be a juicy one. I can hardly wait to hear it!"

"Aye, tell us about it, Slim," Dawnboy begged, grinning with impish delight at his father's discomfort.

Over Ranger's heated protests, Slim began: "It was just after we had seen our first combat, during the civil war between the planets of Castor and Pollux. Our outfit was given a four-day pass to Deepswamp City on the neutral world of Jernia. Naturally, the first thing we did there was look for girls. All of us except Snowy, that is. For some reason, he wouldn't go along with us in that activity. I think it was because he had promised his mother he would remain pure until he married. But on the other hand, he bragged about his ability to hold his liquor. So we decided to find out how good he really was in both those departments."

Slim forked up another large chunk of cake and washed it down with a swig of citroffee, while Dawnboy and Lulu waited impatiently for him to continue. "One night we lured him into the bar at Rita's Pleasure Emporium." Slim sighed nostalgically at the memory. "Now there was a true house of joy for you! They just don't make 'em like Rita anymore. She had the greatest . . ." Slim caught Ranger's warning glare and broke off with an awkward cough. "Well, as I meant to say, we got Snowy in there and bribed one of the girls to challenge him to a strip drinking contest. She was just a frail-looking little thing, but they called her Mary, Queen of Scotch, because she could sure hold a quart of it."

"Wait a minute," Dawnboy interrupted. "What kind of a contest did ye say?"

"A strip drinking contest," Slim replied. "That's where two or more players start drinking from filled glasses at the same time and the last one to finish has to remove an article of his or her clothing. The first one who ends up with no clothes on has to . . . But I'd better wait till I get to that part of the story."

"A strip drinking contest," Lulu repeated with great interest. "That's a new one to me, and I thought *I* had heard everything."

Dawnboy hissed her to silence and urged Slim to go on. Ranger sat rigidly across from his old friend, reminding himself that he could not politely murder the man who had saved his son's life.

"Well, sir," Slim said, savoring the final scrap of frosting from his plate. "Snowy and Mary got right down to business and for a while the competition was neck and neck. Snowy won the first round and off came Mary's shoes. Then she was a split second ahead of him at draining her second glass. That cost Snowy his boots. It went like that until they both were glassy-eyed drunk and peeled down to a single garment each, which modesty prevents me from naming. For the final time their glasses were filled and their trembling hands struggled to raise them to their lips. The moment of truth had arrived! The tension in the bar was so thick that no one hardly dared even to breathe. We waited anxiously to see if our brave comrade would uphold the honor of the Space Rangers, or go down in—if you'll pardon the expression—naked defeat. The glasses slowly and unsteadily rose to the drinking positions. But just as the first drops trickled into their mouths—*Owww!*"

Slim doubled up in pain and reached down to rub his right shin, which had been nearly broken by a hard kick under the table. Ranger looked on innocently as Dawnboy and Lulu pleaded with Slim to finish the story. Slim looked fearfully at Ranger and tried to draw back out of reach of his long legs.

"Well, uh, the fact is . . ." Slim stammered. "Something just jogged my memory. I remember now that it wasn't your father in the contest; it was Flint. And it wasn't in Rita's place; it was some saloon on Tricon. And it wasn't actually a strip drinking contest . . ."

"Oh, please tell us the rest of the story," Ranger pleaded. "We're simply dying to hear it."

Dawnboy glared at Ranger in bitter disappointment. "A fine father ye are! Now I'll never learn what ye were really like at my age."

"That's just as well," Ranger said. "In this family we follow the Eleventh Commandment: Thou shalt do as I say, not as I do."

Ranger's impatient speedup of the *Gayheart*'s overhaul nearly brought him to blows more than once with the painstaking technicians who were accustomed to working at a more leisurely pace. But his demand for haste did produce results. Even Slim was persuaded to help out with some of the heavier work, which he complained was beneath his dignity as a starship pilot.

Dawnboy continued to hope that Slim would agree to accompany them on their treasure hunt, and Slim admitted he was tempted to accept their invitation. But on the day before their scheduled departure, Slim decided to go on to New New America and take the instructor's job at the Merchant Space Academy. After all, he pointed out, it was his humanitarian duty to spread himself around the female population as much as possible and there were many more women in the USA than they were likely to find in the Magellanic Clouds.

Ranger and Dawnboy were disappointed by Slim's decision, but Slim said he would soften the blow by treating them to a farewell dinner in Astropolis's finest restaurant. They finished work late that afternoon and Ranger was about to enjoy a relaxing soak in the soniclaver when Lulu announced the arrival of a technician from the Darwin Institute. Dr. Gitlow had sent him to make final adjustments on the scientific instruments that had been installed in one of the ship's unused aft compartments. Ranger grumbled that it was pretty inconsiderate of Gitlow to wait until the last minute to take care of that detail. At that point, Slim said through the ship's intercom system that he would deal with the technician, to enable Ranger and Dawnboy to get cleaned up for the party.

It turned out to be a very successful farewell party, in Slim's opinion. By the time they tottered wearily back to the ship in the early hours of the following morning, Slim had gotten pleasantly drunk, met an especially attractive woman, knocked down two belligerent spacehands and managed to get them thrown out of three bars. Dawnboy emotionally thanked Slim for an evening that he swore he would never forget.

Ranger, on the other hand, said he was sure going to try to forget it.

14

"HEY, DAD," DAWNBOY's voice called through the *Gayheart*'s intercom system. "What's a transvestite?"

Ranger's head, bending over the No. 3 reserve rocket fuel tank, snapped upright so abruptly that it banged painfully into a low transverse beam. "What is a *what?*" he demanded, as Lulu's low chuckle came from the speaker.

"Transvestite," Dawnboy repeated. *"T-r-a-n-s—"*

"I know how it's spelled," Ranger muttered, rubbing his smarting scalp. "But where in space did you find a word like that?"

"I'm reading one o' the old stories about how the *Jealousy* got lost in Wonderwhat with her precious cargo. It says here that her captain, Otiose Oublier, was a crazy transvestite, among other things."

"Oh, yes, I had forgotten about that particular yarn. There's been so much said and recorded about the treasure that it's hard to tell what to believe. Anyway,

THE TREASURE OF WONDERWHAT 115

a transvestite is a . . ." Ranger hesitated uncertainly. "Well, it's kind of hard to explain. Maybe you better come down here with me."

"Okay. Where are ye?"

"In the engine room."

"Be right there."

Ranger stepped back and ran his gaze along the lines attached to the tanks. The lines led to the smoothly purring luxium reactor, which in addition to generating the ship's star-drive and life-support systems, also produced fuel for the rockets used for take-offs, landings and other precision maneuvers. They were seven hours out of Newtonia, making good speed through clear space. The repair crew chief had wanted to put the ship through a shakedown cruise before certifying her as spaceworthy enough for the company's warranty, but Ranger had been too impatient to wait for that. Eythine already had a four-and-a-half-day lead on them, and he was anxious to get under way while there was still a chance that they could reach the Magellanic Clouds not too far behind her. He had to sign a waiver in order to take delivery of the ship, and he carried out his own inspection of her performance while cruising. So far everything seemed to be working very well.

"What's the matter, are you embarrassed to tell your son the facts of life?" Lulu asked.

"No, I just haven't yet had time enough to get to know him thoroughly. I can't guess how well he'll handle certain things. Dawnboy's pretty mature in most ways, but basically he's still just a kid. By the way, why didn't *you* tell him what a transvestite is, since you've volunteered to be his teacher?"

"There are some things a boy should learn from his father," Lulu answered, taking the easy way out. "Besides, it isn't easy for me to explain things pertaining to the human body, when I no longer have one."

"You have a good point," Ranger agreed, as his son came clattering down the ladder to join him.

"Any trouble here?" Dawnboy asked, looking

around at all the spotlessly clean and gleaming mechanical gear in the room.

"Nothing serious. I just had to make a few minor adjustments here and there. It seems to have been an excellent overhaul job."

"I'll say. Have ye noticed the new lepton scanner yet? It's a beauty."

"That was the first thing I checked out." Ranger hesitated, trying to find the right words to answer Dawnboy's original question. "Uh, about that word you discovered . . . Well, you must remember that different societies have different customs and opinions of what is proper conduct for men and women. What some people may think is shamefully unmasculine or unfeminine behavior could be the accepted norm to other people. That's why I've always told you to be tolerant when we visit other worlds and not let the inhabitants' ways embarrass you or cause you to lose respect for them. For example, in your mother's clan on Apache Highlands the traditional male costume is the kilt, because they think it stresses a man's strength and virility. But in other cultures . . ."

Dawnboy cut him off with an impatient wave of his hand. "Dad, if I'd known a simple question would lead to all that rigmarole, I would ha' looked the word up in the computer's dictionary banks."

Ranger smiled helplessly. "You're right; it isn't worth getting all that worked up over. A transvestite is merely someone with a strong compulsion to wear the clothing of the opposite sex. Captain Oublier liked to shock people by dressing up in women's finery, so the story goes. You can imagine how frustrated he was when unisex styles became fashionable on his homeworld. That was why he left it and became a space wanderer, always looking for new worlds where his girlish hobby would attract attention."

"Is that all the word means?" Dawnboy asked disappointedly. "There was a lad like that in the clan. But we didna call him a transvestite."

"Oh? What did you call him?"

"A sissy. But he really wasna one. I had a fight with him when I was eleven and he knocked me down."

Ranger chuckled at the mental image of his son being flattened by a boy in a frilly girl's dress. "I had no idea the clan was so tolerant of noncomformists."

"Well, he didna dress that way by choice," Dawnboy said. "His father made him do it as punishment, because he was always sneaking away from our warrior games to hang around the visiting bards and artists and other unmanly types. Finally, about a year ago, he ran away with one o' them. The last we heard he was in Londonburg studying poetry, much to his father's shame and disgust."

"The clan has harsh standards for manhood," Ranger said, thinking sympathetically of the ostracized lad whose only sin had been an overabundance of artistic sensitivity. "But I'm glad you measured up to it." He looked around the engine room with professional satisfaction. "Well, I'm finished in here for the time being. What say we adjourn to the galley for a bite to eat?"

"I was just there a little while ago," Dawnboy said, patting his stomach. "But I'll go along wi' ye for company, if Lulu doesna need either o' us on the bridge."

"Things are running so smoothly that I only need you to keep me from falling asleep with boredom," Lulu said. "You two go on along and let me enjoy the feel of my refurbished outfit, before you mess it up with your tinkering."

"I'm beginning to worry about Lulu," Ranger said as he and Dawnboy started up the ladder. "As time goes by, she seems to act more like a machine than a human."

"Stop trying to flatter me," Lulu said.

They headed for the galley where Ranger poured out two glasses of cold, genuine cow's milk and Dawnboy made sandwiches from their more perishable grocery supplies. The ship's hydroponics tanks constantly provided them with fresh vegetables and high-protein soybeans that could be synthesized into any form of meat or dairy product. But on a long space voyage even so varied a diet as that could become as monotonous as salt pork and hardtack had been for Columbus's crew. So most star rovers habitually gorged themselves on planet-grown victuals while in port and for as long as they lasted on a cruise.

"The more I learn about the treasure o' Wonderwhat, the more I wonder how much o' it we should believe," Dawnboy remarked as they sat down at the table.

"There certainly is a strong element of unreality about the story," Ranger said. "And about that part of the universe in general. But I am inclined to believe it precisely because it's unlikely that anyone could have dreamed up such a fantastic yarn. No sane starship commander would have risked his vessel and the lives of himself and his crew on a mad venture into the most dangerous part of the ZuJu territory. So Captain Oublier must actually have been as crazy as the accounts indicate."

"Aye, only a madmon would've done what he did," Dawnboy agreed. "Or what we're doing now. No wonder he was nicknamed Midas, if the tales o' his greedy lust for gold are true."

Ranger nodded. "Evidently his greed so unbalanced his mind that he actually believed the fabulous stories about the lost planet Fossick, where huge ants cast up gold dust and precious stones while digging their burrows. But because this is such a mad and unpredictable universe, he actually did find Fossick, loaded his ship with gold and jewels and managed to evade the ZuJus to make his getaway."

"But when he was nearly home free, he threw it all away," Dawnboy said. "I do na understand that part o' the story at all."

Ranger looked reproachfully at his son over his glass of milk. "You didn't do your homework thoroughly," he accused, setting down his glass and picking up his sandwich. "According to the story, as the *Jealousy* was returning to our galaxy, Captain 'Midas' Oublier sighted the comet Wonderwhat on a collision course with a supernova. He knew that wouldn't bother Wonderwhat, which had been observed on other occasions to pass unharmed through the hearts of exploding stars."

"Aye, that would fit in wi' Dr. Gitlow's theory that Wonderwhat was created from the explosion o' a matter star coming together wi' one o' anti-matter."

Ranger had taken a large bite of his sandwich. He nodded in agreement with Dawnboy's statement while he chewed and swallowed. "Right, but Midas had another scientific theory in mind. He recalled from his study of basic physics that the atom-altering activities within a supernova are supposedly capable of generating gold and uranium from iron."

"The philosopher's stone o' the old-time alchemists!" Dawnboy cried, delighted to find something learned from his study of ancient mythology related to modern science.

"Yes, but the transmuted precious elements would not be of much use to people as scattered atoms," Ranger pointed out. "Midas thought perhaps he could get around that problem by using Wonderwhat's peculiar properties to shield a solid object from disintegration as it passed through the supernova. Motivated by his insatiable greed and ignoring his crew's frantic protests that they were already rich enough, Midas insisted on pushing a nearby large nickle-iron meteor into the comet's tail, whereupon the *Jealousy* herself became trapped in the tail."

"That was a fitting end for the greedy slob," Lulu remarked.

"Yes, if that really was the end of Midas," Ranger replied. "When the crew members saw that they couldn't escape being drawn into the exploding star, they panicked and abandoned ship in lifeboats. But Midas was unable to tear himself away from his treasure. He stubbornly remained aboard the *Jealousy* as she disappeared into the supernova. Years later the ship was observed still trapped in the comet's tail, but no one has ever been able to find out what happened to her captain. At least not anyone who has ever seen the ship and returned to tell about it."

Dawnboy, pausing in his voracious attack on his food and drink, asked: "What about the meteor? Was it actually turned into gold?"

"There are conflicting reports on that," Ranger answered. "Some observers claim they've seen the meteor, glowing bright yellow, along with the *Jealousy*. But others say the ship is alone in the comet's tail."

"You pays your money and you takes your choice," Lulu said lightly. "You may as well believe in a golden meteor, to make the story more interesting, since the whole thing is probably just nonsense."

"Another cynic heard from," Ranger grumbled. "You find it easy to sneer at other people's dreams, don't you?"

"It isn't always easy," Lulu replied. "But it's generally worth the effort."

"Pay her no mind," Dawnboy said. "She'll be sorry when we get the treasure and refuse to share it with her." He finished his sandwich and washed it down with the last of his milk.

"If Eythine leaves anything for us to claim," Ranger reminded him, staring at the boy's empty plate and nibbling on the remaining portion of his own sandwich. He still found it hard to believe what a healthy, growing adolescent's appetite could do to a meal.

"Well, if Eythine gets the treasure first, ye can always marry her for it," Dawnboy laughed. Then he blushed as his father's sharp look reminded him that Ranger considered himself irrevocably married to Gay, or rather to what was left of her. "Sorry, Dad," he mumbled.

"That's all right," Ranger smiled. "Eythine is a mighty attractive woman, as were many others I've met in the past several years. I won't deny that I have been tempted sometimes . . ." His voice trailed off wistfully, then he ruthlessly forced the thought out of his mind. "On the other hand, Shyanne impressed me as being quite a girl. If you two kids were just a little older, I might see if I could get something going between you and her."

"Thanks, but I can choose my own girlfriends," Dawnboy said stiffly.

"Don't you like Shyanne?" Ranger asked.

"She's all right," Dawnboy said tolerantly. "She kens a great deal about matter-transporters and other technical things."

"What a romantic basis for a relationship," Lulu observed. "If you and she ever get married, you'll probably spend your honeymoon working in a machine shop."

"He still has plenty of time to think about getting seriously involved," Ranger said, giving his son an understanding look. "There will probably be many women in his life before he settles down. I *know* there will be, if he hangs around with Slim Hinterwald very much. But I have a strong preference for Shyanne. Being with her reminded me of how much your mother and I wanted a daughter."

"Ye mean instead o' *me?*" Dawnboy demanded indignantly.

"No. In addition to you," Ranger explained. "We thought a boy and a girl would be a nice combination to start a family with. But we postponed having a second child, thinking we had plenty of time for that." He stared morosely into space as memories of unfulfilled dreams flickered through his mind.

"I reckon 'tis just as well that ye didna ha' a daughter," Dawnboy said. "My cousin Kathleen made my life as miserable as any sister could. I do na think I could ha' survived the real thing."

"Spoken like a true male animal," Lulu sighed. "You sound more like your father every day. Sometimes I despair of ever getting either one of you married off, so that I can have some peace and quiet around here."

"You can forget about thinking of me in that way,"

Ranger said. "If I can't have the wife I chose, I don't want any woman."

"Do na be too sure about that," Dawnboy said, his lips twitching with a suppressed grin. "Ye might run into Mary, Queen o' Scotch again."

Ranger bared his teeth in mock anger and lunged across the table at his son. Dawnboy dodged away from him, slipped off his chair and ran laughing out of the galley. Ranger started after the boy, then smiled to himself and started clearing the table. "Lulu, why do you always have to act like a nosy, interfering old busybody?" asked Ranger wearily.

"Because I am a nosy, interfering old busybody," the biocomputer replied. "And I love every minute of it. But I don't think I'll have to worry any more about your unattached status, if I can just keep you alive long enough for either Eythine or Helen to get her lonely widow's hooks into you."

Ranger chidingly clucked his tongue. "You should be ashamed of yourself for having such a suspicious mind. Those two women have only recently lost their husbands. They aren't looking to get married again so soon, if ever. They both have careers, you know."

"Dream on, you happy fool," Lulu laughed.

"What's that supposed to mean?"

"It means that, for all your experience, you still don't know the first thing about women."

"Which is . . ."

"Women are marrying animals. It's in their nature and they can't change it even if they wanted to. And for a mere male to try to change it or escape it is the ultimate folly. Sometimes women will even marry men they really don't want, just to keep in practice."

Ranger threw up his hands in exasperation and stalked toward the door. "I'm not going to listen to any more of your nonsense. I've got work to do."

As he walked down the passageway to the bridge, Lulu cheered him on by humming the wedding march.

15

In the following days, Ranger and Dawnboy had little spare time to think about their lack of female companionship, as they were kept busy monitoring the *Gayheart*'s performance. After a week of careful observation, Ranger felt confident that the ship was indeed spaceworthy enough for the long voyage ahead of them. By then Ranger, Dawnboy and Lulu had settled into the repetitious routine of space flight.

The ship's autopilot and other computerized faculties did most of the work; but Ranger and Dawnboy took turns standing watch at the helm, to allow Lulu to rest. Although her brain actually required little sleep because it was relieved of physical stress, Lulu still occasionally needed to distract her attention from the dulling impact of work.

Dawnboy often wondered what Lulu did for relaxation and entertainment, aside from meddling in his and Ranger's lives. Lulu's evasive answers to his queries on that subject aroused Dawnboy's suspicions enough to inspire him to search curiously through her computer banks. He soon discovered that the banks contained, in addition to much serious material, an extensive collection of romantic and erotic audiovisual fiction. When Dawnboy remained unconvinced by Lulu's claims that the tapes' function was strictly educational, she confessed to using them for harmless titillation now and then. After all, Lulu pointed out, she might be over a hundred years old and confined to her tank of cerebrospinal fluid, but she was not completely dead yet.

Ranger explained that although most starships were crewed by members of both sexes, or more in some species, the tapes' entertaining diversion helped relieve tension among crews that were an exception to that rule. There were also drugs and autohypnotic suggestions from the Sleep-Teacher to spare lonely space travelers the discomfort of pent-up frustrations. Everyone had to handle the problem in his own way, Ranger said, but he preferred to keep his mind and body fully occupied with hard work, vigorous exercises in the ship's gym and concentrated studying.

Dawnboy soon learned that it was best to follow his father's example. He also found much satisfaction in his duties as the ship's gardener and cook. Although Lulu's automation system did most of the work required to take care of the crops grown in the hydroponics tanks, the help of human hands was needed to harvest the swift-growing produce and process it through the food synthesizer. Dawnboy derived great pleasure from experimenting with the wide variety of tasty, nourishing dishes that could be concocted with the machine. Most of the meals he turned out were at least edible.

The youth was so proud of his culinary skills that Ranger tried not to complain when his digestion flatly refused what was placed before him on the table. Even on those occasions no food was wasted, thanks to the bottomless pit of Dawnboy's stomach. In fact, food disappeared so rapidly that if Ranger had not seen with his own eyes how his son could pack it away, he would have feared that the *Gayheart* was infested by Arachnean glutguts, the Space Age equivalent of ship's rats.

Recently Dawnboy had acquired a powerful thirst for fruit and vegetable juices, especially tomato juice, judging by the frequency that Ranger found containers of the red liquid in the refrigerator. Ranger did not ordinarily care for juices, but one evening he came off his watch with his dry mouth craving something wet and cold. He went into the galley and opened the refrigerator door, absently looking over the several liter-sized containers of assorted liquids. His hand fell on the container labeled TOMATO JUICE and he raised it to his mouth to take a deep swallow.

An instant later, Ranger leaned over the sink spewing out the salty-tasting stuff in shocked revulsion. After fighting down an urge to retch, he wiped his mouth with a trembling hand and stared blankly at the juice container. What his taste buds told him made no sense, until he thought to examine the food-synthesizer's memory tape to learn what foods it had recently prepared. Then several small, unimportant occurrences of the past few days started to fit meaningfully together in his mind. Ranger did not like the pattern they formed. To double-check his conclusions, Ranger spoke to Lulu and confronted her with the juice container and the food-synthesizer tape.

"You are aware of nearly everything that happens aboard this vessel," Ranger said in his most formal voice of command. "So just answer yes or no: did you know about this and neglect to tell me?"

"Yes, sir," Lulu replied without her usual flippant tone. "But don't think that . . ."

"That will be enough for now," Ranger snapped curtly. "I'll listen to your excuses after I've talked to Dawnboy."

Ranger left the galley and went to the bridge, his jaw set grimly. Lulu tried to speak to him again, but he ordered her to be silent. Dawnboy was slouched down in the pilot seat, his eyes lazily monitoring the viewscreens. Ranger strode over to his son and thrust the container in front of his face. "Where is she?" the starship commander demanded abruptly.

"Huh?" Dawnboy's startled gaze moved jerkily from the container to his father's stern expression. He felt his cheeks flush hotly, but he tried to keep his tone light. "Oh, hullo, Dad. Ye having some o' my tomato juice? I didna think ye liked it, or I would ha' run off a fresh batch."

"Stow the innocent act," Ranger ordered. "You know only one being who drinks pseudoplasma, and the amount of liquids you have synthesized indicates that you have been feeding her for the past several days. I'm already angry enough with you for helping Shyanne stow away in the ship; don't make matters worse for yourself by lying about it."

Dawnboy stared guiltily down at the deck. "She's in the aft compartment wi' Dr. Gitlow's instruments," he mumbled in a small voice.

"There's no intercom speaker in there," Ranger said, "so you go back there and bring her to me."

"Aye, aye, sir." The young Apache stood up and shuffled dispiritedly off the bridge, not daring to return his father's cold stare.

"May I speak now, Captain?" Lulu asked politely when Dawnboy was gone.

"All right, but make it short," Ranger said impatiently.

"I just want to explain that Dawnboy did not help the girl stow away. We were nearly three days out of Newtonia before even I learned that she was aboard. She sneaked into the galley during one of his watches to get some food. I told Dawnboy about her and we decided to keep her presence a secret because we knew you would waste much valuable time taking her back to Newtonia. It was mostly my fault, so don't be too hard on the kids."

Ranger paced rapidly to and fro on the bridge deck, trying to relieve some of his angry frustration. "I might have known you would try to excuse the boy, but it won't wash. Nobody could have possibly gotten aboard without being detected by your alarm system. Someone had to switch off that system long enough for her to get into the ship and hide herself, and only Dawnboy and I have that authority."

"The service crew foreman also had that authority, temporarily," Lulu reminded Ranger. "He shut my system down several times while the overhaul work was going on."

Ranger thought about that for a moment, then shook his head. "No, I don't see how the foreman could have been involved with this, even if he had wanted to get even with you for the time you locked him in Sick Bay. I personally inspected every compartment after the work was finished. She wasn't aboard then."

Lulu started to say something else, but she was interrupted by the arrival of Dawnboy and Shyanne. The Vampirian girl was visibly nervous and apprehensive as she approached Ranger, but she boldly met his hard gaze with an expression that said she was prepared to take her punishment without whining or asking for special consideration.

"I am sorry to impose on you this way, Captain Farstar," Shyanne began quickly before Ranger could speak. "But I had to find some way to safeguard my interest in the Wonderwhat treasure. I promise I won't be any extra trouble to you. I'll work to pay my way and I'll leave as soon as we catch up with my stepmother's ship."

"You may leave sooner than that, if we come across another ship headed for Newtonia," Ranger replied. "But I'll decide about that later. Right now I want to know how my son helped you stow away in my ship."

"But he didn't help me," Shyanne replied with wide-eyed sincerity. "No one helped me. I slipped aboard all by myself, the night before you blasted off. And not even your biocomputer would have spotted me, if I had thought to bring more food along with me."

Ranger took an impulsive step toward Shyanne, causing Dawnboy to flinch for her sake. The youth had never seen his father looking quite so furious before and he was relieved when Ranger managed to control his temper as he spoke calmly to the girl. "Please don't insult my intelligence by lying to me, Shyanne. It won't increase or decrease Dawnboy's punishment if you admit his part in this. I just want to know for my own satisfaction when he decided to betray me."

The words slashed brutally into Dawnboy's deeply sensitive attachment to his father. Dawnboy started to fling back an indignant denial of the charge, but Lulu forestalled him.

"Be careful you don't say something you'll regret, Boss," Lulu cautioned. "I just remembered there was somebody else who had the temporary authority to shut off my alarm system, somebody whom you trusted enough to leave in command of the ship while you and Dawnboy cleaned up for your last night ashore in Astropolis."

"Slim Hinterwald!" Ranger and Dawnboy cried together.

Shyanne frantically tried to deny Slim's involvement, but her guilty blush was far more expressive than her words.

Ranger slammed his right fist into his left palm and laughed humorlessly. "Of course it had to be Slim! This is just the sort of crazy practical joke that would appeal to his twisted sense of humor. I'll bet he's still laughing about it."

"Thank goodness we've settled that," Lulu sighed. "Now I think you owe Dawnboy an apology for unjustly accusing him."

Ranger's expression softened only slightly as he met Dawnboy's hopeful smile. "You aren't entirely off the hook, Son," Ranger soberly informed the youth. "You should have told me about Shyanne as soon as you found out she was aboard. I might have decided to return her to Newtonia, or I might have allowed her to continue with us. But only a ship's captain can make such a decision. It is a serious breach of discipline for a crew member to withhold important information about a ship's condition from her captain."

Dawnboy hung his head shamefully. "Ye're right, sir. I'm sorry for what I did. But I could na tell ye about Shyanne because among my clanspeople there be nothing lower than an informer or a mon who breaks his word."

"I'm sorry I didn't tell you about her, too, Skipper," Lulu said contritely.

"It was my fault," Shyanne insisted. "I had no right to ask them not to report me to you."

"Don't fight over the blame; there's plenty of it to go around," Ranger told his three companions. "Maybe each of you thought you had good reasons for acting as you did. But no skipper can run an efficient ship with a crew he can't trust. We must restore that trust if we are to survive the dangerous voyage ahead of us. Therefore, we are going to operate strictly according to the book from now on. Understood?"

"Yes, sir," Dawnboy, Shyanne and Lulu replied obediently.

"All right. Dawnboy, I've had to discipline you in this manner before, so you know what to expect. Shyanne, you will be given duties commensurate with your abilities. Lulu, I want you to give both of them intensive training and educational exercises during their off-duty hours. All of you will bear in mind constantly that *I* am the master of this vessel; you will obey my orders instantly and unquestioningly; and you will keep me informed of everything—and I mean everything—that occurs aboard the *Gayheart*."

Ranger studied the two youngsters' tensely set faces and hoped they were sufficiently impressed by his gruff manner. Lulu said respectfully: "Captain, I think the first thing we should do is find more suitable quarters for the new crew member. She hasn't been very comfortable back there in the instrument compartment."

"Yes, of course." Ranger gave the problem a moment's thought and said, "You can have the second mate's cabin, Shyanne. That will put my cabin between you and Dawnboy. I'll keep my door open and I'm a light sleeper, in case either of you should get restless."

Dawnboy and Shyanne blushed and shot indignant glares at their captain, but neither of them dared to speak without permission.

"Very well, then," Ranger said when he could think of no further business to discuss just then. "Shyanne, go collect your gear and I'll show you your new quarters. Dawnboy, carry on with your watch. Lulu, I'm

counting on you to keep these two kids in line. It may
be too late for us to turn back to Newtonia, but I can
always drop both of them off at the nearest civilized
planet with enough money to pay their fares back on a
commercial liner. So see to it that they don't put any
more pressure on my already overstrained patience."

"Yes, sir. I'll take care of them," Lulu promised.

Dawnboy watched his father and Shyanne leave the
bridge. Then he sank down in the pilot seat with a
tired sigh. He was truly sorry that he had incurred
Ranger's disapproval. He should have realized from
the beginning that Shyanne was so much like his pesty
cousin Kathleen that she was bound to end up getting
him into trouble. But while he had been helping Shyanne keep her secret, he had enjoyed their conspiracy
as a childish prank to put one over on a grown-up.
Now he could not decide if the thought of having Shyanne aboard for companionship gave him more
pleasure or dread. He wished he would hurry up and
get old enough to find out if women were actually
worth all the trouble they caused men. Slim Hinterwald
had said they were, but at that moment Dawnboy seriously doubted it.

16

As THE UNEVENTFUL days of their cruise flowed into
weeks, Lulu assiduously fulfilled her promise to keep
Dawnboy and Shyanne too busy to cause any further
disharmony aboard the *Gayheart*. For their part, the
two youngsters greatly eased Lulu's labors by behaving
themselves and seriously concentrating on their work
and on their studies. They both were so bright and ea-

ger to learn that Lulu derived more satisfaction from instructing them than she had experienced during her long career as a teacher.

Ranger also observed his youthful crew's progress with a growing pride he was careful to conceal behind his new role of stern disciplinarian. He was especially relieved to note that Dawnboy displayed little indication of being physically interested in Shyanne. Not that Ranger prudishly begrudged his son a little fun; as he had said, he regarded Dawnboy as being mature enough to make his own decisions in such matters. But it would have offended any ethical starship commander's personal and professional honor if a sentient female were treated disrespectfully while she was a guest—however uninvited—aboard his vessel. Ranger was glad that Dawnboy was able to control himself so well with a highly desirable member of a species that many thought was the ideal biological counterpart of Homo sapiens. Vampirians and humans were similar enough to mate with one another, but different enough to be unable to produce offspring.

Ranger need not have worried about his son's maturing libido, which had undergone considerable stress in the past few months. Dawnboy had felt quite manly and sure of himself when he had left his Apache Highlands home to go star-roving with his father. Then he had met Alexia Ustich. Like many another overconfident youth who had been ruthlessly used and betrayed by an experienced older woman, Dawnboy had retreated in humiliation from the Battle of the Sexes. Now he was determined to stay out of that strange conflict until he had acquired enough knowledge and courage to sally forth with more hope of victory.

Therefore Dawnboy had slipped back into his childhood habit of thinking of girls as sexless chatterboxes who could be fun to have around as long as they did not think they were equal to those of his own gender. Of course there had to be some physical attraction and emotional clashes between two lively teen-agers rushing headlong into adulthood. But by and large Dawnboy and Shyanne were able to relieve their tensions through harmless teasing and other youthful tomfoolery. For the most part, Dawnboy was delighted to have a companion whose intelligence and absorbing interest in technical matters matched his own. As he once remarked privately to Lulu, being with Shyanne was almost as enjoyable as being with another boy. Lulu could not decide if that statement should make her rejoice or despair for Dawnboy's future.

Ranger, anxious to cut down Eythine's lead, kept the *Gayheart* at maximum cruising speed as they raced across the galaxy. With the ship fueled and provisioned for a voyage of a year or more, there was no need for them to stop on their way to the rim world called Pandemo, the last inhabited planet of the Milky Way at its nearest point to the Magellanic Clouds. There they would take the famous Pandemo Channel through the dangerous currents of anti-matter that surrounded the Milky Way and would hopefully pass on safely to the fairly clear space beyond.

Dawnboy and Shyanne were fascinated by the story of the Pandemo Channel, which was justifiably reputed to be the greatest engineering feat in the history of space technology. From the Channel Authority's main base on Pandemo's moon, huge luxium reactors transmitted power to relay stations strung along a ten-mile-wide corridor that stretched nearly half a light-year through the dense concentration of anti-particles along the galaxy's outer edge. The relay stations converted the power to force-fields that formed an interlocking shield of matter/energy stronger than the attacking anti-matter/anti-energy. The resulting clear path through furious waves of annihilation was an accomplishment worthy of the pride its builders had expressed over it. For years afterward even the lowliest construction technician could settle any argument about space mechanics with the simple statement: "I worked on the channel."

The building of the channel had started some two and a half centuries ago, just after the first—and thus far the only—intergalactic war in the Milky Way's known history. That conflict had begun when the war-like ZuJus of the Magellanic Clouds had learned the secret of the star-drive from early human explorers. The ZuJus, being the most numerous and fastest breeding of all the intelligent species, had hurled wave after wave of combat vessels against the Milky Way's feeble outer defenses. Many of the invaders were destroyed by the deadly anti-matter currents. But enough of them survived to subdue and occupy several important rim worlds, including Pandemo.

The long bitter war dragged on until finally the combined space forces of most of the Milky Way's civilized worlds managed to drive out the ZuJu aggressors and negotiate a peace treaty with their emperor. The Unified Systems of Aquila fleet, carrying the brunt of the battle, had liberated Pandemo. The Aquilans, wanting to establish a safe passage through the anti-matter barrier, had obtained an agreement from the grateful Pandemonians that permitted the USA to construct the channel and operate it in perpetuity.

Prior to the opening of the channel, only a few daring space pioneers had braved the anti-matter seas to challenge the awesome unknown of intergalactic voyaging. Some of them, such as Captain "Midas" Oublier, had been ruthless opportunists bent on finding the gold of Fossick, engaging in illicit trade with the ZuJus or otherwise exploiting the rich but hostile Magellanic Clouds. Others, motivated by the age-old lust for discovery that is sometimes an even stronger drive in sentient beings than greed, had pushed on to explore and establish colonies in the Andromeda Galaxy.

Now the channel enabled the Milky Wayans to maintain fairly reliable contact with their growing settlements on the Andromedan worlds and exploratory efforts to reach even more distant star clusters. While the original trickle of traffic between galaxies had not yet become a torrent, it had increased enough to attract space pirates and raiders from the ZuJu worlds that had never ratified their emperor's treaty with the Milky

Way governments. That in turn had brought loud demands from intergalactic travelers for defensive action by the Sentient Species Association's Protectorate Patrol. Civilization, for better or worse, continued its inexorable spread through the universe.

When Dawnboy viewed his first educational tape about Pandemo, he made a startling discovery. It excited him so much that he rushed from the ship's library to Ranger's cabin, where he found his father shaving with a straight razor in his tiny sanitation chamber. Ranger was often tempted to use electrolysis to eliminate the necessity of caring for his facial hair. But his business sometimes took him to societies where beards were considered a preeminent sign of manhood, so he suffered the inconvenience of shaving regularly. That was a bothersome ritual that Dawnboy would soon have to adopt, Ranger reflected as he glanced at the dark fuzz on his son's cheeks and chin.

"Dad, why did ye na tell me that the Pandemonians are Satyr folk?" Dawnboy demanded breathlessly.

"Why, I thought you already knew that," Ranger replied. "They are descended from early Panish settlers from the Capricorn worlds, although the aristocratic Capricornians hate to admit it. They claim the Pandemonians are degenerate mongrels produced by unnatural mating with humans. That's a biological impossibility, but it makes an effective insult to both Pandemonians and humans."

Dawnboy was too preoccupied with his own thoughts to follow his father's words. "But 'tis important," he insisted. "The Satyr who was with the mon who left me to freeze on Newtonia might have actually been a Pandemonian. But I thought he was from one o' the Capricorn worlds."

Ranger finished shaving and rinsed the leftover lather from his face. Tomorrow he would go back to using his laser depilator, which did a safer and more comfortable job, he thought, dabbing at a glistening red ooze from his nicked chin. He did not want to get carried away with his hobby of collecting and using quaint artifacts from the backward worlds he visited.

"Yes, I suppose he could have been a Pandemonian," Ranger agreed. "But what difference would that make, since the police weren't able to find him?"

That reminder reduced Dawnboy's excitement, but not very much. "I've been trying to remember everything I can about the attempt to kidnap Shyanne," he explained. "To see if there was some clue that linked the kidnappers to Captain Zairundi. If we could ha' found out that Zairundi had recently been to Pandemo . . ."

"I don't see how that could have proved anything," Ranger cut in. "But keep thinking about it. You might come up with something."

Dawnboy did continue to think about the matter, but several more days passed before he turned up another clue worth mentioning. In the meantime, he regretted their necessary haste. Though Dawnboy was as eager as Ranger and Shyanne to reach Wonderwhat, he wished they could linger over the points of interest along the way. A few days after Ranger discovered Shyanne's presence aboard the *Gayheart,* they passed near Puerto Miami, a resort world reputed to have the most beautiful and widely varied natural scenery in the galaxy. Dawnboy was particularly interested in seeing that planet because Ranger had told him that was where he and Gay had spent their honeymoon.

"Come to think of it, you may have been conceived there," Ranger added as a casual afterthought.

"Yes, accidents happen even in the best of families," Shyanne said, keeping her face expressionless except for her impishly dancing eyes.

The quip brought a half-smile to Ranger's lips. Dawnboy, determined not to indicate that a mere girl could get under his skin, condescended only to give Shyanne a withering glance. Then he stalked haughtily off to the galley to salve his injured pride with food.

A week or so later, the ship's lepton scanner detected the first VIP that Dawnboy and Shyanne had ever encountered. They stared curiously through the forward bulkhead telescope as the *Gayheart* veered off to avoid the strange object, but there was nothing to see. Only the scanner's ability to register a high concentration of positrons indicated that anything at all existed in an apparently empty patch of space. Most anti-matter particles found in the galaxy existed in small, widely scattered amounts that were easily disposed of by a starship's energy shield, which also protected a spacecraft from collisions with stray meteors and other cosmic debris.

But the things that Dr. Wage Gitlow had labeled Very Interesting Phenomena were something else indeed. Evidently VIP's were unaware of the scientific laws that rendered it impossible for matter and antimatter to coexist peacefully together. Every material object that had been observed to touch a VIP had simply disappeared. There was no flash of released energy, no measurable reduction of the VIP's anti-matter, nor any other evidence of particle destruction.

The apparent lack of particle annihilation in such encounters had led Dr. Gitlow and other scientists to speculate that VIP's were doorways to the theoretical anti-matter universe that was the mirror image of the known universe. If there actually were such a universe, that would explain the age-old riddle of what exactly is existence. A matter universe and an anti-matter universe that matched each other perfectly could exchange, through their VIP-doorways, particles and anti-particles that became the building materials of new stars and anti-stars as old ones burned out. Such an arrangement would be a perfect perpetual motion machine, with no energy or matter ever lost and with no beginning or end for either universe.

Dawnboy and Shyanne had fun discussing what might be found in an anti-matter parallel universe, and they concluded that while it might be a nice place to visit, they would certainly not want to stay there permanently. Ranger reminded them that only Wonderwhat had been known to make two-way trips through

VIP's, so he preferred to stay well clear of them. In Ranger's opinion, the only good thing that could be said for VIP's was that they were relatively rare and had never been known to come near a sun or planet, which—for all anyone knew—the VIPs were capable of swallowing up as easily as they ingested starships.

Dawnboy came to appreciate Shyanne's company even more when he discovered that she shared his interest in printed literature. Although advanced electronics had extended the use of audiovisual recording devices throughout the known universe, elementary reading and writing were still taught in most human societies. Those two basic skills were little used by the more "civilized" peoples, but on backward worlds such as Apache Highlands and Vampiria, the graphic arts continued to be the predominant tools of culture.

The *Gayheart*'s library contained a sizable collection of printed books, which Dawnboy and Shyanne used to improve their knowledge of Unilingo while they pursued their other studies. Unilingo, derived mainly from the ancient English of the first star-traveling Earthlings, had become a cosmic root language with countless dialects spoken by the widely scattered human races and other intelligent beings who had dealings with them. Time and distance had wrought vast differences in the dialects, but they were held together by the easily mastered Basic Unilingo, consisting of the tongue's four thousand most commonly used words. Classical Unilingo, with a far more elaborate vocabulary and grammar, was reserved for poetry and other specialized literary works. Dawnboy had been pleasantly surprised to learn that he and his mother's clanspeople on Apache Highlands spoke one of the oldest and most colorful dialects. Up till then, he had thought that he spoke pure Unilingo and everybody else used dialects.

Dawnboy's command of Unilingo was superior to Shyanne's, and he sometimes derived spiteful pleasure from correcting her grammar and pronunciation mistakes. That was the only way he had found to even the score for the merciless teasing that he suffered from her quick wit and tongue. But, thanks to Lulu's supervision, their boy-girl bickering never became too heated.

One evening Shyanne, feeling in the mood for company, went to the bridge during Dawnboy's watch at the helm. To make conversation, she tried to tell Dawnboy about an old romantic novel she was reading. Shyanne said she liked the book, but it was written in such flowery, confusing Classical Unilingo prose that she was not sure how much of it she understood. Dawnboy listened half-attentively, until Shyanne described one of the book's characters as a coopmaker.

"He was a what?" Dawnboy demanded.

"The author called him a cooper," Shyanne replied. "Obviously that means someone who builds coops for poultry and other domesticated creatures."

Dawnboy laughed derisively. "D'ye na know anything, ye empty-headed lass? A cooper is a mon who makes wooden tubs and barrels. One o' the families in my mother's clan is named Cooper, because that has been their trade for centuries."

"Well, how could I possibly know that?" Shyanne flared defensively. "The word isn't in any of the Unilingo dialects spoken on Vampiria."

"Don't be so smug about it, Dawnboy," Lulu said in a mildly scolding tone. "You still have a lot to learn, too. You only knew what sort of work a cooper does because that trade is still practiced where you grew up. I've always been interested in surnames that can be traced back to ancient or obsolete occupations. For example, someone named Smith may have had ancestors who worked with metal. And a Wagoner was originally one who built or drove wagons."

"Aye, and a Thatcher still makes thatched roofs on Apache Highlands," Dawnboy said. "And a . . ." He suddenly sat bolt upright in the pilot seat and snapped his fingers. "That's it!" he cried. "That has to be it! How could I ha' been so stupid na' to see it before?"

"What are you talking about?" Shyanne asked.

"Is something wrong?" Lulu inquired worriedly.

But Dawnboy was calling excitedly into the intercom system: "Dad, can ye hear me? I ha' some important news."

After several moments Ranger's voice, sounding as if he had just been roused from a sound sleep, muttered thickly, "Wh-what is it, Son?"

"I just thought o' something," Dawnboy went on. "Those two kidnappers I saw on Newtonia: the Satyr and the human. One o' them mentioned somebody called The Arrow. Well, an arrow-maker is a fletcher, and Fletcher is Captain Zairundi's first name, and . . . and . . ."

The others waited for Dawnboy to continue, but he had run out of deductions. Ranger considered Dawnboy's words while he yawned himself further awake. "I think you may be onto something," Ranger finally said thoughtfully. "It fits in with my impression of Zairundi as an egomaniac who likes to play cat-and-mouse games with his victims. I'm sure it greatly amused him to give us such an obvious clue to his identity, then wait to see how long it took us to figure it out."

Danwboy, feeling immensely pleased with himself, sank back in the pilot's seat and gave Shyanne a superior but tolerant smile. Shyanne quickly deflated his vanity by asking: "What good does that information do us now that we have it?"

"That's a good point," Lulu agreed. "Even if we could establish beyond all doubt that Zairundi was behind the kidnap attempt and is now trying to catch up with Eythine before we do, there's nothing we can do to stop him. That is, unless you want to seek out his ship and vap it."

"No, we can't very well kill him and his crew on mere suspicion," Ranger replied. "Besides, it would take too much time to find the *Seven Deadly Sins*. But by the way, Lulu, have you noticed any suspicious-appearing spacecraft following us since we left Newtonia?"

"That's impossible to say for sure," Lulu answered.

"We've been using fairly well-traveled space lanes, so naturally my scanners have detected several other ships around us. But we would have to get close enough for visual contact to identify each of them."

"Well, keep your scanners alert anyway," Ranger ordered. "Now that we know who the enemy is, we can at least be on guard against anything he might try to pull on us."

"I will, Boss," Lulu promised. "But from what you've told me about Zairundi, he seems too stupid to be very dangerous."

"He's not stupid, just overconfident," Ranger corrected her. "That seems to be a common trait among racial bigots. But it is something that can be used against him, if we keep our heads."

"D'ye really think he's a bigot?" Dawnboy asked.

"Yes, but I don't think it's his fault," Ranger answered. "I've noticed that most people who grow up in isolated societies with little contact with the rest of the universe acquire an exaggerated impression of their own group's importance. That's one of the few things I dislike about your mother's people."

"Oh, but that's different," Dawnboy said blandly. "We *know* that we're better than everybody else."

Ranger laughed. "Well, after this, try to use your superior abilities to judge when it's really necessary to wake up your poor, old, decrepit father."

"Aye, sir. Sorry about that," Dawnboy muttered sheepishly. "Go back to sleep. I'll na bother ye again."

"And I'll see that he doesn't," Shyanne promised.

Ranger bade the two youngsters good night, fluffed up his pillow and wiggled into a more comfortable position on his bunk.

"Well, your resolution to get stricter with your crew sure didn't last very long," Lulu remarked, speaking through Ranger's earphone for privacy.

"Oh, you know what a softie I am," Ranger sighed. "Besides, they're good kids. They don't need me constantly on their backs to make them do the right things. But when this cruise is over, I want you to add up all the new gray hairs those two have put in my head."

"Don't blame me for that," Lulu said. "You were the one who said you wished you had a daughter."

Ranger smiled warmly at the thought of his growing affection for Shyanne. "She's quite a girl. It's nice to have a real feminine influence around here for a change."

"All right, I know when I've been insulted," Lulu snapped huffily.

"That's good. I was afraid I might have to explain it to you," Ranger said as he closed his eyes and tried to get back to sleep.

17

SHYANNE WAS JUST about to blast an enemy starship with laser fire, when Lulu announced that she was ready to begin decelerating for their approach to Pandemo. The interruption distracted Shyanne's aim, causing her to miss her target. She muttered an unladylike curse and looked over at Ranger, who was seated at the controls of the combat simulator in the *Gayheart*'s gym.

Ranger smiled and said, "I think you've had enough target practice for now. Let's join Dawnboy in the bridge and strap ourselves down. It isn't going to be very comfortable for us to slow down enough from this speed to orbit a planet in just two or three hours."

Shyanne switched off the simulator's visiscreen and followed Ranger out of the gym. Ranger was pleased with the way Dawnboy and Shyanne had improved their astronautical skills, including the operation of the ship's laser banks, nuclear cannon and other heavy weapons. He hoped they would never have to use the arms in actual combat, but they had to be prepared for anything in the untamed and largely unexplored part of the universe they were bound for. Even in the more civilized areas patrolled by war vessels of the advanced space powers, most independent star traders preferred to carry their own defensive armament. That practice was often condemned by government officials on the worlds where star traders did business. But hardly anyone took much notice of local anti-gun laws, since it was common knowledge that the officials who protested loudest against honest merchants being armed for self-protection often had secret agreements with space pirates to purchase their stolen goods at bargain prices.

"How did I do today?" Shyanne asked as she walked beside Ranger toward the bridge.

"Very good," Ranger complimented her. "Much better than before."

"Better than Dawnboy?"

"Well, you must remember that he grew up in a more warlike society than you did," Ranger replied tactfully. "He has been handling bows, lances and other primitive weapons since early childhood. That was bound to give him a big advantage in developing swift reflexes and other combat skills. But you're coming along just fine, for a . . ."

"For a girl?" Shyanne speculated, giving him a disdainful scowl. "Don't worry about that. I'll do my share of the work, and then some."

Ranger laughed and gave her slim shoulder a fatherly squeeze. "I never doubted that for a moment. I was going to say for a stowaway."

Shyanne glanced sharply at him, saw by his grin that he was joking and grinned back. They entered the bridge and saw that Dawnboy had already moved over to one of the pneumatic couches that were used to relieve the strain of heavy-G maneuvers. Shyanne took the couch next to his and pulled the straps of the safety harness around her. Before joining the two youngsters,

Ranger carefully looked over the instrument panel to assure himself that Lulu was firmly in control of the ship. Psychedelus, Pandemo's red sun, glowered dully at them through the electron telescope lens.

When everyone was safely strapped down, Lulu fired the *Gayheart*'s retro-rockets, crushing them deeply into their couches. Ordinarily a starship approaching planetfall would spend at least twelve hours gradually decelerating from hyperlight speed. That way, the ship's antigravity unit could maintain nearly normal interior conditions for the comfort of those aboard. But because of Ranger's haste, the *Gayheart* had continued at maximum speed until the last possible moment. Even now Ranger regretted the time they would unavoidably lose while waiting for official clearance to use the channel.

Lulu's brain, cushioned in liquid, was unaffected by the torturous G-pressures as she deftly applied the brakes at a rate that her flesh-bound companions could tolerate. Their lungs labored for breath, and after several minutes Dawnboy noticed that Shyanne's face had turned so pale that he feared she was losing consciousness. But the girl smiled bravely and said she was all right when Dawnboy called out to her.

To take his mind off his discomfort, Dawnboy reviewed what he had learned about Pandemo and its Satyr inhabitants. The planet's surface consisted of four major oceans, five continents and numerous islands. Because of its remote location and scarce industrial resources, Pandemo's economy was based almost entirely on agriculture. That would have provided the hundred million or so Pandemonians with comfortable existences, if their political systems had been as productive as their farming methods. But the Pandemonians were notoriously emotional, and there was usually at least one war or some other disturbance in progress among the many similar but antagonistic social groups.

The largest continent, Norolda was loosely unified and ruled along feudalistic lines from its capital city, Phrekowt. The despotic head of the Noroldan government called himself the Proletariat of all the Pandemonians. The title was derived from an ancient, long-forgotten Earth religion that contained the phrase "Dictatorship of the Proletariat." No one knew much about the religion or what a Proletariat was, but the Pandemonians figured that if it had something to do with dictatorship, they were all for it.

It was with the first Proletariat, because he commanded the strongest government and military force on the planet, that the Aquilans had negotiated the agreement permitting them to build the channel's power plants on Pandemo's moon. Since then Pandemonian leaders had often complained about their satellite being used so profitably by otherworlders who paid only a token rental fee to the Proletariat. Most of the time those complaints could be ignored because the political situation on the planet was too unstable for the Pandemonians to speak with a united voice.

But gradually the Noroldan government had strengthened its position until Oreamnos, the present Proletariat, could credibly claim to speak for all Pandemonians when he demanded the right to control the channel. At the urging of the Sentient Species Association, the Aquilans had begun negotiating a new channel agreement with Oreamnos. Actually the negotiations were just window dressing to cover up the fact that the Aquilans were keeping Oreamnos and his henchmen happy with secret bribes. Meanwhile the totalitarian IFIB and PHAP empires, being eager to snatch control of the channel away from the USA, had infiltrated revolutionary agents provocateurs to keep the Pandemonians stirred up against the Proletariat and his Aquilan supporters.

Dawnboy's thoughts drifted to more diverting subjects as the continued strain of deceleration made it difficult for him to think about serious matters. He had almost dozed off, despite the aching distortion of his facial muscles, when Lulu finally announced that they had slowed down enough to restore normal gravity to the ship's interior. Feeling as weary as if he had just completed a month's hard labor, Dawnboy unfastened his couch harness with cramped muscles and massaged his chilled flesh to stimulate blood circulation. But of course a little physical hardship could not bother an Apache brave, his pride reminded him, as he suppressed a groan and sprang up smiling to help Shyanne to her feet.

"I envy you kids at times like this," Ranger sighed as he staggered ponderously to the pilot seat. "With your young strength and energy to recover quickly from such strenuous activities."

Dawnboy and Shyanne, leaning against one another for support, silently agreed not to refute their captain's favorable opinion of them.

"Have you contacted the Channel Authority yet, Lulu?" Ranger asked.

"I've tried, but there's too much interference from a large cloud of anti-ionized gas arriving from outside the galaxy. Most of it should hit Psychedelus in about thirty seconds. So watch the forward bulkhead, if you want to see a spectacular show."

Ranger, Shyanne and Dawnboy looked up curiously at the star that had grown to a glaring sun in the telescope lens. For a long moment the scene remained unchanged, then bright flashes appeared along the outer edge of the sun's corona. An instant later Psychedelus appeared to be going nova as it erupted into a swirling mass of brilliant colors that was painful to watch, despite the telescope's light-filtering properties. But after the first blush of matter/anti-matter annihilation, the light dimmed to subtly soothing shades that writhingly interwove with each other in beautiful eye-teasing displays of form and texture. A million rainbows danced around and into each other, becoming a hundred million variegated rivers that flowed into a treasure chest of exquisite jewels from whose hearts blossomed flowers of delicately trembling designs. The flowers shattered into dazzling multihued specks that flew apart, dissolved, reformed and kaleidoscoped back together to repeat their enchanting performances with countless variations.

"How beautiful!" Shyanne whispered, releasing her pent-up breath in a long sigh.

"Aye," Dawnboy soberly agreed. "Terrifyingly beautiful, if ye had to live under that sort o' thing all the time."

"It doesn't happen all the time," Ranger said. "But often enough to explain why the Pandemonians are such an emotionally unstable race. Living here at the rim of the galaxy, with vast oceans of anti-matter threatening to overwhelm them, it's understandable that they are nervous and suspicious of outsiders."

"I should be able to contact the Channel Authority now," Lulu said as she prepared to put the ship into orbit around Pandemo. "Wait a moment. I'm picking up an Apollo Thirteen!"

Ranger, Shyanne and Dawnboy looked up sharply at the mention of the universal distress signal, named after a near disaster early in the Space Age. They listened tensely to the loud, repetitive bleat of a recorded message playing to them through the *Gayheart*'s communication system. The mechanical tones asked for immediate help and gave the endangered vessel's identification number.

"It's the *Ram's Revenge!*" Shyanne cried. "Eythine's in trouble!"

"Don't panic," Ranger said calmly. "We'll get to her as quickly as we can. Lulu, have you located where the call is coming from!"

"Someplace in Pandemo's northern hemisphere," Lulu replied. "Give me a few minutes and I should have the signal pinpointed. What in the . . ." Her voice trailed off and Ranger was about to ask what was wrong when she reported: "Skipper, we are being hailed by the Channel Authority. Sounds urgent."

"Put them on," Ranger ordered. "They may have some information about Eythine. Or maybe they've already sent a ship to help her." He switched on his photophone as Dawnboy gallantly allowed Shyanne to rest her G-fatigued body in the copilot seat and stood peering over her shoulder.

The photophone screens filled with the image of a fairly young, fairly attractive and fairly worried-looking human female who introduced herself as Cala Brightly, an official of the Pandemo Channel Authority. After Ranger had identified himself and his vessel, the woman started to tell him to maintain his orbit and await further instructions. But before she could finish, she was impatiently replaced by an older, heavier and more imposing-appearing male official.

"This is Channel Commissioner Williwan," the man began briskly. "We have a rather difficult situation concerning the distress signal that you may have picked up."

"Yes, we've picked up the signal," Ranger affirmed. "It appears to be coming from a ship commanded by Archguardess Eythine dara Gildenfang, a personal friend. So we would appreciate any information you can give us about her present condition."

"I'm afraid the only news about her that I have isn't very encouraging," Commissioner Williwan said, causing Shyanne to gasp and bite her lip apprehensively. But the Commissioner added quickly: "She is alive and well, as far as we have been able to determine. But unfortunately her ship is down in the rugged mountainous southeastern area of Norolda, which is controlled by Mosseater rebels."

"By what?" Ranger asked blankly.

The commissioner looked apologetic. "Excuse me. Of course you're not familiar with the local political situation. I'll give you a brief summary. The wild Mosseater tribes of southeastern Norolda have long wanted to be free of the central government in Phrekowt. But they were unable to organize an effective independence movement until a year and a half ago, when they found an able leader in Proletariat Oreamnos's half-brother, Nos-Nos. Since then Nos-Nos has built up a formidable military force. The Proletariat's troops have superior numbers and weapons, but the Mosseaters are masters of the rough terrain. So far they have more than held their own against the government forces sent out to subdue them."

"But what has that got to do with Eythine?" Shyanne demanded.

"I was getting to that," Commissioner Williwan replied. "Three days ago the archguardess's ship arrived here and went into orbit awaiting clearance to use the Channel. Then she received a radio message from the Hunchback Mountains—a Mosseater stronghold—broadcast by someone claiming to be her husband. We tried to warn her against entering that dangerous area, but she disregarded us and landed her ship there. The Mosseaters took her prisoner, but not before she had set off her automatic distress signal and locked her ship up tight."

Shyanne nodded grimly. "Yes, that surely would be the only thing that could make Eythine drop her guard and act impulsively. She loved my father so much that she would *want* to believe he's still alive, even when her common sense told her it couldn't be true."

Dawnboy patted Shyanne's shoulder in an awkward effort to comfort her. "Do na worry about yer stepmother, lass. As long as she is still alive, as the mon said, we'll find a way to get her out o' there."

"Commissioner, what has been done so far to obtain the lady's release?" Ranger inquired. "After all, she *is* a citizen of the USA, the same as you."

The channel commissioner replied with the confident smile of an official who believed that everything would be all right as long as he remained in control of his own little piece of the bureaucracy. "You can rest assured that the Aquilan embassy in Phrekowt is doing everything possible to obtain the release of the archguardess and her ship. But this is an extremely delicate situation. We can hardly blame the Noroldan government for crimes committed by rebel outlaws. Nor can we endanger our already uneasy relations with the Pandemonians by threatening intervention. We must be patient and handle this with diplomatic care."

"What all of that double-talk really means," Lulu sarcastically interjected, "is that all of you political-minded desk jockeys are so scared witless of sticking your necks out that you'll keep kicking the problem back and forth until either the rebels get tired of holding Eythine or she dies of old age. In my day, if a pipsqueak world like this endangered the life or property of an Aquilan, a punitive expedition would be sent to teach them better manners."

Commissioner Williwan drew himself up and stared coldly at Ranger. "Perhaps, Captain, you should teach your crew better manners than to interrupt their superiors. The Unified Systems of Aquila have progressed beyond the age of gunship diplomacy, I'm happy to say. Now we use more civilized methods to settle our interstellar difficulties."

"That's okay if you're dealing with civilized beings," Lulu said. "But with half-crazy savages like these . . ."

Ranger told Lulu to be quiet and apologized to the commissioner for her impudent remarks. He forced himself to smile cordially as he thanked Williwan for apprising them of the situation. The two men discussed the matter further without reaching any definite conclusions, then Ranger said he wanted to think about it on his own for a while. He promised to keep in touch with the Channel Authority and ended the communication.

18

RANGER TURNED TO Dawnboy and Shyanne and asked what they thought of Eythine's predicament. The youngsters told him what they thought so loudly and demandingly that he had to hold up his hand for silence.

"All right," Ranger said. "We all seem to be agreed that we should do something to help free Eythine, instead of waiting for the overcautious Aquilans to act. But first let's do some hard thinking about what we know about the situation and what conclusions we can logically draw from that knowledge."

"To begin with," Lulu said, "we know that Zairundi must be behind the scheme to capture Eythine. I don't have to feed a bunch of data into my computer banks to figure that out."

Ranger nodded. "The evidence is pretty circumstantial, but it does seem to add up that way. Thanks to Dawnboy's good memory and sharp wits, we can be reasonably sure that Zairundi was the leader of the gang that tried to kidnap Shyanne." Ranger left the pilot seat for his habitual practice of pacing aimlessly while he thought over a problem. "One of the kidnappers was a Satyr, probably a Pandemonian. That links Zairundi with some outlaw leader on Pandemo, who is probably this Nos-Nos character. Now, what would Zairundi be most likely to do after he failed to get Shyanne or Eythine in his power?"

"He would send a sub-ether message torpedo ahead," Shyanne guessed eagerly, "telling Nos-Nos that Eythine's ship was bound for Pandemo. And he would tell Nos-Nos how to trick Eythine into landing there."

"Right." Ranger smiled approvingly at the girl. "For further evidence, consider the radio transmitter that had to be powerful enough to reach Eythine's orbiting ship and lure her down there. That's highly sophisticated equipment for a backward world like this. It had to be supplied by someone with access to interstellar trade goods." He turned to Dawnboy. "But what is the motive? Why did Zairundi and Nos-Nos, who obviously have little in common, agree to work together to capture Eythine?"

"For the treasure, o' course," Dawnboy answered quickly. "Nos-Nos needs lots o' money to finance his revolt agin the Proletariat, and Zairundi needed a powerful partner out here to better his chances o' getting the *Jealousy*'s cargo."

"Exactly!" Ranger proudly clapped his son's shoulder. "That means we can't afford to waste time. Zairundi must be on his way to pick up Eythine and force her to help him find the treasure ship. He could arrive here at any moment."

"No, Skipper," Lulu disagreed. "I'm positive there are no other ships within twenty-four-hours' cruising time behind us."

"So, we have a full day in which to free Eythine," Ranger mused. "What have your scanners revealed about the place where she is being held, Lulu?"

"Nothing very encouraging," Lulu replied. "The *Ram's Revenge* is parked in a small mountain valley. The mountains around it are honeycombed with caves, which are apparently occupied by the rebel army. I've already contacted Tombolo, the *Ram's Revenge* biocomputer. He said the ship is still securely locked against anyone except Eythine; but he can take no action without orders from her, and her captors evidently were smart enough to disable her throat mike as soon as they caught her. The rebel stronghold seems to be impregnable to anything but an air attack and we can't blast them without endangering Eythine."

Ranger halted his pacing to absorb Lulu's new data. "Then our task is simple," he said with a wry smile. "One of us will have to go down there in a small vehicle, find a way to get Eythine away from the rebels and return her to her ship—all within twenty-four hours."

"Let *me* go, Dad," Dawnboy quickly volunteered. "We canna risk losing someone as important as ye are to the *Gayheart*."

"No, I should be the one to go," Shyanne insisted. "I'm closest to Eythine. Besides, I'm just a stowaway on your ship, so you won't lose anything if I don't come back."

Ranger looked at their bright, eager faces and tried

not to smile. He could not tell if he was more pleased by their youthful courage or amused by their naïve unawareness of how many other abilities the rescue mission required. "Thanks. I'm proud of you both for offering to go," he said, "but I think this is a job that I had better handle." He turned on his heel and walked rapidly toward the door. "Come down to the main cargo hold with me. You can help me prepare our little survey boat for action."

"D'ye have a plan?" Dawnboy asked, running after his father.

"Part of one," Ranger replied. "I'll have to improvise the rest of it after I've sized up the situation down there. The odds are against it, but it's better than doing nothing."

Shyanne followed the two men out of the bridge, her heart swelling with worshipful admiration for Ranger. She had been grateful to Dawnboy and Slim for fighting off the men who had tried to kidnap her, but what Ranger was doing for Eythine was even braver and nobler than that. He did not owe Eythine any favors. On the contrary, she was his rival for the treasure of Wonderwhat. Under those circumstances, Ranger would be fully justified in turning his back on Eythine and going off to seek the treasure for himself. Shyanne doubted that any other man, even her father, would have risked so much for a woman who meant nothing to him beyond the fact that she needed his help. At that moment, Shyanne gladly would have died for Ranger.

Dawnboy, on the other hand, saw nothing out of the ordinary in Ranger's actions. It simply never occurred to the young Apache that he could have been fathered by someone who was not superior to all other men.

Ranger wondered if he had been too rash in deciding to help Eythine when, a half hour later, he piloted his small two-seat survey craft into Pandemo's upper stratosphere to make his final landing orbit. The boat was similar to, though not nearly as powerful as, the sleek scout ships he had operated as a youthful Space

Ranger, long ago. But he did not feel very much like a dashing star warrior lusting for action and glory now.

A heavy cloud cover obscured most of the planet surface below him, but he knew that the weather over the Hunchback Mountains was clear. A casual survey of the instrument panel assured him that everything was normal enough for him to leave the controls on autopilot. He could have used the antigravity drive to lose altitude quickly, but he preferred to let the boat make a long gliding approach with its retractable wings. That way he could study the terrain before landing and go over his plan, what there was of it, a few more times.

The slower descent also gave him time to worry about details that he had overlooked before. Among other things, he suddenly remembered the radio set that the rebel leader Nos-Nos had used to lure Eythine into a trap. It was quite possible that the radio had enabled Nos-Nos to overhear Ranger's conversation with the channel commissioner. If that had actually happened, the rebels would be highly suspicious, at the very least, of Ranger's sudden arrival among them. Ranger tried to ease his fear by reminding himself that most of the cheap radio sets carried by star traders for sale on backward worlds were incapable of picking up the higher frequencies of photophone communications. Eythine had received the rebels' transmission only because, Ranger hoped, a starship's equipment is far more sophisticated than the average radio set.

Anyway, it was too late to fret about that now. Still, Ranger could not resist thinking that it might be best all around for him to return immediately to the *Gayheart*. Dawnboy and Shyanne would be greatly disappointed in him, not to mention his own self-loathing, for letting Eythine down. But at least he would still be alive to get the youngsters safely out of this. It was one thing for a man to gamble with his own life, which Ranger had gotten in the habit of doing during his years alone, but quite another matter when his son and a pretty teen-aged girl that he almost wished was his daughter were involved.

Ranger had tried to safeguard the kids as best he could by secretly ordering Lulu to wait only twenty-four hours for him. If he had not managed to rescue Eythine by then, he would probably be dead, in which case Lulu was to take the *Gayheart* back to Newtonia without delay. But Ranger strongly doubted that the biocomputer would obey him in this instance, especially if Dawnboy countermanded his orders, which was most likely what the young hothead would do. It was a shame that the lad had not inherited more of his own good sense and instinct for self-preservation, Ranger thought sadly, as he left his boat on course for the Hunchback Mountains and again reviewed his plan for rescuing Eythine.

It was late afternoon in Norolda's southeastern region when Ranger's boat finally glided over the rugged terrain. Ranger looked around curiously and did not care for what he saw. There were numerous mountain peaks in view, but he would have recognized the Hunchbacks even if his craft's instruments were not homing in on Eythine's distress signal. The Hunchbacks towered over their neighboring mountains, thrusting up their rocky bald crests so steeply that Ranger could hardly believe there was enough level ground among them for a starship to land on. He hoped that nothing would happen to his boat while he was down there; it would be a rough place to have to walk out of.

Ranger missed seeing the *Ram's Revenge* when he first passed over it. Then his autopilot turned his boat in a steeply banked circle, and he looked down on a boulder-strewn alpine clearing that seemed barely large enough to accommodate the starship nestled in it. Ranger could see several cave entrances in the surrounding mountain walls. Evidently the report that the rebel army lived in the caves was true, because several manlike figures came running out of the entrances to peer up at the machine circling over them. Ranger decided not to give them time to organize a reception for him. He took over the controls and dropped his boat straight down, landing a few meters away from the forlorn-looking *Ram's Revenge*.

If the valley's defenders were taken off-guard by Ranger's abrupt arrival, they recovered quickly. As Ranger opened his canopy to dismount, about a dozen Pandemonians, riding beasts that vaguely resembled mountain goats, came charging down the least perpendicular side of the valley. They were armed with crude bolt-action rifles, which they deftly brought to their shoulders as their surefooted mounts bore them along.

For a moment Ranger regretted that he had not brought heavy weapons with him. He had decided to do most of his fighting with his wits, but just then he began to think that something more impressive was required. He pulled the synapse disrupter from his belt, set it for stun and made a sweeping pass at the odd-looking cavalry force bearing down on him.

Riders and mounts alike went tumbling head over hooves to the valley floor. When the dust settled, not one of them remained conscious. Some of their companions in the cave entrances fired a few shots that struck uncomfortably near Ranger, but when he pointed his disrupter at them, they fled back into the caves. So much for impressing the superstitious natives with superior weaponry, Ranger thought, as he activated his boat's loudspeaker system.

"Nos-Nos, can you hear me?" Ranger asked, his amplified voice echoing back from the high rocky walls. "I am The Arrow's replacement. Call off your troops and we'll talk things over peacefully."

He waited tensely, but only silence as harsh and lonely as the forbidding mountain peaks around him responded. Good. His unexpected actions had evidently so taken the rebels by surprise that they had withdrawn in confusion to decide what to do next. Ranger did not think he would have to wait very long. Pandemonians were not renowned for their patience.

A few minutes after repeating his message, Ranger spotted movement at one of the cave entrances. As

Ranger waited with the disrupter handy, a Pandemonian riding one of the strangely agile beasts and leading another one, saddled but riderless, came cautiously down the steep slope. Ranger, seeing that the goatlike being was unarmed, climbed out of his boat and walked over to meet him as his animals picked their way over the crumpled forms of those who had imprudently charged Ranger. The Pandemonian grinned brokenly and gestured with his hands for Ranger to mount the beast he was leading.

"The Master say you come," the Pandemonian said in poor but understanble Unilingo. "You be safe. We not kill you, yet."

Ranger uneasily regarded the saddled animal, which appeared to be sneering at him with a mouthful of wicked-looking teeth. The closer Ranger approached the animal, the more threatening it looked. But Ranger could see no alternative to riding the ugly thing, as he doubted that he could scramble up the steep slope on foot and he had neglected to bring an antigravity pack along.

Finally Ranger summoned up his courage, dashed around the animal's snapping teeth, grabbed the saddle horn and clambered aboard. Once he was safely on the beast's back, it became quite docile and nimbly followed the Pandemonian's mount up the slope. When they reached the first cave entrance, Ranger saw that narrow paths had been cut into the vertical mountain face. The guide led the way along one of these trails past several cave entrances where many Pandemonian males, females and children stared curiously at the visiting human. Most of the adult males wore the sort of ragged, nondescript clothing that is common among irregular, poorly paid military forces. Their arms consisted of rifles, spears, swords and other primitive weapons. Obviously Nos-Nos could use part of the treasure of Wonderwhat to get his army properly outfitted. But at least everyone looked well-fed and cheerful.

Ranger's guide turned into a cave illuminated by

smoky torches in wall brackets. Ranger looked around carefully to be sure he would be able to find his way back to his boat, before following him. Inside the cave, they dismounted and turned their animals over to two other Pandemonians. Ranger watched with a relieved sigh as his mount was led away, still baring its teeth at him.

The Pandemonian ushered Ranger down a long, twisting tunnel with several large rooms opening off to each side. One of the rooms was guarded by two rifle-toting rebel soldiers, who stepped aside and motioned for Ranger and his guide to enter. As Ranger walked into the cavern, he heard the precautionary clicking of the safety catches being released on the guards' rifles and he knew without looking around that the guns were aimed at his back.

Ranger understood the reason for that when he observed that the room had the Spartan, businesslike appearance of a general's field headquarters. A long wooden table flanked by several chairs stood in the middle of the room, and the walls were festooned with maps. Even more revealing than those clues was the tall Pandemonian who stood at the head of the table. He wore a colorful, well-tailored uniform and held himself with such poise that Ranger knew he must be Nos-Nos or one of his high-ranking officers.

There were other Pandemonians and a human male in the room, but Ranger had little time to notice them when he saw who was seated at the table. Eythine sprang out of her chair and ran to Ranger with a hysterical cry of happiness.

"It's so good to see a friendly face again!" Eythine sobbed, laughing through her tears as she flung herself into Ranger's arms and clung to him. "How did you find me? No, that's not important. I'm just so relieved that it's you. When they said a man had arrived, I thought it was Zairundi."

This is the toughest part, Ranger grimly told himself. It would be hard for him to do it convincingly, but if he pulled it off he had a fair chance of getting

Eythine out of here alive. His performance would have to be just right to get the desired reaction from her. He held the woman at arm's length and looked her over with a smug leer.

"Zairundi couldn't make it," Ranger said in a harsh voice. "So I'm taking his place. But don't let that make you think you're going to have it easy. I'll give you the same treatment he would have, if you don't lead me to the treasure ship."

19

EYTHINE STARED AT Ranger with shocked disbelief. For a long agonizing moment Ranger feared that she might not accept his cover story. If Eythine had serious doubts about Ranger's pretended criminality, Nos-Nos might also remain unconvinced. Ranger briefly considered whipping out his disrupter, stunning everyone in the room and making a run for it with Eythine. But the odds against such actions were too great. Ranger's only hope of success lay in his original plan to win the rebel leader's confidence.

Before Eythine could regain her composure, the splendidly uniformed Satyr walked over to Ranger, while the other Pandemonians protectively placed their hands on their side arms. "Welcome to our humble planet, good sir," the being whom Ranger assumed to be Nos-Nos said in excellent Unilingo tinged by the mechanical accent that many nonhumans acquired from Sleep-Teacher language lessons. "I do not believe we have been made acquainted with one another. I am Nos-Nos, the true Proletariat of all the Pandemonians."

"I'm Farstar," Ranger said curtly. "An associate of

Captain Zairundi or The Arrow or whatever he told you his name was. He was unable to come for the woman himself, so I will take her off your hands."

Nos-Nos thoughtfully stroked his neatly trimmed goatee. "The Arrow? Captain Zairundi? Would you please explain just what you are conversing about, good sir?" he politely inquired.

Ranger experienced an instant of blind panic as he thought that he might have guessed wrong about Zairundi being behind the intrigue against Eythine and Shyanne. If that was the case, then he and Eythine were doomed. Then he remembered that Eythine had mentioned Zairundi when she greeted him, and he decided to brazen his way out of the uncertain situation.

"Don't play games with me, Nos-Nos," Ranger snapped. "I know Zairundi was your partner in the scheme to hijack the lady's gold. That was why Zairundi left one of his crewmen here—" Ranger jerked his head toward the human male standing with the other Pandemonians— "to send a radio message to trick her into landing here." It was a shot in the dark, but Ranger could think of no other reason why the man would be with Nos-Nos. The man's sullen glare told Ranger he had guessed right about him.

Nos-Nos displayed a thin smile that might have reflected amusement or cruelty, if indeed he distinguished between those two emotions. "You seem to know a great deal about this Zairundi person, good Sir Farstar. You say he is your associate? Will he be joining us also?"

Ranger flashed an enigmatic smile of his own. "I'm afraid not. Zairundi told me all about his plans to get the treasure of Wonderwhat and split it with you. But unfortunately he failed to survive my, ah, methods of persuasion."

Nos-Nos raised his eyebrows in mock alarm. But before he could speak, the man standing with the other Pandemonians stalked over to confront Ranger.

"You're a liar, whoever you are," the man snarled in Ranger's face. "Cap'n Zairundi wouldn't have talked under the worst torture in the universe. What are you really up to?"

"I admire your loyalty to your late captain," Ranger replied calmly. "If you can transfer it to me, I may have a place for you aboard my ship."

Eythine, who had been observing Ranger's act in a dazed stupor, suddenly snapped out of it and sprang furiously at Ranger. "You filthy swine!" she raged, trying to claw Ranger's face. "I trusted you, thought you were a decent human being, and all the while you were planning to betray me. I'll kill you!"

Two Pandemonians caught Eythine's arms and pulled her back, as she kicked and spat curses at Ranger. Nos-Nos regarded her with a reproving frown and said: "Please control yourself, my dear Archguardess. You will upset your digestive organs just as we are about to have dinner."

"I'd rather starve than stay with this double-dealing space scum," Eythine snarled, glaring at Ranger. "Take me back to my cell. Even the vermin there are better company than he is."

"As you wish," Nos-Nos said, nodding to the two Satyrs holding Eythine's arms.

Ranger watched them escort Eythine out of the room with what he hoped was a lecherous smirk. "There's a woman with spirit, just the way I like 'em," he said. "I'm going to have fun taming her, when I get her in my ship."

Nos-Nos continued studying Ranger curiously. "Now I must decide what to do about you, my good sir. If what you say about Zairundi is true . . ."

"I tell you he's lying," the man from Zairundi's crew insisted. "If he knows so much about Cap'n Zairundi, then ask him what's my name, and what's my job aboard the *Seven Deadly Sins*."

Nos-Nos looked inquiringly at Ranger, who gave the crewman a contemptuous sneer. "I don't waste my time learning the names of insignificant underlings," Ranger said arrogantly.

The crewman grinned triumphantly, but Nos-Nos

still appeared undecided. The rebel leader scratched the short bristly hair between his horns and moved his jaws ruminatingly. "This is indeed a tough cud that requires much careful chewing," Nos-Nos said, turning to his officers and asking for their opinions.

The Pandemonians exchanged many words in their own language, but evidently none of their suggestions appealed to the would-be Proletariat. Ranger kept his eyes on the other man, who wore a holstered blaster and sheath knife on his belt. But the man held his hands well away from his weapons, probably because he knew as well as Ranger the suicidal folly of starting a fight around the highly emotional, violence-loving Pandemonians.

"Hey, I've got an idea," the man said suddenly, drawing Nos-Nos's attention to him. "This big-mouthed interloper claims he killed Cap'n Zairundi, but I say he's bluffing to get the woman away from us. If I'm right, Cap'n Zairundi will be here in another two or three days. So why don't we all just wait out those three days and see what happens then?"

Nos-Nos beamed delightedly at the man. "An excellent solution, my good Sir Lakdaw. Now, if the good Sir Farstar is agreeable . . ."

Ranger could have killed the good Sir Lakdaw for being much smarter than he looked, but he managed to shrug indifferently. "It's all the same to me," Ranger said. "I've waited this long to get my hands on the treasure, so a few more days won't matter."

"Good, good," Nos-Nos smiled. Then he held out his hands with an apologetic expression. "Since you both are under my protection here, there is no need for you to carry weapons."

Ranger obediently surrendered his synapse disrupter and allowed himself to be frisked for other weapons. The man called Lakdaw was reluctant to give up his blaster and knife, but he also knew when the odds were against him.

"Now we can have dinner," Nos-Nos said happily. "I regret that the fair archguardess chose not to join us. But if you two gentlemales will be gracious enough to partake of our unworthy repast, we can have the pleasure of elevating our relationship to more intimate levels."

Ranger was too tense to be hungry, but experience had taught him never to risk offending alien hosts by refusing their hospitality. He knew that Pandemonians were vegetarians, so it was unlikely that any of their foods would be poisonous or too repulsive to human taste. When they all were seated around the table, Nos-Nos nodded to one of his guards, who shouted an order down the tunnel. Soon several female Pandemonians marched silently into the room bearing crude serving and eating implements. The meal's main course turned out to be, appropriately enough for a tribe named Mosseaters, boiled moss. Ranger found it bland but edible, as were most of the dishes placed before him. The others were made tolerable by a pale yellow liquid served in artfully designed goblets. Ranger hesitantly sipped his first serving of the beverage and found it strongly alcoholic but not unpleasant to his palate or stomach.

"Does our *nusk-brir* please you, good Sir Farstar?" Nos-Nos asked.

"It's very good," Ranger answered politely. "What is it?"

"The fermented and distilled milk of the *nusk*."

"Forgive my ignorance, but what is a *nusk?*" Ranger further inquired.

"You rode up here on one."

Ranger's respect for the Pandemonians rose several points, as he thought of the nasty-tempered beast that had tried to bite a chunk out of him. Anybody with the courage to milk one of those things was certainly no pushover. Lakdaw swilled down his *nusk-brir* with the haste of a man with a grudge against sobriety. Ranger soon understood the reason for that. The cave's atmosphere—rendered oppressive by smoky lamps and torches, poor ventilation, cooking smells and the Pandemonians' musky body odors—became less noticeable as the alcohol dulled one's senses.

A few of the other Pandemonian officers also spoke Unilingo, but their loquacious leader gave them little opportunity to converse with their two human guests. At first Nos-Nos curiously questioned Ranger about his encounter with Zairundi and other details of his assumed career as a space pirate. Ranger answered cautiously, fearful that the rebel leader might be trying to trick him into revealing the real reason why he was there. But that worry was soon put to rest as Nos-Nos quickly transformed the conversation into a rambling monologue about the idealistic cause he was fighting for and the great things he would do for Norolda and the entire planet when he had supplanted his evil half-brother as the rightful Proletariat. Like all political megalomaniacs, Nos-Nos was a simple soul who asked only one thing from life—to have his own way all the time. The primitive Mosseaters, who were obviously overawed by Nos-Nos's regal bearing and cultured airs, appeared eager to grant him that wish.

For a while Ranger enjoyed the ambitious Satyr's histrionic performance. But as the evening wore on, with the meal long finished and Nos-Nos showing no sign of tiring, Ranger began to wonder if he would ever have an opportunity to get Eythine out of here. Finally a messenger arrived to whisper something of evident importance to his leader. Nos-Nos rose from the table and excused himself, saying that duty required his presence elsewhere and assuring Ranger that he would be provided comfortable quarters for the night.

Several other Pandemonians departed with Nos-Nos, leaving Ranger and Lakdaw at the table with five younger officers. The latter, obviously relieved to be free of their superiors' observation, quickly got down to some serious drinking. As the *nusk-brir* flowed freely, Lackdaw became more chummy with Ranger, saying that maybe he had been too hasty in not believing Ranger's story that Zairundi was dead.

Ranger had no illusions as to Lakdaw's true intentions. The space pirate obviously hoped to get his opponent helplessly drunk and pump him for information. Maybe, Ranger thought, Lakdaw would even try to murder him after the liquor had rendered him unconscious. Therefore Ranger's only hope for survival was to win the drinking bout that Lakdaw had surreptitiously started between them. Ranger ruefully wished that he actually did possess the prodigious capacity for hard liquor that Slim Hinterwald's imagination had credited him with, especially since Lakdaw had the florid-faced look of a heavy drinking man.

But, as things were, Ranger had no choice but to grit his teeth and go to it. Time after time the two men filled each other's goblets and toasted anything that came to mind, until Ranger vowed that he would never touch another glass of milk in any form. The five Pandemonians, working more conscientiously to incapacitate themselves, were the first to succumb. One by one their glassy eyes drooped closed and they sprawled facedown over the table or slid silently under it. Even the two guards who had been left on duty at the doorway managed to sneak enough drinks to be nodding over their rifles.

Ranger decided it was time for him to make his move, if he could still move. His head was reeling and he couldn't be sure how many of his voluntary muscles he still controlled. But at least Lakdaw did not appear to be in much better shape. Ranger leaned forward and slipped his arm affectionately around the space pirate's shoulders. "Lakdaw, ol' shipmate," he slurred. "This's the mos' fun night I ever had in m' whole life."

"Tha' goss for me, too," Lakdaw solemnly replied.

"Only one thing could make it more perfek." Ranger grinned lewdly. "A woman."

"Yeah." Lakdaw licked his lips hungrily. "Too bad thersh only these hairy ol' she-goats here."

"There's one good-lookin' human female here," Ranger reminded him. "If only we knew how to find her."

"I know where she ish," Lakdaw replied secretively. "But I don' think . . ."

"Don' waste time thinkin'; lead me to 'er!" Ranger ordered. "Unless you aren't man enough for it."

"I'll show you whosh a man," Lakdaw growled, struggling to his feet. "C'mon."

Gripping the table with both hands, Ranger managed to stand up unsteadily. Both men had trouble getting their feet moving in the right direction. But finally, leaning against each other for support, they staggered out the doorway between the dozing guards. Lakdaw guided them down the main tunnel for several meters, then turned off into a side passage. The light was dimmer here and the rough floor almost tripped them up in several places. Eventually they came to another armed guard standing before a heavily barred wooden door set in the tunnel wall.

"Open the door for us, goat-face!" Lakdaw bellowed. "We wanna go in an' play with the woman."

The guard, speaking angrily in Pandemonian, blocked their way with his rifle. Lakdaw argued back at him. Ranger, first making sure that his own balance was secure, stuck his right foot between Lakdaw's legs and shoved hard against his back. Lakdaw fell heavily on his belly at the guard's feet, groaning and struggling weakly to rise on his hands and knees. Ranger bent over with his face to the wall, pretending to be sick. The guard hesitated uncertainly, then leaned down to help Lakdaw to his feet.

Ranger turned quickly, swinging his arm in a wide arc. The edge of his hand caught the back of the guard's neck and he fell without a sound over Lakdaw's back. Ranger picked up the fallen rifle and used its butt to make sure that the guard and Lakdaw were quite unconscious. With fumbling hands, he unbarred the door and swung it open to a pitch-dark cell.

"Eythine, it's me—Ranger," he whispered. "I've come to . . ."

"Keep away from me!" Eythine snarled bitterly. "I'll kill myself before I'll let you touch me!"

"You don't understand." Ranger groped in his fuddled mind for the right words to tell her he was really on her side. "Come on out and we'll . . ."

Suddenly a figure hurtled out of the darkness and slammed into Ranger's chest, knocking him halfway around. Fighting to keep his balance, Ranger saw Eythine running swiftly toward the main tunnel. "Wait! Let me explain!" he cried desperately.

But Eythine only ran faster. Ranger stumbled after her, using the rifle as a crutch to keep his feet under him. He saw her turn into the main tunnel, and it seemed to take him forever to reach the spot where she had disappeared. Then he saw her speeding toward the cave entrance. She passed the room that served as Nos-Nos's headquarters, shaking the two drunken guards out of their stupor. They blinked in confusion, then moved out into the middle of the tunnel to aim their rifles at the fleeing woman. Ranger came up behind the first guard just as he was about to fire and clubbed him down with his captured rifle. The second guard turned around in time to catch Ranger's rifle butt in his face.

Ranger tottered on after Eythine. She was out of the tunnel and out of sight down the trail by the time Ranger stepped out into the cold night air and paused to get his bearings. He thought he remembered the way back to the valley where his survey boat and Eythine's ship were parked, but he was still too intoxicated to be absolutely sure of anything. Fortunately Pandemo's moon was up, providing enough illumination for him to pick his way safely down the trail. He encountered no one on the trail and finally came to the top of the steep slope down to the valley floor.

He squinted at the dim shape of the *Ram's Revenge* and saw its main air lock open. Eythine was briefly silhouetted against the ship's interior lighting, as she hurried into the air lock and closed it behind her. Ranger plunged down the slope. As he tumbled and rolled over the loose soil and rocks, he prayed that Eythine would use her ship's antigravity drive to lift off. If she used her rockets, the backblast would burn him and his boat to cinders. He struck the bottom of the slope, getting the breath knocked out of his lungs, and lay gasping as he gratefully heard the smooth hum of the *Ram's Revenge*'s antigravity engine.

Under the swiftly rising starship, Ranger got back on his feet and limped on toward his own boat. Confused voices were calling out from the cave entrances and several rifles fired blindly in the darkness. Ranger reached his boat and gave it a quick visual inspection. It appeared to be undamaged, thanks to Nos-Nos's consideration for his guest. Ranger scrambled into the cockpit and shoved the lift throttle wide open.

The boat leaped into the air with such brain-rattling force that Ranger nearly blacked out. Even as he recovered from that, sickening waves of G-pressure and drunkenness swept over him. He struggled to clear his head, but he could feel consciousness slipping away from him as he opened a communication channel to contact the *Gayheart*. He just had time to switch on the autopilot and order the craft into orbit before the universe blinked out of his awareness.

20

RANGER REVIVED SLOWLY. He managed to pry his eyes open on the third attempt and saw Dawnboy's face peering anxiously down at him. A shift of his gaze located Shyanne looking equally concerned on his other side. He was lying supine on the examination table in the *Gayheart*'s Sick Bay.

"Are ye all right now, Dad?" Dawnboy asked gently.

"Yeah, I think so," Ranger muttered. His tongue

was thick and the interior of his mouth felt as if it had been sandpapered raw, but otherwise he seemed to be in fair shape. "What am I ..." Suddenly the full memory of his escapade on Pandemo came back and he excitedly started to sit up.

"Just rest until you get your strength back," Shyanne urged, her cool fingers pressing down on his flushed forehead.

"Aye, we ha' everything under control," Dawnboy assured his father. "So do na worry yerself about anything."

"But what's become of Eythine?" Ranger demanded. "And how did I get back here? I don't recall contacting you before I blacked out."

"You didn't," Lulu said. "My scanners detected the *Ram's Revenge* lifting off and I hailed her, but got no response. We started to follow her, then I scanned your boat going into orbit. I tried to contact you, but you didn't answer, either. We figured that you must be in more trouble than Eythine, so we tracked your boat down and picked you up."

"But where is Eythine?" Ranger repeated.

"Gone through the channel," Shyanne answered.

"Through the channel?" Ranger cried. "Why didn't the Channel Authority stop her?"

"Why should they have?" Lulu asked matter-of-factly. "She had done nothing wrong, as far as they knew. She already had clearance to use the Channel, and there was no law against her spending a few days on Pandemo before continuing her voyage."

Ranger saw the logic of Lulu's explanation. But it was frustrating to know that Eythine still thought of him as her enemy. "How long have I been unconscious?" he asked.

"About five hours, I think," Shyanne informed him.

"Five hours!" Ranger started to rise again. "We have to go after her!"

"Ye better take it easy, Dad," Dawnboy cautioned him. "Ye were carrying quite a load o' happy juice when we picked ye up." His eyes twinkled mischievously. "There must be quite a story behind that, I'll wager."

"Don't make any sudden moves," Lulu warned Ranger. "I've been pumping you full of detoxicants, but you haven't had time to recover fully from your hangover yet."

"I'm okay," Ranger insisted, sitting up and swinging his legs over the edge of the table. But when he stood up his head started to throb and his stomach felt as if it wanted to divorce his body. Dawnboy and Shyanne caught his swaying body and would have eased him back down on the table, but Ranger insisted that they help him get to the bridge.

Seated in the pilot seat and gulping a mug of hot citroffee, Ranger gave his shipmates a brief summary of his adventures among the Pandemonian rebels. Dawnboy derived much amusement from the account of his father's drinking bout with Lakdaw; he thought that it was the most unique method of rescuing a lady in distress that he had ever heard of. Ranger grumbled that young people had no appreciation for the hardships their elders often had to endure.

By then, Lulu had contacted the Pandemo Channel Authority and obtained clearance for the *Gayheart* to pass through the channel. She gave the authority Farstar & Son, Inc.'s credit-code listing, which would enable the Aquilans to collect the ship's passage fee from the company's bank account. The official on duty thanked them for their patronage. Then he asked Ranger if he would mind taking along a shipment of supplies and mail for the *Sandwich Islands,* an SSA survey ship operating on the route that the *Gayheart* would most likely travel to the Magellanic Clouds.

Ranger hesitated, thinking that it might cost them precious time to locate the survey ship and make the delivery. But, being an old startramp himself, he knew how anxiously men on long cruises look forward to receiving news from home. Besides, a visit with the *Sandwich Islands'* crew might pay off with some useful information about the area where they hoped to find Wonderwhat.

The shipment was already packed in a rocket capsule. As the *Gayheart* approached the moon base, the rocket was launched and guided by remote control to rendezvous with the starship. Lulu deftly caught the capsule with a tow beam and hauled it into the ship's cargo hold without losing a moment's travel time.

The *Gayheart* began rapidly reaccelerating as they left Pandemo and headed toward the channel, which some hard-bitten space jockeys sardonically called "Snake Alley," along with some less genteel names. Dawnboy and Shyanne, again strapped to their couches, soon learned the reason for that nickname when they entered the long tube of nothingness that crackled and writhed like a fiery serpent through the bowels of space. As they were moving at multiple-light speed, it was impossible for them to see any of the power relay stations they passed. All around them the titanic battle between matter and anti-matter swirled by in explosive rivers of light that had the two youngsters constantly breathless with astonishment. It was like plunging down a bottomless pit of fire and always managing to avoid the flames at the last possible instant.

The show seemed to go on forever. Dawnboy wanted it to go on forever as he stared transfixed at the bulkhead telescope and lost all awareness of the ship and those around him. The spellbinding spectacle made him feel almost godlike, as if he had become free of all physical restraints and existed as a naked entity capable of reaching any place or time in the universe instantly by a mere effort of will. He supposed this must be the rapture of the cosmos, a strange sensation somewhat akin to religious ecstasy that sometimes seized star voyagers who had been alone too long in space. Like a joyful but drawn-out melody, the sensual and spiritual pleasure of the experience continued to build up within the young Apache's soul to an intolerable pressure.

But finally the mounting sensation climaxed as they

hurtled out of the channel's opposite end. Before them the great black emptiness of intergalactic space was punctuated only by the bright flashes of the ship's force-screen burning off stray bits of anti-matter and the distant glow of the Magellanic Clouds and the Andromeda Galaxy. Dawnboy, feeling physically and emotionally drained, relaxed and exchanged tired grins with Shyanne. After the fantastic visual impact of the channel passage and the clash of anti-ionized gas with Psychedelus, Dawnboy wondered if the remainder of their voyage could possibly hold any more surprises for them.

When Dawnboy voiced that thought, his father assured him that their real problems had only just begun. "In the wildest parts of our galaxy, at least some semblance of law and order usually exists," Ranger said. "But out here anything can happen, and often does. In some cases, even the laws of nature don't function in ways that rational minds would expect them to."

"Well, we aren't entirely on our own out here," Shyanne remarked. "There are the patrol ships—few though they are—of the SSA and the friendly ZuJu worlds, that we can call on for help."

"Yes, but don't hold your breath until the SSA's Protectorate Patrol arrives," Lulu said cynically. "Most of the SSA's financing comes from the Unified Systems of Aquila taxpayers. That means that most of the patrol's ships are commanded by Aquilan officers, who used to be gutsy and resourceful enough to provide good protection to honest star travelers. But if that namby-pamby channel commissioner is typical of our new breed of officials, I wouldn't give a lead stellar for the USA's chances of surviving much longer as the leading democratic power in the Milky Way."

"Aye, ye Aquilans are a strange folk to understand," Dawnboy said, thinking of those he had met, including Eythine and Dr. Wage Gitlow, as well as Lulu. "What makes ye so contrary?"

"Too much freedom," Lulu answered promptly. "In earlier times we had strict moral and social training that enabled us to become strong individualists, without neglecting our responsibilities to others. But these later generations think they are born knowing everything and don't need discipline to make them well-rounded sentient beings."

"Oh, don't be such a sanctimonious old prude," Ranger chided. "The degeneration and decline of great civilizations is a highly complex subject that philosophers and historians have pondered for thousands of years. In my opinion, the USA is still strong enough to continue as the leading galactic power for a long time to come. It's certainly no worse than any of the other countless Yankee reincarnations."

"What do you mean?" Shyanne asked.

Ranger replied: "As you probably know from your studies of history, most of the interstellar colonists came from the original America on Old Earth. When they established a new society and government, they naturally tried to base them on what they thought were the best qualities of their ex-homeland. Of course they failed, but their descendants have never stopped trying to achieve that impossible goal. Nearly every human settlement has claimed, at one time or another, to embody the 'true American ideals.' And since nobody actually knows what those ideals were, they each have an equal right to make that claim."

"We Aquilans came closest to realizing those ideals," Lulu insisted with unashamed patriotism. "And we might have succeeded, if our younger generations hadn't gone softhearted and softheaded."

"I agree with you," Ranger said. "And I think it will be a tragic blow to all civilized beings if the USA is ever defeated by the IFIB or PHAP totalitarians. But we can worry about that some other time." He rose from the pilot seat on legs that were still wobbly. "Now see if you three can keep us on course and out of trouble for a few hours. I'm going to my cabin to sleep off what has to be the worst hangover ever suffered by living protoplasm."

21

ONCE FREE OF her native galaxy, the *Gayheart* raced ahead to make up for lost time. Even in the emptiest areas of the Milky Way, the stars' gravitational fields exerted some retarding influence on a space vehicle's progress. But between the galaxies, the frictionless vacuum of space was absolute, and a moving body obeyed Newton's laws of motion with a vengeance.

Out here the Jarles Effect, which made it possible for starships to travel at hyperlight speeds, really rolled up its sleeves and went to work in a way that would have gladdened Harlington Jarles's flabby old heart, if he had lived long enough to see his theory achieve practical application. Even the dim light from the most distant stars was efficiently utilized by the *Gayheart*'s light-energy conversion system to produce the propulsive matter/anti-matter explosions. With immeasurable throw-power behind and nothing before her, the ship plunged forward until she was squaring the speed of light every few seconds, just as Jarles had predicted from his study of the way a light-hulled sailboat with a big spinnaker could be made to move faster than the actual speed of the wind that propelled it.

But even the Jarles Effect left much to be desired in covering the incredibly vast distances between galaxies. It was an average six-week cruise for a ship of the *Gayheart*'s class just to reach the Magellanic Clouds, the Milky Way's nearest neighboring star clusters. Ranger, wanting to reduce that time as much as possible, ordered Lulu to push the ship onward at the maximum safe speed while he, Dawnboy and Shyanne spent hours sunk deep into their acceleration couches.

At the same time, Lulu's scanners constantly but futilely searched for some trace of the *Ram's Revenge*. Ranger suspected that Eythine had altered her course after emerging from the Pandemo Channel to throw off pursuit, but there was not much he could do about that. If the *Gayheart* zigzagged to cover a wide area of space, she would most likely lose much precious time without succeeding in finding Eythine's ship. So Ranger kept his ship on a direct course to the midpoint between the two Magellanic Clouds, where Wonderwhat had been most frequently observed. Also, on the off chance that Eythine might pick up a communication beam from the *Gayheart*, Shyanne made a tape appealing to her stepmother to contact them. The tape was broadcast continuously from the *Gayheart*, but there was no response to it. Lulu speculated that even if Eythine heard the message, she might think it was just another of Ranger's underhanded tricks to lure her into his power.

Dawnboy, although he shared his father's and Shyanne's concern for Eythine's safety, thought they had more serious problems to worry about. The lepton scanner and other astronavigational aids enabled them to avoid the frequent VIP's they encountered. But the area abounded in other hazards, most notably space pirates from the Milky Way and renegade ZuJu marauders. The pirates generally did not bother to take prisoners when they captured a space vessel, as they considered it too much trouble to transport captives back to civilization where they could be ransomed or sold as slaves. The ZuJus, on the other hand, liked nothing better than to introduce human and other sentient beings to their peculiar form of bondage.

Dawnboy had first learned of the ZuJus' practice of using living humans as money in Rothfeller Hughes's Currency Museum on Capitalia, where he had seen a facsimile of a man with his monetary value branded on his forehead. The practice had begun when the ZuJus had learned that the odd-looking species from the

Milky Way highly valued the lives and freedoms of their individual members. That enabled the ZuJus to trade prisoners of war for the technological products they desired from the more advanced humans. Eventually nearly the entire ZuJu economy came to be based upon the use of human "money."

The strange monetary system had officially ended when the ZuJu emperor signed a peace treaty with the Milky Way races, agreeing to release all their citizens then being held captive in his empire. But humans were still captured and traded among the ZuJus living outside of the emperor's jurisdiction. Because the renegade ZuJu worlds were so numerous and widely scattered, not even the imperial space fleet had been able to stamp out their unique slave trade. Ranger said that was the main reason why he was so anxious to catch up with Eythine; even after all the trouble she had caused him, he would hate to see her end up as part of a ZuJu's bank account.

But thoughts of ZuJu economics were the furthest things from Dawnboy's mind when they encountered their first ZuJus a dozen days after leaving the Milky Way. He was tending his hydroponics garden when the *Gayheart*'s automatic alarm system sounded Red Alert upon detecting the alien spacecraft. Dawnboy dropped everything and raced through the ship to join his father on the bridge, nearly colliding with Shyanne as she emerged from her cabin, sleepily zipping up her utility coverall.

"Take it easy, kids; we're among friends," Lulu's calm voice informed them. "I've just made contact with the SSA survey ship *Sandwich Islands,* which is being escorted by two imperial ZuJu war vessels."

Ranger was on the photophone conversing with the *Sandwich Islands*'s Duty Officer when Dawnboy and Shyanne reached the bridge. The officer expressed great pleasure at having visitors to relieve the long, monotonous cruise that he and his shipmates were enduring. He was even more overjoyed when he learned that the *Gayheart* was carrying supplies and mail for them. The *Sandwich Islands* and her escorts were traveling slower than the *Gayheart* but on a parallel course, so Lulu had to reduce her speed by a few light-years per hour as she drew alongside them.

Dawnboy curiously studied the three vessels as the *Gayheart* approached them. The ZuJu ships appeared to be typical men-o'-war, and they probably would not have attracted his interest had he not known what strange beings occupied them. (In the pictures of ZuJus that he had seen, the species appeared to be a nightmarish cross between giant insects and tentacled sea monsters.) The warships looked sleek, swift and deadly, especially in comparison to the huge SSA vessel. The latter was about ten times the *Gayheart*'s size, and her globular hull bristling with antennae, scanner disks and other apparatus made her look as unattractive and unwieldly as a fat ballerina.

"The kind of ship that only a skipper could love," Ranger remarked under his breath, as the *Sandwich Islands* thrust out a tow beam to take the cargo capsule from the *Gayheart*.

"I heard that," the survey ship's duty officer said from Ranger's photophone screen. He was a plump, four-armed Shivan who for some reason reminded Dawnboy of Slim Hinterwald. "I dare you to come over here and say that. In fact, come on over anyway. We're all so starved for company that we might even be able to get our bluenosed captain to let us have a few drinks with you. That's the least we can do to repay you for bringing this shipment out to us."

"Thanks for the invitation and my compliments to your captain," Ranger said. "But just now we're in too much of a hurry to stop for social visits. Instead, you can repay us with any news you might have about present conditions in the area we're headed for. We are especially interested in learning if you know anything about the *Ram's Revenge*, another human-operated starship that should have passed this way a few days ago."

"You're in luck," the Shivan replied. "We didn't encounter that ship ourselves, but yesterday one of our Brainsponges telecommunicated with a passing cloud of Chemo-Gypsies who mentioned seeing her heading toward the lesser Magellanic Cloud. They said there was only a single female human aboard the ship— something I find hard to believe."

"You better believe it," Ranger said. "Did the Chemo-Gypsies, by any chance, give you any information about the ship's location, speed or direction of flight?"

The duty officer gave Ranger a pained look. "What do you think we're doing out here in the Big Empty, except keeping tabs on space traffic and recording any and all data that come our way, whether we have any use for it or not? Sure, all of that stuff is in our computer banks. Do you want us to pipe it over to yours?"

"If you'd be so kind," Ranger answered, hardly able to control his joy at receiving such a windfall of valuable information. If the data were accurate, Lulu could use it to make an educated guess as to where Eythine would begin her search for Wonderwhat. Of course that was no guarantee that Wonderwhat would actually be in that area, but Ranger had made up his mind that he was going to stick as close as possible to Eythine on this expedition, even if she didn't like it. Two ships searching together would save a lot of wasted effort.

While data were being fed into Lulu's computer banks, Ranger and Dawnboy continued chatting with the survey ship's duty officer. He told them that the *Sandwich Islands* had been ten months on its present cruise and had recently called at Fossick, where Captain Midas had reputedly picked up the *Jealousy*'s rich cargo. But the planet was no longer a fabulous world of gold-digging ants.

When word of Captain Midas's discovery had gotten back to the Milky Way, it had set off a wild gold rush to Fossick. Countless greedy fortune hunters had swarmed over the planet, fighting pirates, ZuJus and each other in their mad scramble to get rich quick and get out. Eventually Fossick's mineral wealth was stripped, and in the process her ecological balance was so badly disturbed that most of her surface was turned into a lifeless desert.

Now the SSA was trying to revive Fossick by using her as a rehabilitation center for humans who were freed from the bondage of serving as ZuJu money. The demonetized people were educated in how to work and live as free, self-responsible beings in human societies. Then, if they wished, they were transported to a human world and helped to make new lives for themselves. But those who feared the competition and other problems of such a drastic readjustment were allowed to remain on Fossick. They were given tools and farm lands and encouraged to help with the planet's development.

The SSA people in charge of the rehabilitation center thought it showed great promise, although it had not yet been operating long enough to have processed very many freed humans.

Ranger thought that news and most of the other things he learned from the duty officer were very interesting, but not too relevant to his search for Wonderwhat. So he was glad when the garrulous Shivan finally seemed to run out of words. Ranger took advantage of the pause to bid the SSA ship a hasty farewell and ordered Lulu to set a course for where she thought they would be most likely to find the *Ram's Revenge*.

Only Dawnboy seemed reluctant to leave the *Sandwich Island*s and her two alien escorts. "We didna get to see any o' the ZuJus on those ships," he said, disappointed.

"You didn't miss much," Lulu told him.

22

THE MAGELLANIC CLOUDS were no longer merely patches of hazy luminescence, as seen through the *Gayheart*'s electron telescope. Dawnboy could clearly distinguish the major stars of the two subgalaxies, and even the less conspicuous suns of the narrow "star bridge" that tenuously connected the Clouds were visible. Fossick was located about midway in the bridge, which served as a somewhat neutral zone between the ZuJu empire of the larger Cloud and the renegade ZuJu worlds of the lesser Cloud.

"This may be the most dangerous part of the universe, but it sure is a beautiful sight, isn't it?" Ranger remarked while he and Dawnboy were on duty on the bridge, two weeks after leaving the SSA survey party.

"It certainly is," Dawnboy agreed. "Have ye ever been out here before?"

"No. In fact, the only other time I was outside the Milky Way was when I worked on a charter cruise taking colonists to the Andromeda Galaxy."

"What was that like?"

"Intolerably dull for the most part. But the pay was good."

"I meant, what were the worlds of Andromeda like?"

"Oh, pretty much the same as the planets in our own galaxy," Ranger answered. "But far less populated. There are enormously rich natural resources and vast potential for development out there, if only we had a practical way of overcoming the high cost in time and energy required for covering the immense distances. As much as I hate to say it, I'm afraid that efficient intergalactic transportation is beyond starships' capabilities. Something radically different is needed for that job."

"Something like the matter-transporter systems?" Dawnboy suggested.

His father nodded. "Someday, I suppose, the entire universe will be tied together by those silly-looking boxes. Then the only starships left will be in museums along with steam locomotives, jet airplanes and other relics from the early history of transportation." Ranger sighed heavily. "What a depressing thought!"

"Well, maybe Shyanne has the right idea about getting into matter-transporter technology early," Dawnboy said. Then he looked thoughtfully around the interior of the bridge. "But I would sorely miss all o' this. Even Lulu's nagging."

"Your affection is deeply touching," Lulu said. "But now you boys had better get back to work and look at the interesting blip I just picked up on the madar screen. It seems to be another ship, in the approximate area where we expected to find the *Ram's Revenge.*"

Ranger and Dawnboy quickly switched on their monitoring screens of the ship's Microwave Amplified Detecting and Ranging set. At the end of the wide-sweeping arm, a tiny speck of light winked seductively at them. While they waited for the computer to digest all the data that Lulu was collecting about the distant object, Dawnboy summoned Shyanne from the ship's laboratory, where she was conducting a chemistry experiment in the course of her daily study routine. The girl hurriedly joined them on the bridge as Lulu verified that the object was indeed a starship and gave a preliminary estimate of its size and class.

"Yes, I think that's the *Ram's Revenge,*" Ranger said. "Congratulations, Lulu. You haven't lost your touch."

"Thanks, Boss. What do we do now?"

"Let me communicate with Eythine," Shyanne begged, with more than the usual amount of happy deviltry in her face. "I can't wait to see her expression when she learns that I was able to get out here in spite of everything she did to keep me on Newtonia!"

But Ranger vetoed the girl's request. "I don't think we should contact Eythine until we are in a better position to prevent her from running away, in case she refuses to believe that I'm not really the dirty villain she thinks I am. She's moving considerably slower than we are, which probably means that she has already started her search for Wonderwhat. So let's tail her for a while at a safe distance. If we're lucky, maybe she'll locate the comet even before she realizes we're here."

"But what if 'tis na the *Ram's Revenge*, but a pirate or ZuJu ship?" Dawnboy asked.

"Then that's all the more reason for us to stay well away from it," was his father's sensible reply. "We can't be too cautious in this cosmic wilderness."

For the next twenty-four hours they followed Ranger's plan, stealthily shadowing the other ship as it methodically zigzagged through space. By then Ranger was all but positive that the ship was Eythine's, and his admiration for her spacemanship was increased by her efficiency in covering as wide an area as possible in her search. To extend the range of the search even more, Lulu kept the *Gayheart*'s scanner beams on maximum sweep as they trailed the *Ram's Revenge*. But the space they covered remained remarkably empty. They came across a few more VIP's and random clumps of anti-matter, but they found no sign of Wonderwhat or any other comet.

Finally Ranger decided that they might as well inform Eythine of their presence, as Shyanne was anxious to rejoin her stepmother. But when Lulu tried to hail the *Ram's Revenge*, the blip on their madar screen abruptly plunged into a series of erratic movements and sped away from them.

"I'm afraid the lady is in no mood for company," Lulu reported. "As soon as I gave Eythine's biocomputer our identity, she ordered him to break contact with us."

"Stay with her, Lulu," Ranger ordered. "Shyanne,

strap yourself down on one of the couches, then keep trying to communicate with Eythine. We may have to chase her halfway across the universe, but when she finally gets it through her head that she can't shake us, maybe she will listen to reason."

"Maybe she's just coy and wants to play hard to get," Dawnboy suggested with a teasing grin at his father.

Lulu added, with a suppressed giggle, "Yes, remember what I told you about marriage-minded widows."

Ranger bluntly told his son and biocomputer to keep their minds on their work. That proved to be sound advice, as the pursuit of the fleeing starship became a grim test of piloting skill and dogged persistence for both Ranger and Lulu. For more than two hours Eythine whipped her vessel through tortuously unpredictable maneuvers that enabled the *Gayheart* to gain but little distance on her. Then, as they were following Eythine through an especially complicated maneuver, Ranger spotted two more blips far off the *Ram's Revenge*'s starboard stern.

Ranger swore angrily. "I was afraid our wild cavorting might attract unwanted attention. What do you make them out to be, Lulu?"

"I can't say for sure yet at this distance," Lulu replied. "Probably ZuJu ships, judging from their speeds. Their bodies can take more G's of acceleration than humans."

"That's all we needed to make this trip complete," Ranger groaned, watching the two blips rapidly closing in on the *Ram's Revenge*, despite Eythine's continued evasive action. "Give us all the power we've got, Lulu, and release the safeties on our laser banks and nuclear cannon. I want to be ready to fire the instant we have their range."

"But we do na ken for sure if they are enemies," Dawnboy pointed out.

"They'll have ample time to tell us if they aren't," Lulu assured him. "I'm hailing them on all frequencies, but they haven't responded yet."

The silence from the two strange ships continued as the *Gayheart* gradually edged up on them. It seemed to take Eythine forever to realize her danger, whereupon she decided she would be better off if she reversed her course and joined the ship that had previously been pursuing her. But by then it was too late; the two intruders were in position to block her efforts to come about and head for the *Gayheart*. Ranger and Dawnboy, waiting eagerly for the ships to come within reach of their electron telescope, watched the two well-coordinated blips try to work their way up on the third one's flanks.

"Good girl!" Ranger cheered, as Eythine desperately weaved about to keep one of the pursuers between her and the other one. "Don't let them catch you in their cross fire."

"Well, their hostile intentions are now official," Lulu reported. "They've just fired a laser blast at her. A clean miss, fortunately."

"More likely a warning shot to induce her to surrender," Ranger surmised. "If they're renegade ZuJus, they'll try to take the ship intact, so as not to injure the illegal tender in it."

"Why does one o' them na turn around to fight us?" Dawnboy wondered. "Surely they must know we're on their tails."

"They also know how long it will take us to catch up to them," Ranger said. "They no doubt think they have enough time to use their combined firepower to cripple Eythine's ship, if they have to. Then they can turn their two-to-one advantage against us. Say what you want about the ZuJus' ugliness and other faults, but when it comes to fighting they're real pros."

Dawnboy remembered his Grandfather MacCochise saying something similar to that when discussing hand-to-hand combat in the clan's wars. "When ye've the advantage o' numbers on yer side, always try to outflank the enemy and crush 'em between yer two wings," the old Laird had said. "But when it's t'other way 'round, then try to divide yer enemy and defeat his smaller forces one at a time. 'Tis na as honorable and glorious as standing up to yer foes and battling them mon to mon, but 'tis a far easier way to win a war."

The lesson was vividly reimpressed on Dawnboy's mind by Ranger's words, as he thought of how unchanged basic military tactics were even when war was made complicated and mechanized by the highest efforts of civilization.

"Score one for Eythine," Lulu said. "Her lasers got a hit on the ZuJu ship to our right."

"It doesn't seem to have slowed them down any," Ranger said. "They must have strong deflector screens. When we get within range, I think our best bet will be to come up under their bellies and aim for their propulsion units. Damn! I wish I had a good military craft under me, instead of this old cargo tub with delusions of grandeur."

"No sweat, Skipper, we'll vap 'em out of existence in no time at all," Lulu said optimistically.

"Do you really believe that?" Shyanne asked.

"No, but it's the best way I can think of to hide my fear," Lulu answered.

"Well, get a grip on yourself," Ranger said.

"You, too. We're coming in telescope range of them now."

Ranger and Dawnboy watched tensely as the blurred shapes of the three distant ships appeared in the telescope lens. As they steadily drew closer, one of the ZuJu ships fired an energy blast that hit the *Ram's Revenge* astern, causing it to wobble and lose speed. That enabled the ZuJus to complete their outflanking maneuver and bracket Eythine's ship between them. Eythine's lasers blazed away at them, to little noticeable effect, save to spoil the aim of the shots they fired at her.

Ranger cursed in frustration as they swiftly closed with the battle scene. "She told me she had the latest weapons installed on her ship, so why the hell doesn't she give them a taste of her nuclear cannon?"

"Maybe she . . ." Dawnboy began.

"We're almost in firing range," Lulu interrupted.

"Good." Ranger leaned forward, his attention divided between the telescope and his instrument panel. His hands were poised rock-steady over the firing studs of the *Gayheart*'s heavy weapons. "The ZuJu ship on our portside is slightly closer, so it will be our first target. Lulu, stand by to dive steeply at my command, then pull up under the ship as close as you can get."

"Yes, sir."

"Is there anything I can do?" Dawnboy asked.

"Just sit tight and watch closely. If any of my instruments are knocked out, you'll have to take charge until I can change seats with you."

"Aye, aye, sir."

Dawnboy licked his dry lips and stared in trembling fascination as the ZuJu ship grew ominously until it nearly filled the entire telescope lens. The ship's stern laser banks fired a full salvo that jolted them roughly as their deflector screen absorbed it.

"*Now*, Lulu!" Ranger snapped.

The *Gayheart* nosed down so abruptly that the two men were thrown painfully against their seat harnesses. Another blast from the ZuJu ship skimmed over them, but Ranger continued to hold his fire. The *Gayheart* reached the pit of her dive and angled up sharply, crushing Ranger and Dawnboy back into their seats. Ranger's fingers flicked deftly over the firing studs as his sights zeroed in on the ZuJu ship's underbelly. The laser beams splattered light particles against the ZuJu's deflector screen, while the nuclear cannon, firing on full automatic, pumped one megaton round after another into the area of the ZuJu's hull where Lulu had located its propulsion unit.

The ZuJu ship dashed away in jerky rolls and twists, trying to shake off its tormentor. But Lulu skillfully held the ship in Ranger's sights while he continued to pour fire into it. The twelfth round from his cannon broke through the ZuJu's screen, ruptured its hull and caused its luxium pile to go critical. The ship flared up as blindingly as a supernova, then faded gently away as its atomized remains began their long journey throughout the universe.

"Now what about the other one?" Ranger asked calmly as the *Gayheart* came smartly about to face the remaining ZuJu ship, which answered his question by breaking away from the *Ram's Revenge* to come speeding toward them.

Ranger launched a broad pattern of space depth charges and ordered, "Dive, Lulu!"

The ZuJu ship plowed through the exploding charges that did no damage but kept the ZuJus thrown off-guard for the few precious moments it took the *Gayheart* to plunge below and bring her nose up to get her weapons locked on the enemy's belly. Just as Ranger started to repeat his performance that had worked so well with the first ZuJu ship, he saw a smaller craft dart away from the remaining enemy.

"Watch it, Lulu," Ranger warned. "That may be a parasite fighter making a suicide run on us."

"No, I think it's a lifeboat trying to get away," Lulu said. "At least somebody in that ship seems to have had enough of the fight."

"The others haven't," Ranger said, as the ZuJu ship tried to twist away and fire back at them. "So let's finish 'em off!"

Once more his fingers played their deadly symphony on the weapons' controls, rocking the ZuJu ship with well-coordinated laser and cannon fire, while Lulu kept them stubbornly fastened to their wildly plunging quarry. Like the first fight, this one lasted only a few minutes though it seemed to go on forever. Ranger bit the inside of his mouth bloody in his struggle to fight off the nerve exhaustion of total concentration. Finally, just as the ZuJu's deflector screens were starting to crumble, one of the *Gayheart*'s overloaded laser banks shorted out. For an instant it looked as if the enemy ship would get away; then a nuclear warhead struck her hull and once again a miniature supernova brightened the cosmic blackness for a few brief moments.

"That'll teach you to be more polite to a lady!"

Ranger shouted, his voice cracking with laughter. He sank back in his seat, his whole body shaking convulsively, then turned an embarrassed smile to Dawnboy. "Sorry about that, Son. Just a touch of delayed panic. It always happens to me after a fight."

"Just so it never happens *during* a fight," Lulu said, then added admiringly: "Well done, Skipper. I don't know if Eythine will appreciate it, but you can be *my* hero anytime."

"Aye, ye were magnificent, Dad," Dawnboy said, gazing proudly at his father. He wiped his sweaty hands on his shirt and wondered if he could have handled the action with the same clearheaded self-control that Ranger had displayed.

"Are you still scanning the area around us, Lulu?" Ranger asked. "I don't want any more surprises, in case those two had friends within calling distance."

"Relax, there's nothing but clear space out there now," Lulu assured him. "But the lifeboat is still within our range and moving quite slowly."

"Let it go; we've killed enough ZuJus for one day," Ranger said wearily. "Let's go back and see if Eythine's ship is still in one piece."

"Wait—something is going on out there," Lulu reported. "The lifeboat isn't trying to get away from us. It's trailing along after us and sending out signals that seem to indicate that those aboard want to surrender."

Ranger frowned suspiciously. "I've never heard of that happening before. ZuJus are such dedicated warriors that they would rather self-destruct than suffer the shame of captivity. It must be a trick."

"I don't think so," Lulu said. "I've just established photophonic contact with the lifeboat and I think you had better have a look at what's in it."

"All right, but . . ." Ranger switched on his photophone screen, then stared, speechless, at the face of another human male.

23

"I CAN'T MAKE any sense out of what he's saying," Ranger said a few minutes later, as the man in the lifeboat continued to gesture excitedly and speak rapidly in an odd-sounding language. "Can you, Lulu?"

"Just a few words here and there," the biocomputer answered. "It sounds like an archaic Unilingo dialect that has been cut off from the rest of humanity for so long that it has become almost a separate language of its own. It also seems to have some ZuJu words and grammar mixed in with it."

"Well, we can't waste any more time trying to understand him," Ranger decided. "Feed his words into your translator banks and see if they can figure him out."

"Are ye going to take him aboard?" Dawnboy asked, curiously watching the man's well-shaped head and shoulders. His torso was bare, revealing an exceptionally good-looking and muscular specimen. The high cheekbones and epicanthic folds over his wide brown eyes were well matched with his cleft chin and broad forehead that was mostly covered by a shock of thick black hair.

"Of course not," Ranger snapped impatiently at Dawnboy. "We've just been fighting for our lives against creatures who, for all we know, were his friends. It isn't unknown for humans to turn against their own kind and join hostile aliens. Lulu, bring the boat along with a tow beam, at a safe distance, until we can learn more about this fellow. If he tries anything funny, vap him. Now, let's get back to where we last saw Eythine."

"Aye, aye, Cap'n," Lulu said.

Dawnboy flushed at his father's sharp tone, but he knew he deserved the rebuke. The harsh war lessons he had learned on Apache Highlands should have taught him not to approach someone who could be a dangerous enemy, however innocent and helpless he appeared. Besides, Ranger had told him often enough that caution must become second nature to him, if he hoped to survive long as a spaceman. But even so, he couldn't resist a strong urge to get to know more about the strangely unexpected occupant of the lifeboat. He continued watching the man on his viewscreen until Lulu announced that she had finally located the *Ram's Revenge*.

The *Gayheart* came up swiftly on the slow-moving starship that wobbled aimlessly along. A long tail of shattered metal debris was strung out from a ragged hole in the *Ram's Revenge*'s hull near the engine compartment. As Ranger watched the scene on his viewscreen, a large object that he identified as a ruptured rocket fuel tank came floating out of the hole to join the other trailing wreckage.

"Any response from Eythine yet?" Ranger asked Lulu.

"No, but the ship's force-screen is off and I can detect signs of human life aboard her. Could be Eythine or her biocomputer brain, or both."

"Maybe she's hurt and unconscious," Shyanne said worriedly, rising from her couch. "I'll suit up and grav over to see if I can help her."

"Not until we know how safe it is," Ranger said firmly.

"He's right, Shyanne," Lulu said. "I'm getting strong radiation readings over there. The luxium reactor must be damaged and leaking. Oh, wait . . . I'm picking up a broadcast from Eythine. I can't get a picture of her, but here she is on audio."

". . . off my starboard bow. *Ram's Revenge* calling

unidentified starship off my starboard bow. Come in, please. *Ram's Revenge* calling . . ." Eythine's strained but calm voice repeated from the photophone speaker.

"*Ram's Revenge*, this is the *Gayheart*," Ranger responded. "Hello, Eythine. Glad to hear you're still alive. How are you doing over there?"

"I thought that was you," Eythine said angrily, "after Tombolo told me you had tried to contact us earlier. I hope you're happy, now that you've finally beaten me. But at least I can deny you the pleasure of torturing my knowledge of Wonderwhat out of me, because my ship will disintegrate before you can get over here to capture me."

"Don't be stupid!" Ranger snapped. "I'm not your enemy. Get away from there in a lifeboat as quickly as you can. We'll pick you up."

"No, thanks," Eythine replied with a frightened but defiant laugh. "I've never wanted to be a dead heroine, but even that is more appealing than what I'm sure you have in store for me."

"Please, listen to me," Ranger began desperately.

"I would advise both of you not to waste time arguing," Lulu cut in. "My instrument readings indicate that your radiation is increasing rapidly, Eythine. Your ship could blow at any moment."

"That is also my conclusion," said a deep masculine voice that Ranger assumed came from Tombolo, the *Ram's Revenge*'s biocomputer.

"Did you hear that, Eythine?" Ranger demanded. "Get out of that death trap before it's too late!"

"Forget it," Eythine said hopelessly. "I couldn't abandon ship even if I wanted to. All of my small vehicles were destroyed or crippled by the blast that did this damage."

"Then bail out in your vac-suit and antigrav pack," Ranger ordered. "We'll come in as close as we dare and catch you with a tow beam. You can bring your biocomputer brain with you. The lining of his tank should protect him till you get here."

"All right, I'll send Tombolo over to you," Eythine relented. "But I'm staying here."

"Begging your pardon, Archguardess," Tombolo said respectfully, "but I strongly urge you to reconsider your decision."

Ranger signaled to Shyanne. "If you won't believe me, Eythine, there's somebody else here who may be able to get through to you."

"Eythine, this is Shyanne," the girl said anxiously. "Please do as Captain Farstar says. He only wants to help you."

"Shyanne!" Eythine cried in dismay. "How did you . . . ? Oh, no! Were they able to kidnap you after all?"

"I'm not a prisoner," Shyanne insisted. "But there isn't time for me to explain it to you. Please trust me when I say you won't be in any danger over here." She waited tensely for several moments while only silence came from the photophone speaker. Then she said tearfully, "Oh, please, Eythine! You're the only one I have left. I don't want to lose you, too, Mother."

Eythine made a sound that Ranger took to be a sigh of resignation. "All right," she said tiredly. "We're coming over. Stand by to pick us up."

"Thank the gods for that," Dawnboy whispered.

Ranger nodded jerkily. The similarity between Eythine's situation and the accident that had taken his wife from him stirred up nightmare memories that tied his nerves in knots. He fought stubbornly against overwhelming terror as he helped Lulu jockey the *Gayheart* close alongside the doomed *Ram's Revenge*. For several anxious minutes he, Dawnboy and Shyanne stared intently at the other starship, but they could detect no further activity on it.

"Come on, come on!" Ranger muttered urgently. "What's the delay?"

"I don't know," Lulu said, "but all indications are that the ship's luxium pile is about to go critical. If Eythine doesn't get out within the next sixty seconds, we'll have to veer off to save ourselves from the blast."

Each of those seconds fell agonizingly on their raw

nerves like drops of acid. When the minute was finally gone and still there was no sign of anyone bailing out of the *Ram's Revenge,* Lulu announced that she was altering the *Gayheart's* course.

"Belay that!" Ranger snarled.

"But, Skipper . . ."

"Don't argue; just hold your position!" Ranger's face was a sickly pale mask of fear and determination. Dawnboy watched him with a silent scream caught in his throat and Shyanne nervously bit her knuckles, as Ranger shouted into his photophone: "Eythine! Can you read me? What's holding you up there?"

Only a cruelly mocking silence answered him.

"Skipper, I really think . . ." Lulu began uneasily.

"Look there!" Dawnboy and Shyanne cried together, pointing at the bulkhead telescope.

A tiny object had emerged from the hole in the *Ram's Revenge* and was moving swiftly toward the *Gayheart.* Ranger could barely distinguish a human figure in a vac-suit towing a large metal container on a short cable.

"It's about time," Ranger breathed. "Get a tow beam on them and veer off, Lulu."

"With pleasure," Lulu replied, her relay switches clicking frantically to carry out the command. "Another moment's delay would have given even my iron constitution a heart attack."

Dawnboy was so relieved to be escaping the danger that he did not think to ask Lulu how a disembodied brain could have a heart attack. The *Gayheart* sped sharply away from the damaged ship, hauling in the two survivors like fish caught at the end of a long line. Lulu brought them up to the main air lock and got them safely inside just as the *Ram's Revenge* followed the two ZuJu ships to blazing oblivion. Even at that distance, the *Gayheart* was rocked by the explosion. When she had settled back on even keel, Ranger turned to his son and Shyanne with a weak smile.

"I wish I could think of some funny remark to show you what a tough old space pilot I am," Ranger said.

"But the only thing that comes to mind is: Thank God or luck or whatever helped us get out of that mess alive. I hope we never have to go through anything like it again."

"Amen to that," Dawnboy sighed, as Shyanne smiled radiantly at the two men, too overcome with emotion to speak.

"Well, now back to business," Ranger said briskly. "Are Eythine and her friend all right, Lulu?"

"Affirmative. I'm giving them a good spraying with radiation decontaminants. You can talk to her, if you want to."

"No, first I think Shyanne should explain the situation here to Eythine, to put her mind at ease," Ranger said. As Shyanne hurried toward the door, he called after her: "Take them to Sick Bay first, so that the computer's medical banks can give them a complete checkup. Then ask her to join us here on the bridge."

"Good thinking, Skipper," Lulu said. "Now, about our other visitor . . ."

"Who?" Ranger looked puzzled, then brightened. "Oh, the man in the lifeboat. I almost forgot about him. Have you been able to understand him yet?"

"Pretty much so, I think," Lulu answered. "His language wasn't very difficult for my translator banks to sort out."

"Well, what does he ha' to say for himself?" Dawnboy asked.

"He says that his name is S'Hun and he was a money slave to the captain of the second ZuJu ship that we vaped."

"He must be a pretty smart slave to know how to operate a lifeboat," Ranger observed suspiciously.

"He has an explanation for that," Lulu continued. "He claims that although he was born and has lived all of his life as a unit of ZuJu money, he has always yearned to escape to freedom. He fawningly played up to his master and became his favorite pet, so that his master would take him along on raiding cruises. Then S'Hun secretly studied the operation of his master's ship, hoping that someday he would have a chance to seize control of it. He hoped he could reach Fossick, which is the only free, humanly dominated planet known to his people. When we started fighting the ZuJus, S'Hun had no idea which side would win, but he decided to take advantage of the confusion and make a break for it anyway. He got to one of the lifeboats and, well, you know the rest. Now he is appealing to us as fellow human beings to take him aboard and help him get to Fossick."

"So that's his story?" Ranger said musingly.

"D'ye believe him?" Dawnboy asked.

"I don't know. I suppose it could be true, but I can't help feeling leery of him. People who have spent long periods in captivity sometimes come to identify more closely with their captors than with their own people."

"Then what shall we do," Lulu inquired, "leave him out there to fend for himself?"

"No. He couldn't possibly reach Fossick in that little boat, even if he knew how to get there. If he managed to survive at all, he would probably be recaptured by other ZuJus." Ranger sighed and muttered something about how complicated their lives had suddenly become. "We will bring him aboard and do what we can to help him, but only under the most restricted conditions."

"What are ye going to do?" Dawnboy asked. "Keep him locked in the brig?"

"We don't have a brig," Ranger reminded him. "But that's a good idea. We'll rig an outside lock on one of the passenger staterooms and take his meals to him. He isn't to be allowed out unless one of us is around to guard him. I especially don't want him on the bridge, if he was able to learn how to operate a ZuJu ship with the intention of taking it over."

"That seems a rough way to treat a poor mon who has just escaped from slavery," Dawnboy said. "But I can see that 'tis necessary. We do na want a potential enemy in our midst when we ha' so much at stake."

"Right. You can bring him aboard, Lulu. No, wait

until Eythine is finished in Sick Bay. Then we can give him a full physical, too, although the ZuJus generally keep their money-slaves in excellent condition. And one more thing—just to make sure he's harmless, tell this . . . what's-his-name?"

"S'Hun," Lulu supplied.

"Tell him I want him stripped stark naked when he comes aboard."

"That's not necessary, since he has never worn clothes in his life," Lulu said. "The ZuJus don't believe in covering up their wealth."

And naked came the stranger, when he stepped out of the air lock thirty minutes later, to be covered by synapse disrupters held by Ranger and Dawnboy. S'Hun's nudity apparently caused him neither embarrassment nor discomfort, probably because his superbly developed physique and limbs matched his handsome face to make him an exceptionally attractive young man. Indeed, he seemed proud to show off his attributes, as he smiled and bowed gratefully to Ranger and Dawnboy. Evidently he was so happy to have been rescued that he didn't even mind his rescuers pointing weapons at him. He continued smiling as they escorted him to Sick Bay and then to the stateroom they had prepared for him.

S'Hun kept up a constant stream of chatter, but most of it was still gibberish to Ranger and Dawnboy. Once in the stateroom, Ranger used sign language to explain the accommodations to the newcomer. Then he gestured for S'Hun to lie down on the bed and placed the Sleep-Teacher headset on his head, indicating that he was to keep it on while the computer's translator banks attempted to teach him some modern Unilingo.

Finally Ranger and Dawnboy left their uninvited guest, who gazed after them, as he puzzled over the strange sounds in his ears.

"I wish we could be more friendly with him," Dawnboy said wistfully, "since we're the first free humans he has ever met."

"He'll be all right," Ranger said confidently, "as

soon as he learns that freedom has its drawbacks, too."

They returned to the bridge to find Eythine and Shyanne waiting for them. Eythine wore an ankle-length robe of green velvet and matching slippers, which struck Dawnboy as an attractively feminine but impractical costume for a starship commander. She was as beautiful as he remembered her, and she seemed to have recovered sufficiently from her ordeal to greet them with a warm smile.

"I'm sorry we couldn't save your ship," Ranger said, coming forward to welcome Eythine. "But we'll try to make you as comfortable as possible here."

"Thank you," Eythine said with humble sincerity. "Shyanne has explained everything to me, so I want to apologize for the unfair hostility I expressed toward you. I'm very grateful to you for helping me escape from the Pandemonian rebels, and for saving me from the ZuJus."

Ranger dismissed her thanks with a careless gesture. "Forget it. Just having the charming company of your stepdaughter during this cruise has been payment enough for any debt you might feel you owe me."

Eythine exchanged fond glances with Shyanne. "I'm still not sure how I feel about the way she disobeyed me by stowing away to get out here. I'll probably want to give her a good spanking for it, when I get over being so happy to have her with me again."

"We can fight about that later," Shyanne laughed.

"Yes, dear." Eythine turned back to Ranger. "We have attached Tombolo's tank to your biocomputer's life-support system and he is resting now. But I would appreciate it if you'll plug him into your computer and give him some useful work to keep him occupied. He could be a big help to Lulu in operating your ship."

"I think I can manage that well enough on my own, thank you," Lulu remarked coolly.

"I'll see what I can do about it," Ranger promised Eythine. "First we have to reach an agreement on what our relationship regarding the treasure of the *Jealousy* will be."

Eythine's mouth and shoulders drooped dejectedly. "I'm completely at your mercy. I've lost my ship and nearly everything else of value that I owned. As uninvited guests aboard your ship, Shyanne and I will have to be content with whatever treatment you choose to give us."

"You still have your secret information about Wonderwhat," Ranger reminded her. "That should entitle you to a share of the treasure, if you'll help us find and recover it."

"How big a share?" Eythine asked, once again the shrewd businesswoman ready to bargain.

"How about fifty percent?" Ranger offered.

Eythine smiled and thrust out her hand. "You've got yourself a deal, partner. That's a far more generous offer than I had any right to expect."

Ranger shook her hand. "I figure there ought to be enough profit in this venture to please both of us, if the treasure actually exists. Now, to make it all legal and aboveboard, I'll have Lulu draw up a contract recording and we'll sign it with our voiceprints."

"Never mind; your word is good enough for me," Eythine said, looking squarely into Ranger's eyes.

Ranger appreciated the compliment to his honesty. It further increased his growing respect for Eythine's high level of professionalism. In fact, her exceptional combination of brains, beauty, skill and character made him uncomfortably aware of how much a woman such as she had to offer a man. His gaze drifted down over her shapely figure, noticing her robe for the first time.

"That's a very pretty outfit," he said. "But don't tell me you were wearing it when the ZuJus attacked you."

"No, I brought a few of my own things along," Eythine replied. "I knew Shyanne's clothes wouldn't fit me, and I doubted if you'd have any other women's gear aboard."

Ranger stared incredulously at her. "Do you mean that you took time to pack a bag before abandoning ship? When you knew that your luxium reactor could blow at any moment and maybe kill all of us? That's the most idiotic, scatterbrained, selfishly inconsiderate thing I've ever heard of!"

"Take it easy, Boss," Lulu said, as Eythine flushed and dropped her gaze before Ranger's angry glare.

"And just when I was starting to respect your intelligence," Ranger said disgustedly. "How would you feel if someone had endangered *your* ship and crew, just to pick up a few totally unnecessary personal items?"

Shyanne moved over to Eythine and put an arm protectively around her stepmother's shoulders. "Please, hasn't she already been through enough today?" the girl said imploringly to Ranger.

"No, he's right, Shyanne," Eythine said guiltily. "What I did was stupid and thoughtless. I had no right to risk all of your lives. I'm sorry." She looked directly at Ranger again. "Now if you don't mind, Captain, I would like to be excused. I'm very tired."

"All right," Ranger said, his gruffness softening a bit. "You can have the cabin next to Shyanne's. Show her where it is, Shyanne."

Dawnboy sympathetically watched the two women leave the bridge, then turned to his father and cleared his throat. "Do ye na think ye were a mite too hard on her, Dad? After all, she's only a woman, so she's bound to do foolish female things."

"Oh, you men!" Lulu fumed. "You actually don't understand why it was important for Eythine to bring her clothes and other personal things with her, do you?"

"Important?" Ranger asked in bewilderment. "What could have possibly been more important to her than saving human lives? She's a starship commander, after all, and she was the owner of a business employing several people. That should have given her a good sense of responsibility."

"She is also a woman," Lulu said with as much patience as she could muster. "With our sex's need to be reminded occasionally that she *is* a woman. I know that probably doesn't make any sense to you strong, practical-minded men, who always behave reasonably and never become emotional, but that's the way we are."

"If that's true, then I'm more glad than ever that I'm a mon," Dawnboy said, happily oblivious to Lulu's biting sarcasm. "Now if ye do na need me around here for a while, Dad, I'd like to go for a bite to eat. All o' this excitement has gi'n me an atrocious appetite."

"Me, too," Ranger said. "See if you can whip up an especially tasty meal, and we'll serve it to Eythine and Shyanne as a peace offering."

"Hold it," Lulu said, as Dawnboy started to leave the bridge. "I hate to spoil the fun, but I think you had better get back to your battle stations."

"What is it?" Ranger asked, hurrying to the pilot seat. "More ZuJus?"

"Worse than that, I'm afraid," Lulu replied. "Captain Zairundi of the *Seven Deadly Sins* is hailing us."

"Zairundi!" Dawnboy cried. "How did he find us?"

"It would be hard for him to miss us," Ranger answered, "with three starships blowing up like interstellar flares nearby. But he's going to play hell keeping track of us. Strap yourself in and tell the women to do the same. I'm going to show you some *real* evasive flying."

"Don't be too hasty, Skipper," Lulu said. "Zairundi wants to talk to you and I think you should take the call."

"The only talking I'll do to him will be with our nuclear cannon, if he comes within range," Ranger said grimly. "That double-dealing pirate is . . ."

Lulu activated Ranger's photophone and for the second time that day he stared speechlessly at the viewscreen. Fletcher Zairundi's handsome black face peered smilingly at him, along with the unhappy visage of Dr. Wage Gitlow, the Newtonian luxiumwright.

24

"HELLO, CAPTAIN FARSTAR. I'm very happy to see you again," Dr. Gitlow said, with a sickly attempt at a smile. "But I regret the circumstances of our meeting this time."

"So do I," Ranger said, trying to clear his confused mind. "What are you doing with that pirate? You haven't joined forces with him, have you?"

"No, I . . ." Gitlow began.

"I kidnapped him," Zairundi said matter-of-factly. "After my men failed to abduct the young lady. I decided to take another important hostage as additional insurance, in case my colleagues on Pandemo were also unable to detain the beautiful archguardess. I first thought of taking your friend, Mr. Hinterwald, but we had no opportunity to catch him alone."

"Lucky for ye that ye didna get Slim," Dawnboy said flatly. "He probably would ha' taken ye and yer ship apart by now."

Ranger waved his son to silence and stared levelly at the black captain. "All right, Zairundi, you seem to have the advantage in whatever game you're playing. So what's your next move?"

"I propose a simple business transaction," Zairundi replied promptly. "As we both are experienced star traders who know the value of our merchandise, I offer you Dr. Gitlow, safe and sound, in exchange for Archguardess dara Gildenfang, in the same condition."

"I couldn't make that trade even if I wanted to," Ranger lied blandly, "because Eythine was killed when her ship vaporized a short while ago."

Zairundi gazed reproachfully at Ranger. "Please don't insult my intelligence with such a childish ploy, Farstar. I overheard your communications with Eythine when you urged her to abandon her doomed vessel and come over to your ship. If you don't believe me, I'll play back the tape I made of your conversations."

"Never mind; I admit she's here," Ranger conceded. "But I have no intention of turning her over to you without a fight."

"I hope it won't come to that," Zairundi said sincerely. "There would be no profit in us destroying each other. But since you seem so stubborn about this, I'm afraid I'll have to test my evaluation of your character in a very unpleasant manner. I am betting that you won't be able to resist my demands when you see Dr. Gitlow slowly tortured to the point of madness."

Gitlow turned pale at the threat and tried to speak, but only a frightened croak came from his dry throat. Ranger glared scornfully at Zairundi. "And I'll bet that not even you are rotten enough to do that to a man who has never harmed you, and has probably contributed more to civilization than the entire populations of some worlds."

"I'm glad you have such a high opinion of the doctor," Zairundi smiled. "That is exactly what I'm counting on to make you see things my way. But there is really only one way to determine which of us is bluffing." He made a sharp gesture with his right hand and one of his crew members appeared beside Gitlow, holding what Ranger recognized was a modified synapse disrupter. Such an instrument could hold a victim paralyzed while increasing his neural sensitivity until the slightest touch or sound produced agonizing pain.

Gitlow looked pleadingly at Ranger. "I wish I could tell you not to give in to this madman, no matter what he does to me," the scientist said in a trembling voice. "But I'm afraid physical courage has never been one of my strong points."

"Don't apologize, Doctor," Ranger said sympathetically. "Anyone in your position would feel the same as you do." He watched the crewman adjust the disrupter and point it at Gitlow's head, then called out: "Wait! Let's do some more bargaining, Zairundi, before you get down to the rough stuff."

"That suits me," Zairundi agreed. "I have plenty of time." He signaled his crewman to step back.

Ranger desperately spurred his mind to think of some way out of the dilemma. "Look, we both want the same thing, don't we—the treasure of the *Jealousy?* Well, why don't we work together to find it? There should be plenty of money in it for all of us. You can have fifty percent. That was the same deal I made with Eythine, but I'm sure she'll agree to go halves with me on the remaining fifty percent, in exchange for Dr. Gitlow's freedom."

Zairundi nodded. "That arrangement seems agreeable to me. How do you propose we go about the search?"

"Our ships flying abreast at maximum scanner range would probably be the best system," Ranger suggested. "That would cover the widest area possible as we travel. Also, if one of us detected ZuJu ships or other hostile forces, he could warn the other in time for him to take defensive action."

Zairundi nodded again. "And a hostile force is less likely to attack if they see us traveling together. I like the way your mind works under pressure, Farstar, as long as you don't try to outsmart me. My ship should reach your vicinity in about twenty minutes. We can commence our search then."

"There's one more thing," Ranger said. "Eythine's information about Wonderwhat will be invaluable when we locate the comet, but finding it is our first big problem. As you may know, I have some of Dr. Gitlow's scientific instruments for obtaining data about Wonderwhat aboard my ship. If he were here to operate the equipment, I think our chances of finding the comet soon would be greatly increased."

"That's right; I would be much more useful with you," Gitlow said, eagerly grasping the straw of hope that Ranger held out to him.

Zairundi laughed humorlessly at Ranger. "I told you not to try to outsmart me. I have no intention of releasing Dr. Gitlow unless I get a hostage of equal value in exchange. Now, if you want to reconsider sending Eythine to me, or perhaps your son . . ."

Dawnboy started to volunteer for the mission, but a hard look from his father made him keep his silence.

"I won't make that sort of deal with you, Zairundi," Ranger said firmly. "However, I want a better guarantee than just your word that Dr. Gitlow will be released unharmed when you have received your share of the treasure."

"I daresay my word is as good as yours, under our present circumstances," Zairundi retorted. He absently stroked his left earlobe with his thumb and forefinger as he stared thoughtfully into space. "I suppose Gitlow would be more useful with you than he is here," the black captain finally decided. "So what do you think of this offer? I still have the two matter-transporter booths that I acquired on Newtonia. I could send one of them over to you, with its controls locked open in such a way that I could freely transport objects to you, but you couldn't reverse the process without my cooperation. Then I would allow Gitlow to transport over to you. I would also keep an armed bomb ready to transport into your ship the instant you showed any indication of attempting to double-cross me. You would have no defense against that. But on the other hand, I would have no reason to vap you as long as you kept your part of our agreement."

Ranger carefully considered the proposition. It was far from being the perfect solution to his problems, but it was probably the best arrangement he could hope to make with the wily Zairundi. Dr. Gitlow continued to stare at Ranger with mounting terror in his eyes. "Please, Captain Farstar," the luxiumwright begged hoarsely.

Ranger's compassion for the scientist finally made his decision for him, proving that Zairundi had correctly appraised his opponent's character. "All right," Ranger said. "Send the booth over as soon as you're close enough for a robot-controlled shuttlecraft to pass between us. Then we can resume our treasure hunt without any more delays."

Zairundi's victorious smile was made tolerable by the look of relief and gratitude that swept over Dr. Gitlow's strained features.

"Now that we have that settled," Ranger went on, "I'm curious to know just how you got involved with the Wonderwhat treasure in the first place, Zairundi. My guess is that you were aboard the pirate ship that destroyed Eythine's husband's ship. Somehow you survived the battle and you've been keeping tabs on Eythine since then."

"That's good guesswork, but not quite accurate," Zairundi replied. "The pirate ship was commanded by my brother Heathcliff, an unsavory fellow with whom I was never very close. In fact, he once pirated a ship from me. I guess he thought he owed me something for that. So when he knew he was dying, he sent off a sub-ether torpedo message to me, telling me about the treasure and his suspicion that Gildenfang had sent a similar message to his wife."

"You claim you're not really a pirate then?" Ranger asked.

Zairundi flashed his engaging smile. "Not a full-time one, at any rate. But who among us is exactly what he appears to be? For the most part I'm just a hardworking businessman on the lookout for a lucrative deal, much like yourself."

Ranger resented the comparison between their ethical standards, but he did not think the point was worth arguing about.

"What did ye do wi' the cargo ye were supposed to take to Sappho?" Dawnboy suddenly blurted, unable to stay out of his elders' conversation any longer. "Did ye jettison it in space when ye turned back to Newtonia?"

"No, I was lucky enough to run across another star trader who was glad to make the delivery for an extra bonus," Zairundi answered, turning back to Ranger. "So you see, I'm not entirely irresponsible when it comes to fulfilling a business agreement. As a matter of fact, I prefer doing things the honest way, when it's convenient."

"Don't we all?" Dr. Gitlow said, emboldened by the promise of freedom from his kidnappers. "The true test of one's character is how much inconvenience he will endure to do the honest thing."

"That's very astute of you, Doctor," Zairundi said admiringly, "but I'm afraid most of us have a very low tolerance for inconvenience, as you have just demonstrated."

Gitlow glared angrily at Zairundi, but could not deny the simple accuracy of his statement.

25

RANGER FINISHED ADJUSTING the woofer and tweeter balance of the loudspeaker on the biocomputer control panel and said, "All right, Tombolo, try it again and see how it sounds to you."

"Testing: one, two, three, four ..." a sonorously deep male voice intoned from the speaker. "Thank you, sir. That sounds very much like my natural voice."

"Fine." Ranger stepped back in the small, well-protected biocomputer compartment to view his handiwork. The living brain from Eythine's ship's biocomputer had been placed on a stand beside Lulu's, and Ranger had just finished connecting it to the *Gayheart*'s computer banks. The two brains floated serenely in their transparent tanks of cerebrospinal fluid, with the blinking lights on their life-support consoles indicating their present states of health and awareness. Ranger wished, with a touch of amusement, it was possible for a brain to use physical expressions. He would have liked to see the jealous glare he was sure Lulu was giving her new workmate.

"As I always say, two brains are better than one." Ranger smiled. "With you two working with Dr. Gitlow, along with the rest of our combined wits, we should be able to handle any problems Wonderwhat or Zairundi might spring on us. Now aren't you glad I had the new cerebral linkage assembly installed when the ship was overhauled, Lulu?"

"I'm overjoyed," Lulu replied tartly. "But remember what I told you—I only share my system with another brain for emergencies. As soon as we can dispense with this mental parasite's services, I want him off my back."

"Madam, I assure you that I regret my unwelcome imposition on your facilities as much as you do," Tombolo's newly adjusted voice said with a fine balance of hauteur and servility developed during his long career as head butler to the dara Gildenfang family. "I promise I will do my very best to make our relationship harmoniously productive and I will always respect your superior status as the rightful mistress of this establishment."

"See that you do," Lulu instructed him.

Ranger laughed at the clash of biocomputer egos. After the tremendous pressures he had been under recently, he was glad to take his amusements wherever he could find them. Nearly four hours had passed since Zairundi's ship had drawn alongside the *Gayheart* and the black captain had sent over the matter-transporter booth in a shuttlecraft. Immediately after Ranger had set up the booth on the bridge, Dr. Gitlow had stepped out of it, tearfully thanking Ranger for rescuing him.

As soon as Gitlow could speak privately with

Ranger, the luxiumwright had offered to break Zairundi's hold on them by disabling the booth. But Ranger had rejected the proposal as being too dangerous. Zairundi had insisted that the booth be placed where he could constantly watch it from the photophone screen and he had threatened to destroy the *Gayheart* if anyone aboard her made any suspicious moves. Therefore, Ranger was resigned to keeping his promise to Zairundi—at least until a good opportunity to dissolve the enforced partnership presented itself.

Ranger gave the compartment a final visual inspection. He had put in a long, hectic day's work and he was looking forward to catching a few hours' sleep now that some semblance of order and efficiency had been restored to the ship. Eythine had been sufficiently refreshed by a short nap to return to the bridge and take charge of the search for Wonderwhat. Dawnboy and Shyanne were still too excited to sleep, so they remained on duty with Eythine, while Dr. Gitlow tinkered with his scientific instruments in the aft compartment. Their combined efforts and the aid Zairundi's ship contributed to the search should keep things running fairly smoothly for a while without Ranger's supervision, he hoped.

"How is the search going, Lulu?" Ranger asked through a yawn as he was about to leave the compartment. "Anything new to report?"

"Not much, Boss," Lulu replied, "unless you're interested in knowing that my scanners have detected a distant object that appears to be a comet; possibly the one we're looking for."

"You mean Wonderwhat?" Ranger demanded, instantly becoming fully alert with nerve-tingling anticipation. "Why didn't you tell me that sooner?"

"You didn't ask me," came Lulu's nonchalant answer. "Besides, I only found the thing a few moments ago. It's moving at sub-lightspeed, which means we will have to decelerate rapidly as we approach it. So you'd better get up to the bridge and strap down."

"I'm on my way," Ranger said, dashing out the door.

When he reached the bridge, Dawnboy and Shyanne were chatting excitedly about their new find as they strapped down for deceleration. Eythine, once again the cool-headed professional spacewoman, was calmly discussing the comet with Dr. Gitlow through the intercom system. The luxiumwright insisted on staying with his instruments until he had determined that the comet was composed of equal amounts of matter and antimatter, thus fitting the description of Wonderwhat. Then he joined the others in the bridge to occupy one of the pneumatic couches.

By then Ranger had taken the pilot seat, and Eythine sat beside him as his copilot. It rankled Dawnboy's pride to have his job taken over by a woman, but he was mature enough to respect Eythine's superior qualifications. Besides, he was glad to have his attention free to observe the comet as they approached it. Before they were within telescope range of the glowing object, Lulu's probing beams identified an unpowered spaceship moving along near the head of the comet's hundred-thousand-mile-long tail.

"It looks like we really have found Wonderwhat, partner," Zairundi said through the photophone. He had brought the *Seven Deadly Sins* close to the *Gayheart*, and the two ships flew together to intercept the comet's course. "I don't know about you, but I'm starting to feel rich already."

"Well, let's not spend it before we get it," Ranger cautioned.

The ships completed their deceleration as they came parallel with the end of the comet's tail and started to move warily up toward its brightly glaring head. As soon as Dr. Gitlow could safely leave his couch, he hurried back to resume monitoring his instruments, as the others anxiously studied the strange starship through the electron telescope lens. It was a needle-nosed, stubby-winged vessel of obsolete design that appeared to be frozen motionless by its glittering surroundings, like a fly preserved in amber.

"You'd better not watch it too long," Lulu warned them. "The comet's head is so bright that it might cause eye damage, in spite of the telescope's light-filtering qualities."

"She's right," Dr. Gitlow concurred. "My instrument readings reveal the comet's head to be a densely packed concentration of matter and anti-matter particles, as well as some other elements that I can't identify. According to all the known laws of physics, such a combination of mutually annihilating forces can't possibly exist, but there it is. It's almost as if . . ."

"As if what?" Ranger asked when the scientist failed to complete his sentence.

"Oh, I just had a wild thought that's too ridiculous to mention," Gitlow answered with an embarrassed laugh. "Forget it." Then his voice rose with childish delight. "But, my God, what a fantastic opportunity this is for research! I'll be the envy of every scientist on Newtonia when I return with this data."

"You go right ahead and enjoy the intellectual rewards of our journey, Doctor," Zairundi said. "While we less idealistic beings try to find a way to get our hands on the *Jealousy*'s gold and jewels."

"That's right," Ranger said. "Okay, Lulu, you can switch off the telescope now." He blinked and rubbed his smarting eyes. "At least we saw enough to verify the story that old Captain Midas had sprayed his ship's hull with gold paint, to symbolize his heart's desire. Did you notice how brilliantly yellow it is?"

"Aye," Dawnboy said eagerly. " 'Tis as if the entire ship is made o' gold!"

"I'm glad the rest of you are so happy to be here," Lulu said. "Whatever the comet is made of, it's putting out such high levels of radiation that I'm not sure our force-screens can protect us from it."

"Then we all will put on lead-lined suits," Ranger decided. "We know it's possible to survive within the comet's radiation field, because the *Jealousy* has been in there all these years without suffering any apparent damage."

"That doesn't prove that *living* things can survive in there," Lulu said, still sounding worried.

"That's what we're going to find out," Shyanne said, exchanging looks of youthful enthusiasm with Dawn-boy.

"My husband's ship survived a passage into and out of the comet's tail," Eythine reminded Lulu. "And I know how he did it."

"There, you have nothing to worry about, Lulu," Ranger said lightly. "You just concentrate on flying this tub and keeping a lookout for pirates and ZuJus and any VIP's that Wonderwhat might pop into."

"Will do, Skipper," Lulu said. "If I can get any help from this useless hunk of protoplasm that you plugged in with me."

"I'll do my best, Madam," Tombolo humbly promised.

Ranger turned his attention to Zairundi's photophone image. "I don't think we should risk both our ships in the comet's tail at the same time. Just one of us should be able to go in and tow out the *Jealousy*, if that's possible. The other ship can stay out here in the clear, in case the towing ship gets into trouble and needs help."

"That's a good plan," Zairundi agreed. "And it's only logical that you should be the one to make the trip, since you have the lady who knows the secret of maneuvering safely in Wonderwhat, as well as Dr. Gitlow and his helpful instruments."

"Hmmm, it looks like I outsmarted myself by insisting on having Eythine and Dr. Gitlow aboard my ship," Ranger reflected. "But I can't dispute that logic is on your side. Besides, I'm pretty curious to have a close look at the *Jealousy*." He looked up at Eythine. "Well, partner, how do we get safely in and out of the comet's tail?"

"I'm interested in hearing about that, too," Zairundi put in. "My brother tried several times to get the treasure. But he said the comet's radiation overloaded his luxium reactor so dangerously that he had to withdraw to clear space to avoid having his ship vaporize."

"Ram also mentioned having that problem," Eythine said. "But he learned through trial and error to avoid it by shutting down his reactor and using only his ship's rockets within Wonderwhat's radiation field."

"Then that's what we'll do," Ranger decided.

"But what about our lepton scanner and other instruments?" Dr. Gitlow demanded. "They will be useless without luxium power."

"I can operate them on reserve energy batteries," Lulu said. "But their ranges will be drastically reduced. If the comet encounters a VIP, we might not be able to detect it in time to escape it."

Ranger looked inquiringly at Eythine, who only shrugged fatalistically. "That's an unavoidable risk we will have to run," Eythine said. "Ram believed it was possible to make a swift dash into Wonderwhat's tail, attach a cable to the treasure ship—because you can't use a tow beam without luxium power—and drag her out before the comet hits a VIP or other space hazard."

"Then why did he na do that?" Dawnboy asked.

"Obviously because the pirate ship attacked him before he could," Shyanne reminded him.

"That's right," Eythine said. "He had made a couple of scouting runs near the *Jealousy* and was waiting out here for his luxium reactor to produce enough rocket fuel to replace what he had used up, when the pirates struck."

"All right then, let's go finish his job," Ranger said, standing up. "I want everyone in lead-lined vac-suits, complete with helmets, in case there's a failure of the ship's life-support system. Dawnboy, take an extra suit down to S'Hun and show him how to use it. And then . . ."

"Wait; I haven't told you the most important thing about Wonderwhat yet," Eythine said. The others stared attentively at her and she continued: "Aside from the comet's radiation—or maybe because of it—there is a strange force that can't be resisted by protective clothing or anything else. It evidently affects the nervous system, because it distorts one's sense of reality, causing hallucinations, memory lapses and other sensory and mental disturbances."

Ranger turned over the new information in his mind, weighing it against his sense of responsibility for his ship and everyone aboard her. "Now I'm not so sure the treasure is worth the gamble after all," he said, "if there's a chance that we all might go mad getting it."

"But the influence is only temporary," Eythine insisted. "Ram was able to survive and function rationally by exerting his willpower and proceeding slowly enough to enable his senses to adjust to the change."

"Yes, I suppose it could be possible to build up an immunity to the force," Gitlow said, "if the mind is gradually exposed to it. The other treasure hunters were probably so impatient that they rushed in and received its full impact."

Ranger continued to ponder the problem. "Well, I don't know . . ." he said uncertainly.

"If the treasure was easy to get to, somebody else would have claimed it by now," Zairundi pointed out. "You have to take big chances for big profits."

Ranger looked around at his three companions' anxious expressions, then he suddenly laughed. "Oh, what the hell? I'm just as eager as all of you to get to the *Jealousy*, now that we've come this far. I guess nothing could drive us any crazier than we already are anyhow. So let's go in and find out if there really is a treasure, or if Captain Midas played the greatest practical joke in history on us."

26

AN HOUR LATER the *Gayheart* had drawn parallel with the *Jealousy* and was standing off about ten thousand miles outside the comet's tail. Even at that distance the radiation from Wonderwhat's semi-solid head was so strong that Lulu had long since shut down their light-energy converter and all other luxium-powered equipment.

While the ship was coasting up to her present position, Ranger and his crew had hurriedly placed extra lead shielding around the deactivated luxium reactor and did everything else they could think of to make the ship secure for their run for the treasure. Now they were back on the bridge, eagerly donning their heavy lead-lined vac-suits and antigrav packs. Even with the ship's artificial gravity unit shut off, the cumbersome outfits made movement awkward as the five of them floated weightlessly around the bridge.

Dawnboy, Eythine, Shyanne and Gitlow turned their helmeted heads to look inquiringly at Ranger. Now that the decision to go for the treasure had been made, they all shared an emotional bond of reckless daring, like soldiers finally committed to battle after a long, boring wait in ranks. Ranger put on what he hoped was a confident grin and ended his companions' suspense with the simple command: "Let's go."

Ranger kicked his right heel against a nearby bulkhead to propel himself across the room, caught the back of the pilot seat and swung himself into it. Eythine took the copilot seat as the others settled down on acceleration couches. Dawnboy no longer resented

Eythine's temporary usurpation of his copilot's position, because Ranger had promised him the important mission of attaching the tow cable to the *Jealousy*, when they reached her.

At Ranger's order, Lulu fired their port rockets. The *Gayheart* executed a smooth right-angle turn and surged ahead with her rocket tubes snorting flames. Without luxium power, the lens magnification of the electron telescope was greatly diminished. But even so, the five treasure hunters had a good view of the scene before them. They kept their eyes averted from the dazzling comet head while they waited for their rapid advance to carry them near enough to the treasure ship for it to become visible again.

Shyanne suddenly had the poetic impression that the comet's glowing tail was like a sequined curtain waiting for them to part its folds and enter the secret world of Wonderwhat. She started to voice the thought, then decided that her companions would probably laugh at her for being so childishly imaginative. It did not occur to her that the mystery, danger and nerve-tingling anticipation of their undertaking had briefly transformed all of them into romantic dreamers.

The feeling of suspended reality slowly left Dawnboy as his well-trained habit of mentally taking stock of himself and his situation reasserted itself. His gloved fingers checked the tools on his belt as he went over the safest procedure of leaving the *Gayheart* and boarding the *Jealousy*. At least he could take comfort in the knowledge that no living enemies would oppose him, no matter how many ghosts of previous treasure seekers might haunt the ancient derelict. . . .

"So ye thought ye'd steal me treasure, eh?" a gravel-voiced roar echoed in Dawnboy's ears. "I'll blast ye all to the flaming pit o' cosmic hell first!"

Dawnboy looked up with a startled cry at the figure of a burly, black-bearded man wearing a gold-colored woman's gown standing in the center of the bridge. The man looked so frighteningly dangerous, with a blaster gripped in each hand, that Dawnboy did not pause to wonder how he could have possibly gotten into the *Gayheart*. He knew instinctively that this must be Captain Midas Oublier, who had somehow returned from the dead to defend his treasure-laden ship. With a shouted warning to the others, the young Apache groped frantically for a weapon, coming up with only his photon torch. It was a simple tool used for welding and other shipboard repair jobs, but he raised it bravely against the threatening intruder.

"What's the matter with you, Son?" Ranger's voice demanded from the communication unit in Dawnboy's helmet. "Put that torch away before you damage something with it."

"But do ye na see ..." Dawnboy began, then blinked at the empty space where the transvestite starship commander had stood. "He was right there—Captain Midas. I saw him as plain as ..."

The others stared at Dawnboy in bewilderment, as Lulu calmly assured him that there had been no new arrivals aboard the ship.

"It was a hallucination," Eythine declared. "We must be entering the comet's psych-electric field, as Ram called it. He said it can take something you're thinking about, consciously or subconsciously, and project it as a realistic image before you. Memory lapses are another type of mental distortion caused by the field. We can expect a lot more of that sort of thing, until our minds have built up a resistance to the field."

"All right then," Ranger said, mustering his willpower to keep his mind clear. "We'll just have to try to be as skeptical as possible. Keep telling yourselves that sentient beings are too smart to be made fools of by an inanimate comet. Don't believe anything you see or hear until you've checked it out with the rest of us. I don't think it's likely that we all could have the same hallucination at the same time."

"All right, but you don't have to shout at us," Eythine said irritably.

"I didn't shout! Get hold of yourself!" Ranger brought his rising voice under control with an effort.

"Lulu, I may not be clearheaded enough to fly the ship for a while, so take control for now."

"Who do you think you're ordering around?" Lulu lashed back angrily. "This is *my* ship and I'll do what I damned well please with it!"

"Now, Lulu, remember your place," Tombolo said gently but firmly to her. "Captain Farstar is the master of this vessel. You and I are only his servants. So let us take pride in serving him humbly and efficiently."

"You're right," Lulu said in a chastened voice. "I'm sorry, Boss."

"Forget it," Ranger said. "I guess Wonderwhat's influence has penetrated even your compartment. But fortunately Tombolo is still able to resist it."

"That must be due to my professional experience, sir," Tombolo said. "Servants are so frequently disillusioned by their employers that eventually nothing can shock them anymore." The ex-butler gasped and quickly added, "Oh, please forgive me, Archguardess! I don't know what made me say that."

"So the truth finally comes out!" Shyanne cried accusingly. "Why, Tombolo, you old faker! Making us think you were such a dummy all these years." She strained at the straps holding her to the couch, her body convulsed by waves of hysterical laughter, as Eythine and Dawnboy tried to calm her with soft words.

"My, you certainly have a masterful way with women," Lulu said coyly to Tombolo. "I've always admired strong, dominant men. I should have known you were that type when I first saw the deep, handsome furrows in your cerebral cortex."

"Why, thank you," Tombolo replied. "And may I say that you have the most attractive pair of frontal lobes that I have ever beheld?"

"Oh, go on!" Lulu simpered. "I'll bet you say that to all the girls."

"That's all we need," Ranger sighed. "A couple of romantic biocomputers. Snap out of it, you two. We have serious work to do."

"As you wish, sir," Tombolo replied, with his proper butler's decorum restored. "I am sure the lady was only amusing herself at my expense, anyhow."

"Of course; it was just the comet's influence over me," Lulu said coldly, but with a strangely wistful note in her voice.

Ranger smiled inwardly at the thought of a love affair between two disembodied brains. That was almost as absurd as his continuing love for what little was left of Gay. If only the accident had not . . .

Happy feminine laughter drew his attention to the copilot seat, where Gay lounged with a teasing smile on her beautiful face. Ranger stared dumbfounded at her. She couldn't be there! Every fiber of his sane, rational mind told him that. But there she was! Somehow a miracle had happened, fulfilling his deepest yearning to be reunited with the one woman who could make him a full man. He had only to reach out and take her in his arms again. But even as he was fumbling to unbuckle his seat harness, something at the back of his mind argued stubbornly that this couldn't be Gay, because Gay was . . .

His wife's beautiful, vibrant flesh started to shrivel and crack before his eyes. The ugly red welts of luxium radiation burns swelled up and ruptured into running sores as her agonized screams tore jaggedly across his nerves.

"Gay! Oh, God, no! Not again!" Ranger sobbed, struggling to reach her in time, but knowing it was already too late.

"Ranger, it's me—Eythine," the woman in the copilot seat said loudly. "You just had a bad dream. It wasn't real. Remember the treasure. Try to hold onto that."

"Yes, yes. I'm all right now," Ranger mumbled, sinking weakly back into his seat. "You are Eythine, not Gay. I understand."

But the memory of Gay was still so strong in his mind that he had to fight to keep it from returning in full force. At last he thought he understood why so many seekers of the *Jealousy*'s treasure had never returned. As long as they had Wonderwhat's strange powers to turn their fondest desires into lifelike illusions, who needed reality? Especially when reality was so much more painful.

That tantalizing opportunity to escape life's cares was presented in the most seductive terms to everyone aboard the *Gayheart* in the next two hours, as one highly appealing hallucination after another assailed their senses. It wasn't easy for them to resist the urge to sink blissfully into the world of apparently instant wish-gratification that Wonderwhat offered them. But by helping each other cling desperately to things that they knew were real, they gradually strengthened their willpower until the tempting illusions faded away to ghostly shadows and whispers that haunted the borders of their perception.

"Well, I'm glad that confusing mess is finally over with," Ranger sighed. "Now maybe we can get back to functioning halfway normally again." He glanced at his blank photophone screen. "How are we doing, Lulu? Couldn't you stay in touch with Zairundi's ship?"

"No, we lost contact with him as soon as we entered the comet's tail," Lulu answered. "So I shut down all of our machinery that we don't absolutely need, to save what little reserve power we have left. We're practically flying blind now, but we'll need all of our reserves to get us out of this."

"You made the right decision," Ranger complimented her, looking up at the electron telescope. The underpowered lens was little better than plain glass, but they no longer needed strong magnification. Through the haze of comet dust and debris, they could see the shining, gold-colored spaceship several miles ahead of them.

"So we've really made it," Eythine said breathlessly, joining the others in staring spellbound at the scene before them. "Even after everything Ram told me, I still didn't completely believe I would ever get this close to the *Jealousy*."

"We still have the most important part of the job ahead of us—bringing back the treasure," Ranger said briskly. "So let's not get careless and lose everything at the last moment. Dawnboy, go to the air lock and prepare to board the *Jealousy* as soon as Lulu brings us alongside her."

"Aye, aye, sir!" Dawnboy said eagerly, releasing the straps holding him down on his couch.

"I want to go, too," Shyanne insisted.

"I do na need yer help," Dawnboy told her curtly.

"Don't question the captain's orders, Shyanne," Eythine said, as her stepdaughter started to argue her case with Ranger.

Shyanne reluctantly fell silent. Ranger tried to cheer her up by telling her to sit tight and wait her turn; they all would have to work efficiently together to accomplish the task ahead of them.

"I think I should go with Dawnboy as far as the air lock," Gitlow said, rising from his couch. "I can act as a relay between you and him, and if he should need help, I'll be all ready to go out to him."

"Good idea," Ranger agreed.

"What about communications?" Lulu asked. "Dawnboy could take along a portable photophone camera to show us what he finds."

"Why bother?" Ranger replied. "He's just going out to attach a towline to the *Jealousy*. The comm unit in his helmet will be enough to keep him in touch with us."

"I'm afraid he might have a problem finding a place to fasten the cable," Lulu said, "because the *Jealousy*'s hull is so streamlined."

"Then he can clamp it on electromagnetically," Ranger suggested.

"That would tax our power reserves," Lulu reminded him. "I thought that perhaps he could enter the ship and let down her landing gear, if the machinery is still operable. Then he could attach the line to the forward landing gear."

"That's a great idea!" Dawnboy cried happily.

"You just want an excuse to get in there and see the

treasure," Ranger accused his son. "But we can't waste time waiting for you to figure out the controls of a three-hundred-year-old ship. Besides, it would be dangerous for you to fumble around with unfamiliar equipment."

"There shouldn't be much danger if he takes a camera with him," Lulu said. "Then he can show me the ship's controls and I can help him find the right buttons to push."

Ranger considered Lulu's proposal for a few moments, then said, "I hate to admit it, but I guess you're right, Lulu." He grinned at Dawnboy. "I'm as curious as you are to see the interior of the *Jealousy*. But you be very careful over there, understand?"

"Aye, aye, sir!" Dawnboy grinned, as he propelled himself over to one of the equipment lockers to get a photophone camera.

Dr. Gitlow's gaze fell on the matter-transporter booth and his face brightened hopefully. "Now that we're no longer in contact with Zairundi, I can deactivate the booth without his knowledge," he said, starting toward the booth. "Or we could put it in one of your small vehicles and send it far out into space, where there would be no danger to us even if he did transport a bomb through it. Why didn't I think of that before?"

"Wait," Ranger said thoughtfully. "We don't know for sure how ignorant of our activities Zairundi is, just because *we* lack the power to maintain two-way communication with him. Besides, I may have a better use for that booth. First, let's see what we can learn about the treasure ship."

Lulu expertly brought the *Gayheart* up to the *Jealousy,* then briefly burned her retrorockets to lay alongside the treasure ship at a distance of about fifty meters. The *Jealousy* was not equipped with the now-standard automatic coupling collar that enabled two spacecraft to join air locks, so Dawnboy was prepared to burn his way into the older ship. But he saw that was unnecessary when he left the *Gayheart*, powered by his antigravity backpack.

The outer and inner hatches of the treasure ship's air lock gaped wide, their fused and scarred edges indicating that a cutting torch had been used to force them open. Dawnboy, hoping the broken hatches did not mean that another treasure hunter had already salvaged the *Jealousy*'s rich cargo, graved through the air lock to the ship's main passageway.

"Can ye see this clearly enough?" Dawnboy asked his crewmates aboard the *Gayheart*, flashing his helmet searchlight over the gleaming deck, bulkheads and overhead, following the beam with his camera lens.

"Yes, the picture is coming through very well," Ranger answered.

Dawnboy moved slowly forward, his pulse racing with an oddly mingled sensation of excitement and fear. " 'Tis an eerie place, this," he remarked uneasily. "There be a fearsome air about it, I think."

"Don't let your superstitious Apache imagination run away with you," his father cautioned. "We've already been frightened enough by the hallucinations the comet gave us."

"If it scares you too much," Shyanne taunted Dawnboy, "come back and I'll take your place."

Dawnboy retorted that girls should stick to their dolls and not interfere with men's work. He drifted on along the corridor, then paused to touch one of the bulkheads. "Dad, there's something strange about this," he muttered.

"You've already told us that," Ranger said shortly. "Go on and see if you can release the ship's landing gear, or I will send Shyanne over to do it."

Spurred on by the ultimate threat to his masculine pride, Dawnboy moved quickly onto the ship's bridge. Then he halted and looked around in growing puzzlement at the ordinary-looking equipment that somehow seemed extraordinary. "Can ye see the bright yellow color o' all this, Dad?" he asked.

"Yes," Ranger said. "I told you that Captain Midas had everything around him painted the color of gold, as an expression of his insatiable greed."

"But this doesna seem to be just . . . Here, let me try something."

Dawnboy searched his tool-belt pouch and brought out his "touchstone," a small energy-cell powered device that gave a spectroscopic analysis of any gold-bearing object brought in contact with it. The gadget had been invented by Newtonian scientists to safeguard the Capitalians' golden stellars from counterfeiting. Dawnboy had brought the touchstone along to see how it would react to the *Jealousy*'s cargo. Now he pressed it to the ship's control panel, the deck and a bulkhead.

"Now what are you up to?" Ranger demanded impatiently.

" 'Tis what I thought before," Dawnboy said excitedly. "I ken that none o' ye are going to believe me, but this entire ship and every metal object in it seems to be made o' pure gold!"

27

"BUT THAT'S IMPOSSIBLE!" Dr. Gitlow protested to Dawnboy's surprising announcement.

"Of course it is," Lulu agreed. "Nevertheless, it appears to be true, if Dawnboy's touchstone isn't malfunctioning. I've been monitoring its readings of the *Jealousy*'s composition, and my computer banks confirm them."

Ranger turned to Eythine. "Did your husband's message say anything about this?"

"No, I'm just as astonished as you are," Eythine answered. "But then, Ram never actually boarded the *Jealousy*."

Shyanne was squirming with excitement inside her

vac-suit as she gazed enviously at Dawnboy's discovery. "A whole starship made of gold! Oh, please let me go over to see it, Captain Farstar!"

"Not until we learn more about this weird situation," Ranger said firmly. "Dawnboy, start searching the ship to see if you can find any clues to explain why it's like that."

"Shall I go over to help him?" Dr. Gitlow asked. "My scientific background may enable me to spot something that he would overlook."

"All right," Ranger agreed. "But both of you be on the alert for any other unexpected developments. Shyanne, you can go to the air lock and take Dr. Gitlow's place."

"Yes, sir!" Shyanne happily shot out of the bridge as if her antigrav pack was rocket-powered.

"Be careful and don't do anything without the captain's permission," Eythine admonished the girl.

Ranger smiled at his temporary copilot. "If I didn't know better, I'd say you sound just like a worried mother."

"Don't be silly," Eythine retorted. "I'm just trying to help you run an efficient ship."

"Sure, sure," Lulu said. "Now if you both will direct your attention back to your photophone screens, you'll see that Dawnboy has found something that I think is rather interesting."

Ranger and Eythine looked at their viewscreens to discover that Dawnboy had moved across the *Jealousy*'s bridge and opened the door to the adjoining captain's cabin. On the narrow bunk lay a shriveled object that appeared to be the remains of a long-dead human. The corpse was recognizably male, but wore a gold-colored woman's gown that Dawnboy recognized from his earlier hallucination. The youth licked his dry lips and said in an unsteady voice, "Captain Midas Oublier, I presume?"

"That's probably who it was," Ranger agreed. "What's your opinion. Lulu?"

"How should I know who he was?" Lulu demanded.

"But judging from the body's well-preserved condition, I would guess that he died while the ship still possessed a breathable atmosphere. Then he slowly dehydrated as his cabin decompressurized. If the process was gradual enough, there would have been no moisture left in the corpse when the interior of the ship became as much a vacuum as the space outside."

"Perfect natural mummification," Ranger concluded. "Well, I suppose there are worse ways to die. What about the rest of the room, Dawnboy? Do you see anything to confirm Lulu's theory?"

"I'm na sure, but there are some papers here wi' strange-looking writing on them." Dawnboy turned his camera to a nearby desk and picked up a sheaf of papers covered with uneven script made of a dry, flaky substance. "It seems to be an old-fashioned Unilingo dialect and the writing is so faint that I can only make out a few words here and there."

"Don't waste your time on it," Ranger ordered. "Scan each page with your camera, so that Lulu can feed their contents into her computer banks and try to decipher them."

"Yes, sir." Dawnboy held the camera steady in his right hand and used his left to turn the manuscript pages.

"Hmmm, very interesting," Lulu mused after a few pages. "No, don't stop; I want to see how the story ends. I just thought it was interesting to find out that it was written with human blood. That's why it's so hard to read."

"But you can read it?" Ranger asked.

"Yes, just barely. Wait till I've had time to digest it, and I should be able to give you a fairly accurate summary of the last days of Captain Midas, who wrote this when he realized he was doomed to die here."

As they waited anxiously for the biocomputer to finish her deciphering, Dr. Gitlow's voice spoke excitedly in their helmets. "Captain, I'm in the *Jealousy*'s main cargo hold. The treasure is here, all right. There seems to be tons and tons of it. I can see huge heaps of bags of different sizes. Some of them have split and gold and jewels have spilled out on the deck. It . . . it is really a breathtaking sight!"

"I can see how it would be," Ranger said, "if it has made even you lose your scientific detachment. Stand fast there and I'll get back to you as soon as Lulu . . ."

"I'm all set now, Skipper," Lulu reported.

"Then don't keep us in suspense any longer," Eythine urged.

"Okay," Lulu said. "It goes something like this: Midas survived the passage through the supernova that he had hoped would transform the meteor into gold. But the process worked *too* successfully. Not just the meteor but every other metal object within Wonderwhat was turned into solid gold. So at last Midas had attained his heart's desire, to his bitter regret."

"Why should he regret being fabulously rich?" Shyanne asked.

"Let me see if I can guess the answer to that," Ranger said. "Pure gold is too soft to make workable machine parts, so the *Jealousy*'s engines failed to function when Midas tried to take his ship and treasure out of the comet's tail. He was trapped here to die of oxygen starvation when his life-support system broke down."

"That's exactly right," Lulu confirmed. "At that point Midas decided to leave a record of his tragic experience, for the benefit of anyone who might someday find his ship. But all his recording instruments were useless. Even the graphite in his pencils had turned to gold. So he opened a vein and used his own blood for ink. When he had finished telling his story, he put on his best dress and took a fatal overdose of sleeping pills."

"Poor, greedy, foolish Captain Midas," Eythine sighed pityingly.

Dawnboy looked from the mummy of the transvestite captain to the papers on the desk. "But what happened to the gold meteor?" he asked. "Did the papers na say something about that, too?"

"I was getting to that," Lulu said. "The last few pages of the manuscript were written by another starship captain, who signed his name as Burno Forchine. He was the one who burned open the air lock, when he reached the *Jealousy* about a century after Midas's death. Evidently he was a religious man who didn't want to desecrate what had become Midas's tomb. So he decided to leave the *Jealousy*'s cargo and take only the meteor with him when he blasted out of Wonderwhat's tail."

"I wonder what became of him?" Eythine mused. "If he had succeeded in reaching any civilized world with such a rich prize, I'm sure there would have been some historical mention of it."

"Maybe the ZuJus got him," Shyanne speculated.

"I can think of another possibility," Dr. Gitlow said. "He may never have returned to *our* universe. If Wonderwhat had entered a VIP without his knowledge, he would have emerged from the comet's tail on the other side, in the anti-matter universe where he, his ship and the golden meteor were instantly and totally annihilated."

"That sounds like a good theory," Ranger said. "If Wonderwhat's strange forces could protect Midas and his ship through the heart of a supernova, I suppose they can also protect people during a journey to and from the anti-matter universe. That is, if there really is such a universe. But I'll let you scientists try to solve that riddle. Right now I'm worried about how *we* are going to know when it's safe to leave here, since Wonderwhat pops in and out of VIP's so frequently."

"I think I can solve that problem, at least once," Lulu said. "We have enough reserve power to operate the lepton scanner for a few minutes. So let me know when you want to leave, and I'll take a reading of the space beyond Wonderwhat's reach."

"Good enough," Ranger said. "Now I want you to maneuver us into a belly-to-belly position with the *Jealousy*, then open our cargo hold hatches. We're going to transfer as much of the treasure as we can to the *Gayheart*."

"But why do we na just tow the *Jealousy* away wi' us, as we originally planned?" Dawnboy asked.

Ranger clucked his tongue reproachfully at his son. "Didn't you learn anything from the story we just heard about Midas and the other captain who took the meteor? It isn't safe to tempt the fates by being too greedy. We'll just take our fair share of the treasure. Besides, I have a good practical reason for wanting to leave the *Jealousy* here. Trust me. I haven't gotten us killed yet, have I?"

"No, not even once," Lulu admitted, as she jockeyed the *Gayheart* into the position against the *Jealousy* that Ranger had ordered.

When the two ships were properly aligned, Ranger, Eythine and Shyanne graved over to join Dawnboy and Dr. Gitlow in the *Jealousy*. They cut open the *Jealousy*'s cargo hold hatches and eagerly went to work manhandling bags of treasure across the several meters of space separating the two vessels. Even in zero gravity their exertions soon had them sweating and panting, but none of them complained or shirked his share of the labor. The incentive of seeing their fortunes rapidly increasing was sufficient to keep them working in a frenzy of avarice. In fact, Dawnboy and Shyanne protested unhappily when Ranger finally called a halt to their efforts.

"But we only ha' a small portion o' the treasure," Dawnboy argued, covetously gazing at the massive wealth remaining aboard the *Jealousy*.

"We have enough to buy Eythine a new ship, cover our other operating expenses and still have a tidy profit left over," Ranger replied. "And I don't think we should push our luck too far when we're dealing with forces that we don't fully understand."

"I know what you mean," Eythine said. "Being near this old ship and her dead captain has given me a spooky feeling. I don't believe in ghosts, of course, but I'd rather not take any chances on seeing one."

Ranger signaled with a wave of his arm. "Back to the ship and strap in, everybody. I have just one more detail to take care of. Then we'll blast out of here as soon as Lulu can find us some clear space."

They graved back to the *Gayheart*'s bridge, and Ranger approached the matter-transporter booth. "Now we'll find out if Zairundi still has any control over this thing," Ranger said, gingerly lifting the booth from the deck. He sighed with relief when the weightless booth floated harmlessly at his touch. As the others watched curiously, Ranger steered the booth out of the bridge and ordered Lulu to open the air lock for him.

A few minutes later, Ranger returned without the booth and settled into the pilot seat. Dawnboy started to ask a question, but Ranger cut him off with a promise to explain his actions later. Then Ranger told Lulu to give him a lepton scanner reading of the space outside the comet's tail.

"It looks like we're still in our own universe," Lulu reported. "I can detect no anti-matter within the scanner's reach."

"Good," Ranger said. "Let's get out of here before that situation changes."

With a blast of rocket power, the *Gayheart* veered away from the *Jealousy* and headed for the outer limits of Wonderwhat's tail. As there was no longer any need for the caution with which they had approached the treasure ship, Ranger ordered Lulu to proceed at maximum rocket speed. Their progress was pitifully slow compared to their hyperlight velocities under stardrive, but even so they moved out of the comet's tail much more rapidly than they had entered it. As soon as the radiation readings aboard the *Gayheart* had dwindled to a safe level, Lulu turned on the luxium reactor and restored the ship's normal gravity and life-support system.

"All right, everyone, get to your battle stations," Ranger said crisply. "Lulu, get our defensive force-screens up and let me know the instant you locate Zairundi's ship."

"I think he has already located us," Lulu said. "A ship is moving toward us at sub-lightspeed. Do you want me to hail her?"

"Yes, we may as well get this over with as soon as we can," Ranger replied. To his crewmates he said: "Stand by to go into action at any moment; I'm going to say some things to Zairundi that may provoke him to fight us."

"We're wi' ye all the way, Dad," Dawnboy said eagerly, as Eythine and Shyanne voiced agreement with him.

"You can count on me, too, Captain," Dr. Gitlow said with a self-conscious smile. "Our recent experience has given even my craven spirit some courage."

Ranger smiled encouragingly at the scientist, then looked at his photophone screen as Zairundi's face appeared on it. "Welcome back, partner," the black captain cordially greeted Ranger. "I'm glad to see that you've returned safely. I became quite worried about you after communication between us was severed."

"I'm deeply moved by your concern for us," Ranger replied with just a touch of sarcasm in his voice.

"I've always been a sentimentalist at heart," Zairundi modestly replied. "I trust that your venture into the comet's tail has produced profitable results?"

"Yes, quite profitable for us." Ranger gave Zairundi a brief account of their journey to the Jealousy and what they had done there, concluding with: "Now we have our share of the treasure and yours is still in there waiting for you to pick it up. So we'll wish you luck and be on our way. I even left your matter-transporter booth aboard the Jealousy to make your work easier for you."

Zairundi gave Ranger a disappointed look. "Really, now, was that fair of you? Our agreement was for you to tow the Jealousy out here, where we could divide the treasure equally between us."

"I know, and it grieves me to break a promise to someone as honorable as yourself," Ranger sighed. "But it occurred to me that even you might be overly tempted by the sight of so much wealth and take advantage of our defenseless condition as we emerged from Wonderwhat's tail. So I decided to play it safe and give you the same opportunity to reach the treasure that we had. In fact, your chances of success are better than ours were, now that you know what to expect in there."

Zairundi thoughtfully studied Ranger for a long moment before speaking again. "Is that your final word on the matter?" he asked flatly.

"Not quite," Ranger said. "As I see it, you have two options; you can try to reach the *Jealousy,* as I've recommended, or you can try to take our share of the treasure away from us. If you choose the latter action, it will mean a fight that could make us both losers. But you'd better make up your mind quickly, because we're leaving now."

Ranger switched off his photophone before Zairundi could respond and said, "Let's go, Lulu. Keep your scanners on Zairundi and let me know if he comes after us."

They waited tensely while Lulu got the ship under way with her rockets, then shifted into star-drive. Finally Lulu said: "It looks like you've won that gamble, Skipper. The *Seven Deadly Sins* has altered her course and is moving toward the *Jealousy.*"

Ranger relaxed and looked around at the happy smiles of his crew. "Well, we still have a long way to go before we're home free," he said. "But for now I want to thank and commend all of you for performing your duties so well. You are a crew that any captain would be proud of and I'm glad to have each one of you aboard, regardless of how you got here."

"It is we who should thank you, sir, for bringing us safely through our ordeals," Tombolo's deep voice intoned. "But if I may ask, how could you be so confident that Captain Zairundi would decide not to attack us?"

"I couldn't be absolutely sure about that," Ranger answered. "But as Zairundi himself said, he is more a businessman than a pirate. So I figured he would choose the least dangerous and most profitable alternative I offered him."

"But we left so much more o' the treasure for him," Dawnboy complained. "As well as the solid gold starship. He'll be the richest humon in the entire universe!"

"Don't waste time envying another's good fortune," Eythine told the boy, "Just be thankful that we came out in such good shape."

"That's right," Ranger said. "Anyhow, maybe things have worked out for the best. If Zairundi makes it back to his homeworld with all that gold, his people might decide that he's black enough to suit them after all."

"Trust you to look on the dark side," Lulu quipped. "Shall I set a course for Fossick, so that we can drop S'Hun off there?"

"Oh, yes, I keep forgetting about him," Ranger said. "How is he doing in his cabin?"

"He seems to be just fine," Lulu answered. "But I suppose he must be pretty hungry, as it has been several hours since he was last fed."

"I think that's true of all of us," Eythine said. "Now that the excitement has abated enough for me to hear my stomach growl. Come on, Shyanne. Let's go to the galley and treat the men to a good home-cooked meal."

Dawnboy watched the two women leave the bridge, suddenly realizing how empty his own stomach felt. He also felt strangely disappointed and let down, now that their treasure hunt was over and they were on their way back to more familiar space. It struck him that none of the really important questions that had confronted him—the problem of his mother's disembodied brain and whether or not he should return to his old life on Apache Highlands—had been resolved even after all they had gone through. Then he thought of something that cheered him up and took his mind off his other concerns.

"Now we'll ha' plenty o' time to calculate the value

o' our treasure and gloat over it," Dawnboy said to Dr. Gitlow. "Ye're entitled to a share o' it, too, sir."

"What? Oh, I'll leave that to your father's discretion," the luxiumwright said absently. "I want to get back to my instruments and review the data they recorded about Wonderwhat. This voyage may prove to be of great value to science after all!"

Dawnboy watched the scientist hurry out of the bridge and sadly shook his head. "I sure hope *I* never get that disinterested in money."

"To each his own," Ranger said tolerantly. "I'm just happy that we all came through this wild venture alive, healthy and prosperous. Best of all, Lulu didn't manage to get me married off to Eythine."

"Yes, but this cruise isn't over yet," Lulu said, with the patient wisdom of all womankind in her voice.